WILLIAM GILMORE SIMMS

WILLIAM GILMORE SIMMS

BY

WILLIAM P. TRENT

PROFESSOR OF HISTORY IN THE UNIVERSITY OF THE SOUTH

HASKELL HOUSE PUBLISHERS Ltd.
Publishers of Scarce Scholarly Books
NEW YORK, N. Y. 10012
1968

First Published 1892

HASKELL HOUSE PUBLISHERS Ltd.
Publishers of Scarce Scholarly Books
280 LAFAYETTE STREET
NEW YORK. N. Y. 10012

Library of Congress Catalog Card Number: 68-24944

Haskell House Catalogue Item # 249

PREFACE.

———

THE following are the chief sources on which I have relied in the preparation of this biography: —

1. About twenty pages of memoranda jotted down by Mr. Simms, probably forming the commencement of the "elaborate autobiography" to which Allibone refers.

2. About one hundred and seventy-five letters addressed by Simms to Hayne, Beverley Tucker, John J. Bockie, W. H. Ferris, W. Porcher Miles, and others.

3. More than one thousand letters addressed to Simms by correspondents from all parts of the Union, covering well the period from 1845 to 1870. These letters were given to Mr. W. Hawkins Ferris, of Brooklyn, N. Y., whose son and namesake kindly placed them at my disposal.

4. Letters written to myself by personal friends of Mr. Simms in answer to various questions.

5. Notes of conversations had with descendants and friends of Mr. Simms.

6. Biographical details extracted from Simms's own writings, from magazines and newspapers, and from other printed sources too numerous to mention. As the plan of this series excludes a frequent use of footnotes, reference has been made to the above sources only when such reference seemed to be specially important.

A word must be said with regard to those portions of this book which are concerned with Simms's environment rather than with the romancer himself. It may seem at first sight that I have too frequently dropped the rôle of the biographer in order to assume that of the historian. This may be the case, for a teacher of history is likely to seize every chance to magnify his office. But I have an excuse for my offense — if offense it be — in the fact that Simms was a typical Southerner, and that it would have been impossible to convey a full idea of his character without constant reference to the history of the Southern people during the first seven decades of the century. This history has been little studied and still less understood, hence an apparently disproportionate fullness of treatment has been required. It is not for me to say how far I have succeeded in throwing light upon the subject, or in treating it with fairness; but I may say that

the extended account I have given of Simms's political career was introduced with no desire to rake
up dead issues or to say unpleasant things. I saw
no way by which a conscientious biographer of
Simms could avoid the mire of ante-bellum politics, so I waded in with very little hope that I
should get through undraggled.

In conclusion, I must return my thanks to the
numerous persons who have kindly assisted me in
the preparation of this volume. It is impossible
to name all, but the following must be specially
mentioned: Mrs. Edward Roach, of Charleston,
and William Gilmore Simms, Esq., of Barnwell,
S. C., — children of Mr. Simms, who have given
every assistance in their power; Mrs. Paul H.
Hayne; Dr. F. Peyre Porcher, Mr. Samuel Lord,
Mr. W. Gibbes Whaley, Mr. Yates Snowden, of
Charleston; Miss Pinckney, of the Charleston Library, and Miss E. L. McCrady for researches
made in the same; Professor George F. Holmes,
of the University of Virginia; Hon. W. Porcher
Miles, of Louisiana; Mr. Charles W. Coleman,
of Williamsburg, Va.; Mrs. John J. Bockie and
Mr. W. H. Ferris, of Brooklyn, N. Y.; the author-
ities of the Virginia State Library, the Peabody
Library, and the Congressional Library, especially
Mr. David Hutcheson of the latter; and lastly

General James Grant Wilson, of New York, for whose unsolicited and unstinted help my warmest thanks are due.

W. P. TRENT.

SEWANEE, TENN., *November* 10, 1891.

WILLIAM GILMORE SIMMS.

CHAPTER I.

EARLY YEARS.

WILLIAM GILMORE SIMMS was born at Charleston, South Carolina, on the 17th of April, 1806. His father, who bore the same name, emigrated to Charleston shortly after the Revolution, from the little town of Larne, in the north of Ireland. He was a mere youth at the time of his coming; and he may have accompanied some one of his brothers, three of whom are known to have sought homes in the new world. Of these Matthew and Eli settled in Tennessee, where they lived long lives and left descendants. James, the third brother, settled in Lancaster District, South Carolina, and was the only one of his uncles, indeed of his father's kinsmen, that the subject of these pages ever saw. He made some impression upon his young nephew by his extreme ugliness, his eternal smiles, and his constant kindness, from which characteristics, and from other facts, it may be inferred that he was an old bachelor.

Little is known of the early life of William Gil-

more Simms the elder. By the beginning of this
century he had engaged in some mercantile pursuit
that was sufficiently remunerative to allow him to
think of marriage; and we accordingly find in
the "Times" of Charleston, for Friday evening,
June 1, 1804, the following brief notice: —

"Married, last evening, by the Rev. Mr. Mal-
comson, Mr. William Simms, merchant, to Miss
Harriet Singleton, both of this place."

There was some disparity between the ages of
the bride and groom, for the former was only nineteen and the latter could not have been far from
forty-two. To her nineteen years Miss Singleton
added three Christian names, — Harriet Ann Augusta. A badly executed portrait, which her son
remembered seeing in his youth, represented her as
a fair young girl of about seventeen, with sweet
and expressive eyes, and an artless, gentle counte-
nance. She had a fine ear for music, which was
doubtless a great source of delight to her husband,
who could not only sing, but also improvise the
songs he sang.

Not much is known of her family, save that she
was the only child of a Mr. John Singleton, who
had been dead five years at the time of her marriage. There were two seemingly distinct families
of Singletons in Charleston, and, curiously enough,
two Harriet Singletons, daughters of two John
Singletons, were married in that city during the
month of May, 1804. The Singletons with whom
we have to deal were a respectable family, that had

removed from Virginia to Carolina some time before the Revolution. One tombstone in the graveyard of old St. Michael's preserves the memory of John Singleton, of his daughter, and of his first grandchild; and perhaps the curious epitaphs, in prose and verse, that adorn it are due to the affection, if not to the genius, of his Scotch-Irish son-in law.

John Singleton left a widow, whose maiden name has escaped discovery. How long she remained a widow is equally a matter of doubt; but it is certain that she eventually married a Mr. Gates, and that as his wife, or widow, she displayed a care and affection for her little grandson which shall be duly commemorated in this chapter.

Of the personal characteristics of Mr. Simms the elder there will be occasion to speak hereafter; but the few events that are known of his married life must be noted here with a brevity proportioned to their sadness. Early in 1805, a first son was born to him, and christened John. In the following spring, as we have seen, came the boy who was to bear and make honorable his father's name. But in the autumn of this year a premonition of the disasters impending upon the family came in the death of the infant John. Then the father's business affairs went wrong, ending in bankruptcy,[1] just at the time that his wife died, along with her third child (January 29, 1808). The merry and

---

[1] The court records of Charleston have been searched in vain for information on this point.

stalwart man ceased making songs and epigrams, and bent beneath these cruel blows. In one week his hair became white, and he resolved to fly from a city which his imagination ever afterward pictured as "a place of tombs." He mounted his horse, and, turning his face toward Tennessee, began a series of wanderings destined to have no little effect upon the imagination of the son he had left behind him.

This motherless and almost fatherless boy found the sympathy of the one and the protection of the other in the guardianship of his grandmother. Although there are hints here and there of some property left him by his mother, this could not have been available at first, for there is abundant testimony to the poverty of the little household. They managed to live, but soon the question of the boy's education presented itself. The wandering father was in no position to help, and the child already showed signs of precocity; a free school, bad as such things then were, must be tried. At the age of six, therefore, his grandmother, with many misgivings, we may imagine, entered him at one of these so-called schools, and for two years the experiment was continued. One year seems to have been fairly employed; but that the common school system, as it then existed in South Carolina, was wretched, the following memoranda, made by Mr. Simms in mature life, abundantly prove: —

"With the exception of one [of the schools] I was an example of their utter worthlessness. They taught me little or nothing. The teachers were generally worthless in morals, and as ignorant as worthless. One old Irishman, during one year, taught me to spell, read tolerably, and write a pretty good hand. He was the best, and he knew little. Not one of them could teach me arithmetic. There was no supervision of the masters or commissioners worth a doit. The teachers, in some cases, never came to the school for three days in the week. We boys *then* thought these the best. When they did come, they were in a hurry to get away. The boys did nothing. Never attempted to work out a rule in arithmetic, but put false proofs which were never discovered. The master had a key, and was satisfied with the figures in the proof. He knew as little as the boys. The whole system, when I was a boy, was worthless and scoundrelly."

These emphatic words suggest a train of unpleasant reflections. The people of South Carolina, and of the South in general, were not insensible to the advantages of a good educational system. However inefficient their early schools and colleges were, the idea that education and culture were desirable things was always present in the minds of thoughtful men. But it is to be feared that few of these thoughtful men saw the necessity for the establishment of a system of schools which should reach high and low alike, which should tend to establish a thrifty middle class, and which, finally, should enlarge the sympathies and widen the views of the dominant aristocracy. The free or common schools were tacitly, or expressly, understood to be the schools of the poor, and schools for the poor alone will always be poor schools. The upper classes had private tutors, private schools, state colleges, New England colleges, and finally European schools and universities, to which their sons could be sent; and these advantages were constantly made use of. But while rich young Carolinians were astonishing sober-minded New England students with their lavish waste of money and time, many a poor lad in the proud city of Charleston was being doomed to a useless, or at best unsatisfying and chequered, career for want of decent schooling and a helping hand.

Returning now to our half-Irish boy and his wholly Irish teacher, it may be remarked that the latter's arithmetical deficiencies seem to have been communicated to his pupil in no slight degree; for in the very memoranda that have just been quoted, Mr. Simms estimates the period of his school life at four years, equally divided between free and private schools, and then in almost the next sentence tells us that his "schooling was at private schools four years out of the six that" he "went to school at all." Figures were generally small things to Southerners of the old *régime*, and perhaps Mr. Simms's arithmetical vagaries never caused him any great trouble. Unfortunately, they have given some trouble to his biographer.

But the reading and writing lessons were emphatically successful. The boy became an omnivorous reader, and as for his writings, one has only to transfer the epithet to Time, which has devoured them all, — numerous verses though they were. From the age of eight, when he employed his precocious talents in celebrating the victories gained by his countrymen in their second war with Great Britain, to the publication of his first little volume in 1825, his pen was rarely idle, and his brain never. When he could not write poetry, he read it; and in all probability, Byron and Scott and Moore had nowhere a more devoted admirer than this little Charleston boy. There is no way of determining what his own stock of books was; but the Charleston Library was open to him, and in those days of direct communication with England, Charleston was well supplied with English books. Although trash was accessible then as now, his tastes seem to have led him along right lines of reading. "I used to glow and shiver in turn," he said once to Paul Hayne, "over 'The Pilgrim's Progress;' and Moses's adventures, in 'The Vicar of Wakefield,' threw me into paroxysms of laughter." Years afterward the recollection of his youthful delight over the pages of Bunyan furnished him with material for one of the most touching scenes in the whole range of his romances.

In the mean time the common schools had been abandoned, and private schools tried for at least two years. These may have been better than the free schools, but they did very little for the boy. He learned no Latin, and late in life was heard to say that he had never read through an English grammar. Perhaps his sickly childhood may account in part for his slight progress; but, whatever the cause, it is evident that school training must count as a very small factor in his development.

Formative influences, however, were not lacking. The grandmother was a shrewd woman, with a stock of stories she was never tired of telling, or the boy of hearing. It was but little more than a generation since Charleston and Carolina had experienced the horrors of a war which was all the more terrible because it was, in the main, a civil war. Mrs. Gates had been a child at the time, but she had an active memory, which must have been quickened by reports of contemporary victories over the ancient enemy. A flood of recollections was doubtless unlocked when her grandson rushed in, as we may imagine he did, one January evening, eager to tell all he had heard about sailing-master Basset's brave defense of the schooner Alligator against a British frigate. Fighting at their very door must have called up the often told story of how her father fought "day and night at the lines of Charleston, armed with the rifle which past experience had rendered a fatal implement in his hands;" of how he had sent his wife and child away from the city; of the wife's anxiety, and her final determination to share her husband's peril; of how, "in an open row-boat, she descends Cooper

River from its sources, and, with muffled oars,
passes, at midnight, through the midst of a fearful cannonade, through the thronging barges of the
British."

Nor was Mrs. Gates confined to exciting stories
of war time. Naturally superstitious, she had collected a large stock of weird and ghastly tales,
which she was wont to repeat to her imaginative
grandson, little fancying that he would one day put
them to very good use. But the boy's curiosity
could not have been confined to the deeds of his
patriotic ancestors, or to the supernatural experiences of the heroes of his grandmother's tales. He
must often have asked and dreamed about the father whose infrequent letters told of perils and pri-
vations endured in warfare with the murderous
Creeks. He must have listened eagerly while his
grandmother told of the family troubles and the
suddenly whitened hair; but just where that father
was now, and when he would come to see his little
son, were questions that Mrs. Gates could not answer, and they were the most important questions
of all to a boy who was about to exchange the freedom of home for the confining precincts of a druggist's shop.

Exactly when Mrs. Gates decided that further
schooling was impracticable cannot be determined.
Nor are the reasons known which prompted her to
apprentice her grandson to a druggist, in the hope
that he might one day become a physician. It is
not even known what master he served, or how

long the apprenticeship lasted. But, whatever his condition, his love of reading and his desire for self-improvement could not be thwarted. During the day he had little opportunity either to read poetry or to write it, and his grandmother did not approve of late hours or a waste of candles. But the end justified the means with the young student, and deception was resorted to. He brought home a large box, and put his candle inside. His head and book followed the candle, and such rays of light as passed these obstacles were dissipated in the rear of the room. Mrs. Gates would see no light shining through the crevices in the door, and could retire in peace.

Books seem to have been his chief companions during these early years. Protracted periods of illness, and the consequent restraint exercised by his grandmother, developed, according to his own confession, a constitutional timidity, which must have made him more and more eager to take refuge with them. This timidity was bravely shaken off in later years; nor did it prevent him from exploring, in his boat, the beautiful harbor that is still Charleston's pride. But he never learned to swim, and his chief pleasure was to lie on the sands at evening, looking out upon the ocean, listening to its mysterious sounds, and longing to take a voyage that would carry him out of sight of land. He did not wish, he says in a manuscript note, to visit foreign lands and see strange sights; he wished to get rid of the land entirely, to be alone with the sea, to commune with it as with a mysterious being, that had affected his imagination more powerfully than had anything else in nature. This sense of the weird power of the sea must have been enhanced by the peculiar features of the Charleston landscape, — the flat stretch of country unbroken by hills, the swamps over which the tide ebbed and flowed, the venerable trees drooping with gray moss. Long into manhood this undefinable influence of the sea kept its hold upon his imagination, and to it may be traced the equally undefinable conceptions that underlay his first elaborate poem, "Atalantis."

About this period an event occurred which deserves a passing notice. The elder Simms, after going through many adventures, had settled down in what was then the territory of Mississippi. His prospects had brightened, and he began to think of the son whom he had not seen for eight years. Some friends, who were about to make a journey to Charleston, were commissioned to bring the boy back with them. According to a tradition in the family, and to the biographical sketch given in "Appleton's New American Cyclopædia," the data for which evidently came from Simms himself, these emissaries caught him in the streets, and, on his refusing to go with them, would have applied force, had not his grandmother, getting wind of the affair, brought the matter into court. There it was determined to give the boy his choice, whether he would go or stay. He decided to remain with his

grandmother. This is the story, and thus far it
has been impossible to throw further light upon it.
The case was not reported,* at least old members of
the Charleston bar have never heard of it; and if
there be a newspaper account, it has escaped notice.

The effect upon the elder Simms was to increase
his desire to see his son. Accordingly, in 1816 or
1817, he came to Charleston for the first time since
his self-enforced banishment. Recognizing the
attachment existing between Mrs. Gates and her
grandson, he forebore to press the question of a removal to Mississippi; but before he himself went
back, he lingered long enough to make a great impression upon his namesake. His affection cheered
the lonely boy, and his little poems and impromptu
epigrams stimulated a poetic faculty already in use,
and possibly produced a shy confession of the box
and candle experiment, and an exposure of the verses
written under so great difficulties. But his father's
tales of adventure were more fascinating than his
own or his father's poetry, even when the latter was
addressed to himself. They would have been interesting told at second hand, but told by the hero
himself, in his impressive Irish manner, they carried
the boy away, and had a profound influence upon
his future career. To the day of his death his
chief interest and his chief power were to lie in descriptions of hairbreadth adventures, of rough bor-
der-life, and of cruel Indian or partisan warfare.

The elder Simms was now a little upwards of
fifty years old, a vigorous man over six feet high,

with a florid complexion and snow-white hair. According to his son, he was not, strictly speaking, an educated man, but he was a great reader and a keen observer, and had a sense for humor, combined with a melancholy and at times poetic temperament. On first settling in Tennessee he had become a friend and admirer of that idol of the sturdy backwoodsmen, Andrew Jackson. When volunteers were called for after the brutal storming of Fort Mimms (August 30, 1813) by the half-breed Weathersford and his Creek warriors, he had at once followed his hero to the field, enlisting in General John Coffee's brigade of Tennessee mounted gun men. What his commission was is not known. He was probably at the battles of Tallahatchie and Tohopeka, and was certainly at New Orleans. The horrors of Florida warfare did not daunt him any more than the questionableness of his authority to make the expedition daunted Jackson; and he left Mississippi (for this was in 1818, two years after his visit to Charleston) to follow his old chieftain. Of course, such a round of experiences furnished many tales of daring and of danger. The man who had killed his own horse for food, and lived on it for seven days, was no ordinary hero in the eyes of his son.

But this pleasant visit soon ended, and before long the father was out in Florida with Jackson, while the young druggist's apprentice was plying his uncongenial trade. We do not know how the years passed, but it is certain that he continued to read and to write verses, some of which were adjudged good enough to be admitted into the daily newspapers. He even attempted a tragedy upon the time-honored subject of Roderick, the last of the Goths, but it was not until later that he mustered courage enough to submit it to a manager.

So matters went on until he was eighteen, when his apprenticeship probably ceased. The irksomeness of his proposed profession, medicine, was apparent, and he resolved to study law. Perhaps by this time his own and his grandmother's circumstances were better, and possibly his father could now contribute something to his support. He entered the law office of Mr. Charles R. Carroll, a friend not greatly older than himself, and there he continued for a while, reading Blackstone and writing Byronic odes whenever important personages like Lafayette honored Charleston with a visit.

But about this time (the close of 1824 or the beginning of 1825), he received an invitation to visit his father in the Southwest. He accordingly embarked on a small trading vessel, and after some trouble with a mutinous crew reached New Orleans in safety. A long and perilous journey lay before him, and he may have wished himself back in Charleston, where there were at least two persons who were thinking of him, — his grandmother and a certain young lady, Miss Anna Malcolm Giles by name, who had promised to be his wife. But the journey had to be made, and it was made, part probably by boat and the rest on horseback. He found his father at his plantation near Georgeville, Mississippi, just at the time when the active old man had returned from a trip of three hundred miles into the heart of the Indian country.

Simms must have remained several months; for so long a journey demanded a proportionate visit in those days of slow traveling. He rode with his father from one small settlement to another, accepting the lavish hospitality offered by the backwoodsmen and narrowly observing their manners. He visited both the Creek and Cherokee "Nations," and wrote poems on Indian subjects during his visits. Twenty years later, when addressing the students of the University of Alabama at Tuscaloosa, he told them that he had once ridden over that very spot when the silence of the primeval forest was only broken by the fall of his horse's feet and the howl of the distant wolf. On one occasion he stopped at noon to rest, and when he awoke his father showed him that his head had been pillowed on a lonely grave. A rudely carved cross suggested to the imaginative boy that this must be the grave of one of De Soto's followers, a notion which his father combated, but which nevertheless furnished material for a poem.

The influence of these journeys upon young Simms cannot be overestimated. They familiarized him with the life of a peculiar people, and enabled him in after years to describe that life as no other writer has done, or in all probability will do. The broken-down aristocrat from the older States, planting his first crop of cotton with the aid of lazy slaves and still lazier Indians; the hardy North Carolina mountaineer, building a cabin similar to the one left behind, and still supporting himself and family on what his rifle could bring down; the half-breed, as slimy as the swamp in which he took up his abode; the flashy gambler compelled to fly from Mobile or New Orleans, and amusing himself while in hiding by practicing on the simple-shrewd inhabitants of a cross-roads settlement; the rascally pettifogger; the pompous and absurd justice of the peace; the Yankee peddler; the Methodist circuit rider; and, finally, the hearty, sensible woodsman, now fighting like a tiger, and now as gentle as a lamb, — all these he rode with, ate with, and slept with, and they live yet in his pages. One can only regret that he never finished certain "Sketches of Personal Adventure," a few fragments of which still exist in manuscript.

Only one incident of this visit has been recorded in detail by Simms himself. On one of their long rides his father began to urge him to take up his abode in the new and fruitful country they were then traversing. Simms declared his purpose of returning to Carolina, marrying his sweetheart and beginning the practice of law. Whereupon his father exclaimed: —

"Return to Charleston! Why should you return to Charleston, where you can never succeed in any profession, where you need what you have

not, — friends, family, and fortune; and without
these your whole life, unless some happy accident
should favor you, will be a mere apprenticeship,
a hopeless drudging after bread. Ho! do not
think of it. Stay here. Study your profession
here, and pursue it with the energy and talent
which you possess, and I will guarantee you a
future, and in ten years a seat in Congress. Do
not think of Charleston. Whatever your talents,
they will there be poured out like water on the
sands. Charleston! *I know it only as a place of
tombs.*" [1]

The son listened to this appeal with respect, but
it did not move him. He had resolved to cast in
his lot with his native State, and neither this nor
any subsequent proposal could change his determination. Thirty years later he regretted that he
had not remained with his father, for reasons which
will become apparent as this narrative proceeds.
Every prediction that the older man made came
true; and if the younger had yielded, the success
that was foreshadowed would, in all probability,
have been attained. But it may be doubted
whether a lucrative practice or a seat in Congress
would ever have satisfied a man who had it in him
to make the heroic fight to lead the higher life that
Simms afterwards made. Waiving all question
of the amount or the permanence of his literary
fame, it may still be believed that he acted wisely
in rejecting his father's proposals. The life of the

---

[1] From Simms's memoranda.

writer and scholar is a noble life, and the man who
feels in himself the desire and the power to lead it
is right in disregarding all worldly allurements and
distractions, although in the end it be proved that
he has merely lived his life, without leaving behind a single line that posterity will care to preserve. It was with some perception of this truth,
although his ostensible purpose was to practice law,
that young Simms took his lonely journey back to
the seaboard and to civilization.

CHAPTER II.

THERE were doubtless other visions than those of
literary fame that hovered before the eyes of our
young traveler as he approached the city of his
birth after so long an absence. The midsummer of
1825 was close at hand, and, whether he made his
journey by land or sea, he must have been glad to
think of the rest and healthful security promised
by the breeze-swept city. Then, too, the regrets
occasioned by the parting with his father must have
been swallowed up by the delight he took in picturing the welcome he would receive from his sweetheart and from his old grandmother.

But these could not have been the only attrac-
tions that Charleston exercised upon him. It
promised him a better chance to lead a literary
life than the rough border country he had just
quitted; it promised him sight and touch of the
two women he loved; but more than all, it drew
him on by the peculiar fascination which alone,
perhaps, of Southern cities it possesses for sons and
strangers alike. He knew that he was a poor and
friendless boy, that the men and women who made
Charleston what it really was did not know him

and did not want to know him; he knew that he and his class were not so much looked upon with disfavor as not looked upon at all; he knew that what his father had said of Charlestonian pride and narrowness was every word true; and yet he was proud of being a Charlestonian. They all are; every man, woman, and child born within its limits is proud of the city, and would hardly exchange a life of poverty in its narrow streets for any assurance of wealth or consideration abroad. "See Charleston, and live to envy her people" is the way they have improved upon the Italian proverb.

It must not be imagined that Simms and the more intellectual men of his class, together with a few far-sighted members of the aristocracy, had not perceived, more or less clearly, that there was much to be reprehended and feared for in the social structure of the city they nevertheless loved. They doubtless rebelled often enough in their secret hearts against the domination of a blind, exclusive, and thoughtless aristocracy. The druggist's apprentice, whose soul had been fired by the strains of Byron inciting the Greeks to throw off their chains, could not but have felt an irresistible desire to burst the social chains that fettered himself; could not but have formed a determination one day to push his way, by the force of his talents and the greatness of his achievements, into the innermost circles of his formal and exclusive city. But just as the barbarian Goth was overawed by the majesty and mystery of the Eternal City, before which he lay encamped, so the cold stateliness and silent pride of the Carolinian metropolis cast a spell upon the rash spirits that yearned for change.

Into the nature of this spell and its workings we must now briefly inquire. In other words, we must consider Simms's environment before we attempt to follow his career as a man and a writer. Without a knowledge of this environment we should be constantly tempted to be unjust to him; in fact, we should hardly understand him at all. But as it is obvious that this environment includes not only Charleston and Carolina, but the whole South, for all Southern men were subjected to very much the same influences, it is equally obvious that we have entered upon a formidable task, — one for which a whole volume would hardly be adequate, much less a few pages.

The population of Charleston was estimated by a census of 1824 at slightly under twenty-eight thousand. Over half of these were slaves and free persons of color; and if the importance of the city had depended upon its white inhabitants merely, that importance would have been slight. Even its commerce would hardly have entitled it to any great respect; for its shipping, though still considerable, no longer sufficed to give the town the distinction it had enjoyed as a prosperous port in the days before the Revolution. Baltimore had already passed it in the race for population and wealth; and at the mouth of the Mississippi a city had sprung up which in size, wealth, and even in picturesque interest threatened to eclipse its fame.

But if the city had sunk in the scale of importance, so had the State, and so had the proud mother of States, Virginia. Not long since, Southern statesmen had dreamed that wealth and population would steadily flow south and keep that section ever in the van of progress and political power. Now the calm observer could see that so far from this being the case, the South had really lost ground, and was losing it every day. Nor would he have failed to reflect with sorrow that this lost ground could never be recovered by the bold schemes of politicians, or by the ostrich policy of blinding the eyes to the true state of the case. But calm observers are rare everywhere, and they are especially rare in a conservative aristocracy. And yet it did not take much observation to see that in wealth and enterprise, and all that goes to make up a material civilization, the Northern States, with their system of free labor, had left the slaveholding States far behind; nor did it require much historical knowledge to infer that before long the centres of wealth and enterprise would become the centres of political power and the centres of culture as well.

But although the Southern States were thus steadily receding from the position they occupied when Washington and Jefferson and Henry and Marion and Rutledge were their representative men, and although for the next forty years the chief interest attaching to their history is the

mournful interest arising from a contemplation of
the evils that flowed from an unsound social and
political system, nevertheless there will be found
in their literary, social, and economic history during this period, much that possesses a picturesque
charm, much that appeals to the deepest sympathies
of our nature, and finally, much that illustrates the
working of the great forces that underlie and control the development of a people.

Now what is true in this regard of the Southern
States in general is preëminently true of the city of
Charleston. What Boston has been to New England that has Charleston been to South Carolina,
one may almost say, to the Southern States. Indeed, it would be nearer the mark, if one may compare small things with great, to say that Charleston
is to South Carolina as London is to England.
Just as English country gentlemen have for generations gone up to London for the season, so have
the Carolina planters made their annual migration
to Charleston. Those who do so no longer have
only changed their habit with their change of
fortune. And just as London has been the literary, social, and political centre of England,
so has Charleston, since its founding, been the
literary, social, and political centre of South Carolina.[1]

Nay, it is to be feared that to most ante-bellum

---

[1] These and the following remarks are more true of the " low
country " than of the " up country," but they are not entirely in-
applicable to the latter.

Carolinians, Charleston was the centre of the universe. They swore by St. Michael's Church, by the statue of Pitt, by the Orphan House, and by the old Broad Street Theatre. They were proud of their Library, of their Battery, of their beautiful harbor. If a stranger remarked on the narrowness of many of their streets, they dilated on their good system of drainage, on their salubrious sea breezes, and on the fact that many invalids from the West India Islands came to Charleston to spend the summer months. If it was hinted that the so-called College, recently founded in a part of the old barracks, was in reality a mere academy, they generally contrived to shift the subject to their two banks, their sixteen churches, their Literary and Philosophical Society, and their three daily newspapers. If the lack of a good market was noted, it was courteously explained that nearly every Charleston gentleman owned a plantation from which he was in the habit of getting frequent supplies. Should the philanthropic stranger have pointed out that this bore hardly on the poorer classes, whose interests, indeed, seemed in few respects to have been considered, his remarks would have elicited some well-bred commonplace or an equally well-bred silence. But should he have gone on to point out that the frequency of incendiary fires indicated a smouldering discontent among the slaves, which the strictness of the patrol kept up must necessarily increase, the silence would have become ominous, unless, indeed, some sharp retort gave him to understand that he was treading on dangerous ground.

But although the Charlestonian had many objects of civic pride to point out to visitors; although he could dilate on the sombre beauty of the landscape, and grow enthusiastic over many a live oak almost as stately and venerable as his own family tree; although Sullivan's Island lay across the blue waves of the harbor ever ready to remind him of Moultrie and the glorious days of '76; nevertheless it was the men Charleston had produced and was producing that furnished the most grateful material for his song of praise. And it was these men whom youths like Simms wondered at and envied, and into whose society they longed to be admitted.

Very stately gentlemen they were, those distinguished Charlestonians. Courtesy sat upon them like a well-fitting garment, albeit they preserved an air of coldness and reserve, reminding one of their unsociable houses which rose behind walls shutting in beautiful gardens, which it would have been a sacrilege for the public to enjoy. Among their number there were not a few who would have been distinguished for their classical attainments even in a European capital, — men who, in the words of one of their descendants,[1] " looked upon literature as the choice recreation of gentlemen, as something fair and good, to be courted in a dainty, amateur fashion, and illustrated by *apropos* quotations from Lucretius, Virgil, or Horace."

[1] Paul Hayne.

Others there were who, though equally stately, cared less for the classics than for the pedigree of the horses that were to run next February over the Washington course. Political races are not alluded to here, but the all-exciting Charleston races, the event of the year, to which everybody went, — clergymen and lawyers; judges, who would have been trying cases had the court-house doors dared to stand open; rural members of the Episcopal Convention, which met in Race Week that it might be sure of a quorum, — the carnival of the year, attended by gentlemen in buckskin breeches and top boots, and by ladies attired in every fashion, riding in coaches of every style. Perhaps these gentlemen of the South Carolina Jockey Club, who sat down to a stately dinner on the Wednesday of Race Week, and danced a stately measure at their ball on the Friday of the same, were more admired and envied by young outsiders than the distinguished classicists mentioned above.

But the mention of the Charleston races brings up the memory of the poet who celebrated them, William Crafts, for many years literary dictator of Charleston, whose "Raciad" is now wellnigh forgotten, but who will deserve further notice in another place. And the mention of Crafts recalls the name of Charleston's next literary light, the learned and just-not-great Legaré, who criticised his predecessor in no gentle manner in the pages of the "Southern Review." With Legaré comes the ablest lawyer of his State, James Louis Petigru,

now, in 1825, a young man of high promise and
some little performance. Others of greater age
and achievements also pass before us. First,
Stephen Elliott, senior, perhaps the most public-
spirited citizen of his day, first president of the
State Bank, founder of the Literary and Philosophical Society, first professor of natural history
and botany in the Medical College he helped to
establish at Charleston, author of a "Botany of
South Carolina and Georgia," advocate of free
schools, and founder and contributor to the famous,
if short-lived, "Southern Review." By his side
stands the Right Reverend John England, Roman
Catholic Bishop of Charleston, beloved by Protes-
tants and Catholics alike, founder of seminaries
and papers, courageous opponent of dueling, pro-
moter of classical learning, and a perfect hero in
times of pestilence and public distress. Beside
these names others shine out with a milder lustre:
Joel R. Poinsett, Thomas Smith Grimké, a heretic
in the matter of the classics, Charles Fraser, the
friend of Allston, who has already left the bar
that he may paint miniatures in peace, and the
Rev. John Bachman, soon to obtain distinction as
a naturalist and a fellow-laborer with Audubon.
A more conspicuous figure than any of these is
Robert Young Hayne, Webster's future opponent,
and last but not least, connecting the present with
the past, is Charles Cotesworth Pinckney, patriot
and statesman, now within a few weeks of his death.
Certainly such a place and such men must have

exercised a fascination upon an imaginative youth like Simms. There was, and is, something unique about the town, an old-world look, an air of conscious individuality such as aged men wear who have been through stirring scenes. Here was nothing new, no mushroom growth. Along these narrow streets men like Marion a l Rutledge and Sumter and Gadsden had walked, and along them their descendants were walking in that year of our Lord, eighteen hundred and twenty-five. Turn where you would, you were reminded of the past, not of the Revolution merely, but of the stately colonial days anterior. Had not the Reverend Commissary Alexander Garden preached in St. Philip's Church for thirty-four years, and had he not cited the famous George Whitefield before the ecclesiastical court of the same parish? Did not the sheriff still escort the judges to open court, and were not gowns and official robes still a thing of the present? Surely, he would have been a rash innovator who thought to change such a people in a day. It was far more likely that he would become proud and sedate like the rest than that he would succeed in disturbing their self-satisfied quiescence.

But, some one will ask, was not this very sedate city thrown into a tumult of confusion only six years later? Did not hostile political factions nearly come to blows in that most respectable of localities, King's Street, near Hasel? Is not a trifle always sufficient to set these people by the ears? How is it, then, that they are represented

as cold, conservative, and slow to move? These
questions must be answered, and in answering them
we shall be compelled to leave Charleston for a
while and to extend our field of view in the manner
indicated at the beginning of this chapter.

South Carolina is often called the "Hotspur
State," and the impression has gone abroad that
every South Carolinian is an arrogant, hectoring
personage, ready to overwhelm you with his courtesy and hospitality at one moment, and at the next
to put a bullet into you from the distance of ten
paces. Even his Southern neighbors look upon
him with some awe, and consider his courtesy a
little stiff, his hospitality a little ceremonious, and
his courage a little too demonstrative and unreflect-
ing. This popular impression is not the result of
more prejudice or ignorance, but is based upon in-
ferences from many undeniable facts. At the
same time no one can sojourn long in South Carolina, or be much thrown with natives of the State,
without perceiving that this popular impression is
very far from being a just estimate of South Carolinian character. The very appellation "Hotspur
State" is a loose one, for who can imagine a com-
placent Hotspur perfectly well satisfied with himself and his circumstances provided only he be let
alone? Yet this complacency, this lack of ambition, is a chief characteristic of the little State and
its people. It cannot, of course, be denied that
Carolina politicians have been dominated at times
by ambitious motives; but the desire to be let alone,

to be by themselves, to be the same to-day, to-morrow, and a century hence, that their fathers were a century ago, was more potent in stirring up the mass of the people to the precipitant rashness of nullification and secession than all the allurements and incitements of the Goddess of Ambition could ever have been, even though Calhoun himself, imitating Peisistratos, had driven with her into the market place of Charleston.

Of course the character of no people is free from inconsistencies, certainly of no interesting people; but it would seem that the inhabitants of South Carolina are preëminently conspicuous in this regard. They have always been ultra-democratic aristocrats. With conservative tendencies so extreme as frequently to hamper development, they have entered upon revolutions with a facility unparalleled outside of France. While countenancing a code of honor that might bring misery upon any family at any moment, they have constantly refused to imperil the family with a law permitting absolute divorce. While professing to hold culture and literary attainments in high repute, they have consistently snubbed or disregarded all efforts that looked toward the creation of a home literature. While chivalrously careful of the sensibilities of their equals, they have ignored, as a rule, the existence of such sensibilities in their inferiors. Can these inconsistencies, which are more or less seen in the people of the other Southern States, be satisfactorily explained, or are they inconsistencies at all?

If there be one fact that stands out before the student of ante-bellum Southern history, it is that the Southern people, down to 1861, were living a primitive life, a life full of survivals. This fact has been often brought out, by no one so clearly, perhaps, as by Professor Shaler, of Harvard, in his admirable article on "The Peculiarities of the South."[1] Approximate explanations of the fact have also been attempted, and these explanations resolve themselves sooner or later into two words, feudalism and slavery. The Southern people were descendants, in the main, of that "portion of the English people who," to quote Professor Shaler, "had been least modernized, who still retained a large element of the feudal notion." Feudal notions were by no means dead in the England of the seventeenth century, and transplantation to a new world gave them a more vigorous growth from the moment that the first slave-ship made its appearance in Virginia waters. Feudal-minded cavaliers were the people of all others to whom overlordship would be natural and grateful. What wonder, then, that slavery struck its roots deep, or that the tree over which it spread its poisonous tendrils should soon show signs of decay? Slavery helped feudalism and feudalism helped slavery, and the Southern people were largely the outcome of the interaction of these two formative principles. A few paragraphs will, perhaps, suffice to show the truth of this statement, as well as to cast some light upon

[1] In the *North American Review* for October, 1890.

the alleged inconsistencies of the Southern character.

Among ante-bellum Southerners the plantation played a part similar to that played of old by the English manor. The planters were the sole repositories of social dignity and of judicial and political power in their respective neighborhoods. They reproduced as far as was possible the life of the English country gentleman, and those fortunate individuals who, besides several plantations, possessed well invested funds were accorded a position not unlike that of an English nobleman. In manners and customs, in education and religion, they resembled that survival of feudalism, the English squire, and they prided themselves upon the resemblance. They were even more tenacious of good old customs than their prototypes : witness the gentlemanly necessity for falling dead drunk under one's host's table, a custom which, although it finally died, seems to have held sway in the South after it had died in England. Like the English squire they were loyal to church and creed, to party chiefs and principles, and this loyalty is a delightful survival from the times described in the "Germania" of Tacitus.

But the conservative and loyal Southerner was feudal minded in other ways. He believed in social distinctions and in the respect due to himself from his inferiors. He acknowledged no superiors, but as every gentleman had to defend his honor as zealously as any knight of old, he saw the necessity of observing a punctilious courtesy. He must also be deferential to women, and guard the honor and welfare of those of his own family. Being woman's guardian and worshiper, he demanded of her charms, graces, and accomplishments, especially those of the housekeeping order. But where was the use of a high education for women, when any Southern gentleman would welcome to his house his old maid fifth cousin, provided she were dependent? He would even welcome ne'er-do-wells of the male sex, for living was cheap, and the presence of such hangers-on was a sign of his own importance as the head of his house; besides, they were agreeable fellows as a rule, who paid for their support much as a court jester did in the Middle Ages.

But his hospitality was not limited to the poor relation, or, indeed, limited at all. It, too, was a relic of feudalism. It was lavish and hearty, and not devoid of elegance, but in many respects it would have suited the tastes of a Norman nobleman better than those of a modern epicure. Abundance was deemed a prime requisite of every entertainment, and one of the chief differences between the Southern baron and his prototype of the twelfth century lay in the fact that the former plundered his own family by his wasteful hospitality, while the latter plundered his neighbors by more open and violent methods. When whole families of relations would migrate from Florida to Virginia, summer after summer, in gigs, in carriages, and on horseback, with baggage wagons and numerous

slaves in attendance; when they would stay month
after month, living upon the fat of the land, the
gods of hospitality were doubtless delighted, but
the gods of thrift and household peace hid their
faces and groaned. And how like a royal progress or a visit from one nobleman to another it
all was !

But a Norman noble would have found more to
remind him of feudal days than the loaded-down
table of his host, had one revisited "the glimpses
of the moon " and become the guest of a Southern
planter. His dignity would not have stood out long
against the hail-fellow-well-met manners of those
around him. Late hours might have told upon
him at first, but the sound of the horn would have
found him ready for the chase, whether of deer or
fox, even though the old muzzle-loader put into his
hand were a cause of considerable bewilderment.
He would have thought that the horses were capar-
isoned rather plainly, but he would have appreci-
ated the horsemanship.of the planter and his sons
as they vaulted into their saddles. The negroes,
who held the hounds and guns, or who hovered in
the neighborhood watching the preparations, might
have created some surprise, with their black faces,
but would instantly have been classed with his own
retainers at home. And finally, when, after a long
day's sport, they stretched a twelve-point buck before the door of the mansion, and the lady of the
house, with her guests and daughters, came out to
welcome the hunters and to admire and pity the

prey, he would have thought of his own noble lady issuing from her bower to welcome her lord home from the battlefield or the chase.

One more feudal characteristic of the South may now be mentioned, and then we shall be at liberty to draw some conclusions as to what the very hackneyed expression, "Southern chivalry," actually means. Primogeniture, although not acknowledged by law, really flourished in the South; for although the head of a house had very few plans for his daughter's future beyond marrying her off to a man of known antecedents, he did have rather definite plans about his sons, and especially about the eldest. This young hero was to become the head of the house, to take the homestead plantation, and, if possible, to marry a neighbor's daughter and increase the estate. He was usually sent to Yale or Harvard, and after that to Europe; at any rate he traveled about the South on horseback, and visited his scattered cousins. It was no great matter if he were not a reading man, but he must ride well, and shoot well, and every manly accomplishment he could add to these was so much the better. The Southern father would hardly have thanked Saint Bothan for the fact that only one of his sons could pen a line, but if one had turned author in a professional way, he would have had a sneaking feeling that the family had been somehow disgraced. The other learned professions were, however, open to the younger sons when there were not plantations enough to go the rounds; but as soon as these sons made enough money, they proceeded to reëstablish their position among the gentry of their native county by the purchase of a plantation. They then slaved the rest of their lives at their professions, trying to make enough money to cover their losses from bad overseers and from a wasteful system of culture.

Little has been said of the pleasant, easy-going side of this life, of the parties and balls, the Christmas romps, the picnics and barbecues, but these things have been sufficiently described time and again. If feudal England was merry England, the feudal South was the merry and the sunny South; nay, more, it was "a nation of men of honor and of cavaliers." The South was never barbarous, for it possessed a picturesque civilization marked by charm of mind and manners both in men and women. But the South had forgotten that, in the words of Burke, "the age of chivalry is gone." It ignored the fact that while chivalry was a good thing in its day, modern civilization is a much higher thing. Even now many otherwise well informed gentlemen do not understand the full meaning of that expression "Southern chivalry," which they use so often. They know that it stands for many bright and high things, but they seem to forget its darker meaning. They forget that it means that the people of the South were leading a primitive life, — a life behind the age. They forget that it means that Southerners were conservative, slow to change, contented with the social distinctions already existing.

They forget all this, but the expression has meanings which probably were never known to them. It means that Southerners lived a life which, though simple and picturesque, was nevertheless calculated to repress many of the best faculties and powers of our nature. It was a life affording few opportunities to talents that did not lie in certain beaten grooves. It was a life gaining its intellectual nourishment, just as it did its material comforts, largely from abroad, — a life that choked all thought and investigation that did not tend to conserve existing institutions and opinions, a life that rendered originality scarcely possible except under the guise of eccentricity. Would not such a life produce peculiarities and seeming inconsistencies in a people, and would not a young man shut out from it long to gain admission into it, and form his ideas and habits largely in accordance with its spirit?

So much has been said about the feudal element in the Southern character that there is little time left for a discussion of the effects of slavery upon that character. But this subject has been so often treated that after all there is little reason to regret the necessity for its slight treatment here. It will, too, inevitably crop up all along the course of our narrative. Suffice it, then, to say that the more Southern history is studied, the more it becomes apparent that slavery was a much greater evil to the master than to the slave. Throughout most of the South, certainly in the older States, harsh and cruel

masters were decidedly rare. Where cruelty was
practiced toward the slave, and *all* of the atrocious
incidents recorded in abolitionist documents could
not have been exaggerated, the master was generally responsible for it only in the way that an ab-
sentee Irish landlord is responsible for the condition of his tenants. The overseer in the one case,
the steward in the other, are the proximate causes
of the suffering, it being perfectly possible for both
slave-owner and landlord to be humane and honorable men. That they should be considered
thoughtful men, alive to a sense of duty, is not
possible; and though we may feel for them when
they have had their duties forcibly thrust upon them
from without, it cannot be denied that such men
must at one time or another be awakened from
their slumbers.

Slavery lifted the African vastly in the scale of
civilization, and there is no telling what social and
economic benefits may in the future flow from it.
But this only palliates the evils of his condition
to the ex-slave and his freed descendants; it does
not affect our judgment of the slavers who captured or of the masters who bought. The only and
sufficient excuse that can be made for these men is
the same excuse that can be made for the English
legislators who allowed thousands of poor wretches
to suffer more under absurd penal statutes than was
ever suffered by an African slave under an overseer's lash, — want of thought and a desire to let
things be.

But if the effects of slavery upon the slave were of a mixed nature, the effects upon the master were almost wholly bad. He became an aristocrat and yet claimed to be a democrat; hence he strove to resist the course of development his country was taking, and was crushed in the attempt. His relations with his aristocratic neighbors developed his chivalric qualities, and made him fall behind his age. His power as a landed and slave proprietor drove out the small yeoman, cowed the tradesman and the mechanic, and deprived the South of that most necessary factor in the development of a nation's greatness, a thrifty middle class. He became day by day more conservative, more inert, more proud. When he was aroused it was oftener by scorn and passion, by a determination to carry his own policy with a high hand, than by the promptings of a generous ambition or a wide-reaching sympathy. Hence he could make a dashing politician of himself, but not a statesman; a vehement and florid orator, but not a poet.

It would be idle to attempt to enumerate all the evils that inured to the Southern gentry from the existence of slavery. It would be equally idle to enumerate the brighter features of the system. That it was wasteful and ruinous; that it was founded upon injustice or blindness, and continued by blindness; that it afforded constant provocation to the indulgence of lowering passions, — these are truths that cannot be gainsaid. That, in spite of foolish and horrible laws, it lifted the status of the

African; that it fostered the beautiful relations of
fidelity and protecting care; that it reproduced in
the new world some of the most picturesque features
of an old-world and old-time civilization, — these
also are truths which some honest persons seem de-
sirous to ignore, and which other honest persons
seem equally anxious to magnify.

There is one point in this connection, however,
that deserves a brief notice. Most of the great
Southerners of the days of Washington were as outspoken about the evils of slavery as their chief;
how was it that forty years later the leading men
of the South wrote and thought of slavery as of an
institution established and blessed by God himself?
One reason is obvious. The trials of the Revolution, and of the times immediately preceding and
following it, had taught Washington and his com-
peers to use their minds. They turned them upon
themselves, nor shrank from the painful but logical
conclusions forced upon them. Seventy years later
this was changed. The stimulus of a great crisis
having been withdrawn, the incapacity of the easy-
going cavalier for grappling with great moral problems became more and more apparent. His pocket
grew larger and his mind narrower, as the market
for his great agricultural staples increased. What
wonder that he forgot the warning words of his wise
forerunners! When the rest of the world woke up
at last, though shamefully late, to the horrors of
the slave system even under its most favorable
aspects, he awoke only to the fact that he was be-

ing criticised; that his critics frequently used harsh words and did not appreciate his good qualities. He felt, but he did not think. At best he thought backwards, and, with his feelings for a guide, began to use his by no means inconsiderable powers of mind in the erection of a system of political and social philosophy which, as an exhibition of what wrong-headed honesty can accomplish in the way of self-stultification, has never had an equal in the world's history.

Now this incapacity to reason clearly, with the direful consequences that flowed from it, — social decay, war, and painful reconstruction, — is chargeable to no one man, and deserves no words of blame. The evils of an institution like slavery are vastly multiplied for each succeeding generation. The economic and selfish interests of the master grow stronger year by year. The dangers arising from domestic insurrection and from foreign interference become more and more imminent. And finally the evil effects, mental and moral, of overlordship — arrogance, contempt for inferiors, inertia of mind and body — continue to sap, with increasing force, the vigor of the individual and of the State. Under such conditions and with his inherited qualities, it is no wonder that the Southerner of the days of nullification was inferior to his revolutionary sire. Slavery and feudalism had combined and done their work effectively.

We are now in a position to see that the inconsistencies pointed out in the character of the South

Carolinian, if inconsistencies at all, were such only in an objective sense. Their existence did not imply a want of consistency of feeling or action on the part of the inhabitants of the little State. It was natural for such a people to be extremely conservative, and yet to be easily swayed in their passions whenever they fancied that they were being insulted or imposed upon. It was natural for them to proclaim themselves to be democrats, and yet not cease to be aristocrats; for every member of that aristocracy claimed equal rights with every other, and no one recognized the lower classes more than was absolutely necessary. It was also natural for the modern representatives of an age that produced the Crusades and the knightly encounter to give their antagonists every opportunity for revenge; it was equally natural for them to look upon an absolute divorce with something like horror. In their contempt for native authors they were simply reproducing a feeling common enough in England a century before. In short, although such causes as the extreme sultriness of his climate, the intermixture of French blood, and the preponderating number of his slaves, may have made the South Carolinian appear a marked man even to his Southern neighbors, it is apparent that his peculiarities were shared with all the Southern people, and that they were just what might have been expected from a man living in his environment and with his inherited qualities.

Such, in the main, were the men whom Simms

was destined to live with, and into whose society he
longed, as a boy, to be admitted. However clearly
he might see their faults and failings, he could not
escape from the fascination which their easy, pleasant life exerted. But while it is both interesting
and important to know something of the influences
by which Simms was surrounded, there is some
danger that, if this discussion be prolonged, the existence of that gentleman will be forgotten. Let
us, therefore, return to him.

That a young man who is destined to make a reputation, great or small, as a prose writer should
begin his career by vainly attempting to write
verse is one of the commonplaces of literary history. The phenomenon needs no comment, and
the biographer of such a man is readily excused
from dwelling upon his hero's metrical failures.
Simms differs from the common run of would-be
bards that eventually find their true place among
prose-men, only by the fact that to the day of his
death he never ceased to write verse, or to feel that
he had been cruelly wronged by a generation that
had refused to hail him as an inspired poet. This
fact will naturally need explanation, and will force
me to allude more often to Simms's poetical ventures than their intrinsic worth would otherwise
warrant. I shall endeavor, however, to confine
myself to such aspects of his forgotten poetry as
have definite relations with his more successful work
as a romancer, and to such as will illustrate the

merits and defects of Southern poetry in general. And I shall dwell upon this last point the more readily because I believe that the best service that can be done to the memory of Simms will be, not to hold him up as an unjustly treated poet, which he was not, or as a partially successful romancer, which he was, but to deal with him as the most conspicuous representative of letters the old South can boast of,[1] as a type of a peculiar people, as, finally, a man who, under harassing conditions, fought a brave fight to lead the higher life.

Probably the first thing that our young aspirant for fame did after his return from the Southwest was to brush the dust from his long abandoned law books. But his study of Blackstone did not have the same effect upon him as the study that went to the making of the great commentaries had upon Blackstone. Simms wrote no Farewell to his Muse. On the contrary, he had not settled down many weeks before he was not only writing new verses, but, what is worse, publishing them. He had some excuse for this conduct, however, for an event had occurred that demanded instant commemoration in song. This event was the death of General Charles Cotesworth Pinckney, which took place on the 16th of August, 1825. A patriotic young poet could have had no more congenial theme than the death of such a man. General Pinckney represented all that was venerable in

[1] Poe is excepted, as the South's claim to him is not unimpeachable.

Carolina's past. He had received or refused almost every honor that a republic could bestow, and once, at least, words had fallen from his lips that his countrymen would not willingly let die.

It is little wonder, then, that the "Courier" of September 14th should have contained a complimentary notice of an anonymous Monody on General Charles Cotesworth Pinckney, which the editor declared to have proceeded from a hand not unknown to his readers. It is also no matter of wonder that the young poet adopted the heroic couplet as his measure, and began by describing a serene sunset. It is some slight matter of surprise, however, that the little volume has so entirely escaped discovery. Collectors of rare *Charlestoniana* have never even heard of it, and catalogues of great public and private libraries have been searched for it in vain. But the cover in which Simms's own copy once resided has been seen, and with that and the extracts furnished by the "Courier" critic, we may well rest content.

In spite of the "Courier's" commendation there is every reason to believe that this patriotic tribute made no impression whatever upon the cultivated circles its author particularly desired to reach. Most of the elegant gentlemen forming those circles were still living, in imagination at least, in the time of Horace. If they had come down the centuries at all, they had certainly stopped at another Augustan age, — that of Pope and Addison. Not a few private libraries in the South will be found,

upon examination, practically to have stopped there
for good, which is one explanation of Mr. Stedman's correct surmise "that standard literature, including poetry, is read with more interest in the
South" than in the North. It is very often all
that a Southern boy with a taste for reading can
lay his hands on, unless he is content with a stray
novel or a contemporary magazine. At the period
here treated of, there were doubtless a considerable
number of book-buyers in Charleston, a class
which, by the way, decreased as men ran deeper in
debt, grew more excited over politics, and finally
lost their property in the war; but they had something better to do, in their own opinion, than to
encourage the efforts of native American genius,
especially of a Charleston nobody. To quote Paul
Hayne: "That any man ignorant of the dead lan-
guages, who could only read Homer through the
medium of old Chapman or Pope, and whose
acquisitions generally were confined to the master-
pieces of his own vulgar mother tongue, should aspire to the honors of *any* of the Muses seemed
monstrous and absurd. The sole arbiters of taste
in a comparatively small provincial town, they
treated the maiden effusions of our author with
good-natured contempt." How Simms repaid them
in kind will be seen hereafter.

These supercilious critics came near having another opportunity to show their scorn of Simms and
his like. The young gentleman devoted many
hours that should have been given to Blackstone to

polishing his precocious play on the fortunes of
Roderick. He then submitted it to a manager, who,
strange to say, accepted, announced, and put it in
rehearsal. A subsequent quarrel with his bene-
factor induced Simms to withdraw the play, and
although he immediately wrote two new ones, he
had the sense to burn them. Had he not quar-
reled with Holman (or Gilfert, that gentleman's
son-in-law and successor) he would have had to run
a very severe critical gauntlet. For those were the
golden days of the drama in Charleston, when
Cooper often drove up to the Broad Street Theatre
in the gig that had carried him from Boston to New
Orleans, and when Crafts and his fellow-connois-
seurs sat in state and weighed out their applause
with judicial hands.

Meanwhile he had himself been acting a rather
serious part in life's drama for a poor young man
of twenty. On October 19, 1826, he had been
married to Miss Anna Malcolm Giles. Little is
known of her family save that she was the daughter of a Mr. Othniel J. Giles, who appears, from
a stray notice gleaned from the " City Gazette "
for 1828, to have been in the city's employ as clerk
to the board of commissioners of streets and lamps.
This would seem to preclude any possibility that
Simms could have bettered his affairs by his marriage, which was probably a true love match with
a girl he had long known. Nothing is known of
the bride herself, save that she was a Charlestonian,
and two years and a half younger than her husband.

There is reason to believe that the young couple took up their residence at Summerville, a suburban village, where board was cheap. Perhaps, however, this was only a summer home.

As several months were to run before he could be admitted to the bar, our poet had abundant leisure to prepare his second volume for the press. On New Year's Day, 1827, therefore, he signed an advertisement to a collection of poems, written for the most part before his nineteenth year, and entitled "Lyrical and Other Poems." As Simms subsequently suppressed his youthful ventures, this volume is now quite rare; but it would have become so even if its author had not lifted a finger for its destruction. Its prevailing tone was of course Byronic, and when the poet grew tired of reciting the woes of the Greeks, he could draw on his own southwestern experiences and recite those of the Creeks. The general impression produced is that the young writer has ability, but not of a poetic order. There is a certain fluency of diction and directness of expression that suggest the possible development of a serviceable prose style, but there is an utter absence of that charm which, according to Matthew Arnold, makes the "song of the poet divine." There is a commonplaceness both of matter and style that more than neutralizes the facility and correctness that mark the verses; and one perceives that this facility and correctness will stand greatly in Simms's way as a poet by making him disdain to take pains with his work.

Whether he would ever have got pleasure out of "poetic pains" may be doubted in spite of Cowper's authority. Southerners did not usually like to work.

But however unsuccessful his poetry, Simms could at least flatter himself that he had striven to relieve his section from the reproach of having done little or nothing toward the creation of a national literature. It was an auspicious moment for such an undertaking. In the North, Cooper and Irving were working like bees, to say nothing of Bryant and Halleck, and Pierpont and Percival, and the lamented Drake. But what could the South show? Maryland could indeed point to a tiny volume containing a few lines of genuine poetry, and declare that even in its crudest portions there were traces of a virility of thought and expression not usually perceptible in the work of American poets. But Pinkney was to die in a year and, worse fate, was to fall into the hands of the Reverend Mr. Griswold. Virginia[1] could say much the same thing of the unfortunate Richard Dabney, who at least escaped Griswold, and who was long credited, and still is, in Virginia, with having written Peacock's "Rhododaphne." And both States could name poets of a single song, like Key and McClurg, and forensic rivals, like the elder Pinkney and Wirt. Besides, had not Marshall and Wirt published standard biographies, and were not the latter's mild Addiso-

[1] Poe's *Tamerlane* (Boston, 1827) would hardly have been cited.

nian essays read in all parts of the land? Then,
too, Georgia could boast of Richard Henry Wilde,
albeit he was foreign born; and South Carolina
had Crafts and Farmer, and Holland and Hasell,
and Muller and Spierin, no matter if the last three
were hardly remembered even in Charleston itself.
They had written prize poems, and therefore they
deserved to be remembered, especially Spierin, who
died at sixteen. So, at least, thought Simms when
twenty years later he dutifully collected their choi-
cest pieces in "The Charleston Book."[1]

But although a few Southern bibliophiles could
have added to this list of names, and perhaps felt
a faint glow of pride in reciting them, a candid
critic, even of the year 1827, would have been compelled to confess that, if America as a whole made a
poor showing in literature, the South made scarcely
any at all. He would, perhaps, have accounted
for this state of things by pointing out the imma-
turity of the country, the absence of towns which
could act as literary centres and furnish publishers,
and the absorption of the upper classes in politics
and in social pleasures. How far slavery accounted
for these facts and how far it had injured the Southern mind, he would hardly have thought it necessary to inquire. Naturally, he could not be expected to know that at that very time New England
was training up certain of her sons whose literary
work would not only redound to the glory of the

---

[1] The only example I know of a Southern "annual" — if the
name be applicable where only one volume is published.

whole country, but would also confute forever the pretensions of Slavery to rank with Freedom as the nurse and guardian of genius.

There was room, then, for a new Southern writer, if Slavery still wished to continue the unequal contest; and the death of Crafts had left an especially good opening in Charleston. But in the opinion of the Charlestonians, this opening could be filled by one man only, — Hugh Swinton Legaré, whose prodigious performances at the new state college were still remembered. Legaré was certainly able to fill, and more than fill, Crafts's place. As we glance over the latter's remains and note the thin quality of his essays and orations, and the still thinner quality of his poetry, we wonder that there could ever have been a time and place when such a man could have been considered a great literary light. But we remember the "Brazen Treasury of Songs and Lyrics" of Mr. Griswold, and are silent. Legaré, who was to keep Simms for years out of his rightful position as the first of Southern authors, — at least in the eyes of the South Carolinians, — was a writer of far more weight than Crafts; but in his case, unfortunately, weight meant, as it so often does, lack of creative power and positive dullness. In spite of all that has been said of his brilliancy, in spite of his remarkable scholarship, which in the special department of the civil law was perhaps superior to that of any other American of his day, I have to confess that I laid down the two thick volumes of his works with a sigh of relief and regret.

Of relief, because I had discharged the duty I owed to one of the few classic writers of my section; of regret, because I could not but acknowledge that here was another instance of the fact that great industry and great learning cannot of themselves make a man a great writer. His scholarship was not even of service in popularizing the scholarly work of others; for who of his luxuriously inclined Southern readers could have read without napping his long essays on Athenian and Roman history in the " Southern Review"? If they were read through, then our ancestors were more patient and long-suffering than they are usually supposed to have been.

But after all, the Charlestonians were perhaps right in putting Legaré into the vacant seat of honor and in coupling his name with that of the far from heavy and scholarly Wirt. Certainly no one could have foretold from the "Lyrical and Other Poems " that a youngster who had frequently carried pill boxes and medicine bottles through the streets of Charleston would at no distant day stand forth to the world as the chief, if not the sole literary man of his State and the recognized delineator of her manners and customs.

On April 17, 1827, his twenty-first birthday, Simms was admitted to the bar. That he was speedily successful, for a beginner, may be inferred from the fact that his receipts from his first year's practice amounted to six hundred dollars. Most young married men in his position would probably

have stuck to the law and let poetry go; but
Simms thought otherwise. It was well enough to
be able to defend a murderer in a style which a
bystander has described as "vehement, earnest,
dramatic;" but his earnestness and his dramatic
talents ought to be reserved for higher things. He
accordingly celebrated the close of the year with
another still more daringly Byronic volume, entitled "Early Lays."

In this he actually gave his own "Apostrophe to
Ocean" in orthodox Spenserian stanzas, and then
proceeded to sing the praises of another favorite,
Thomas Jefferson. It can be seen, however, that
the history and legends of his State and section are
beginning to fascinate him, and one is willing to
read a poem on "The Last of the Yemassees," in
consideration of the pleasure already derived from
what is, perhaps, the most popular of his romances.

Meanwhile a daughter had been born to him
(November 11, 1827), and christened Anna Augusta. She was the only child his first wife
brought him, and for this reason she became especially dear to him. But the addition to his family
made him doubly anxious to add to his income, and
as many a fond dreamer had done before him, he
resolved to rely solely on his pen. His law books
were abandoned; and in June, 1828, he issued a
prospectus for a new literary magazine in conjunc-
tion with James W. Simmons. It may be gathered from this prospectus that a paper called
"The Tablet" had been running for some time in

Charleston, probably under the editorship of Mr.
Simmons, who was not only a friend of Simms's,
but also a brother poet in a small way. It was now
proposed to enlarge this paper to a monthly magazine of sixty-four pages, to be entitled "The
Tablet, or Southern Monthly Literary Gazette."
On Saturday, September 6th, the first number was
issued and was complimented in "The City Gazette." The experiment was continued through
two half-yearly volumes; but as each number fell
dead from the press, and as the pockets of both
partners began to suffer, it was considered that
enough had been done for the glory of Southern
literature, and publication was discontinued.

It has been impossible, so far, to discover a
complete set of this short-lived periodical, but a few
of Simms's contributions have been preserved.
One, a notice of a long-forgotten book, is characterized by a successful assumption of the omni-
scient tone of an Edinburgh reviewer; another crit-
icises the prying tendencies of modern biographers
with a vim and directness which, if not convincing,
are at least refreshing — to a biographer. The
readers of the number for July 1, 1829, were also
treated to some fragments of an oration delivered
the previous year by Mr. Simms, on the occasion of
the fifty-second anniversary of the battle of Fort
Moultrie. The Palmetto Society, before which it
was delivered, appears to have languished after
the anniversary just mentioned; but this fact is to
be attributed to the proximity of the Fourth of

July, and not to the character of Simms's oration,
which seems to have been as patriotic and florid as
the tastes of his hearers could well have demanded.
The fact that he was selected as orator shows that
he was not absolutely ignored in his native city;
and it is interesting to think that he may have had
among his hearers no less a personage than Edgar
Allan Poe, who was at that time serving as E. A.
Perry in Battery H, First Artillery, stationed at
Fort Moultrie.

But our two co-workers in behalf of Southern
literature were not alone either in their efforts or
in their failures. Older men of greater distinction
and resources had awakened to the fact that the
South had no proper medium through which the few
writers and thinkers she possessed could make their
ideas public. But these gentlemen had the true
Southern contempt for small things. Nothing but
a quarterly review of the approved English type
would comport with the dignity of Charleston; for
did not Boston glory in that decorous periodical
the "North American Review"? What New England could do, the South could do; so Elliott and
Legaré set to work with a will, and launched the
"Southern Review."

The first number of this child of many prayers
saw the light in February, 1828. All the pride
and all the talent of South Carolina were interested
in its success. Not only would it give Southern
writers an organ, and show the rest of the world
what things they could do: it would also dissemi-

nate the true and only political doctrine of the divine rights of States. But alas! not even an orthodox quarterly review, conducted by brilliant men, backed by public sentiment, and supported by such contributors as Cooper, Nott, and Henry, of the College, and McCord, Grimké, Trumbull, William Elliott, and the two editors from the city and State at large, could "create a soul under the ribs of death," a Southern literature under the shadow of slavery. Even in Boston the "North American" was dragging along in a dull and weary way; and it was not at all certain that such stately periodicals could flourish anywhere on this side of the water. To expect one to flourish in a small city, in an isolated section, where the people read little and were disinclined to trouble themselves about such a trifling thing as paying a subscription, argued an ingenuousness on the part of the editors as noble as it was chimerical. One is not surprised, therefore, to read a conspicuous notice in the fifteenth number, requesting subscribers to pay up, or to find Elliott and Legaré withdrawing and leaving their bantling to die on the hands of the former's son, Stephen Elliott, Junior, afterwards first bishop of Georgia.

But they had made a gallant struggle for four years, and their review had been a credit to them in many ways. If the articles look long and dry to us, it must be remembered that such will before long be the fate of the article we read only yesterday in our favorite English review; if they seem

to bristle with quotations, we must remember that
the South was not yet awake to the fact that the
eighteenth century was defunct; and if some lucubrations of not the least length are unmistakably
padded, we must remember that not infrequently
one man (Legaré) had to furnish half the contents
of a number. It is not likely that many individuals, even of the most loyal class of Southerners,
have ever been tempted to look inside the covers
of the eight formidable volumes that represent the
labors of Legaré and his friends. The present
writer does not pretend to have mastered their contents, but he has read enough to make him respect
the zeal and talents of editors and contributors
alike, fully enough to make him regret that such
zeal and such talents were practically thrown away
from causes over which their possessors had little or
no control. But where Elliott and Legaré failed,
how could Simms and Simmons hope to succeed?

With the failure of his magazine Simms was
under the necessity of seeking fresh employment.
It so happened that a daily newspaper of long
standing, the "City Gazette," was for sale, and he
determined to invest in this manner the remains of
the small property that had come to him through
his mother. A practical printer, E. S. Duryea
by name, was found who was willing to form a
partnership; and the new firm began issuing their
paper on the first of the new year (1830). A cursory comparison of the first volume issued under
Simms's editorship with those that immediately

preceded it reveals the fact that the local news is more fully reported, and that more attention is paid to current literature. Strange to say there is not a great deal of poetry, and there is a corresponding paucity of editorial comment on passing events.

But if Simms did not publish much poetry in his newspaper, he did not let his previous failures deter him from issuing two fresh volumes. One, entitled "Cortes, Cain, and Other Poems" (1829), was only remarkable as containing "The Lost Pleiad," the single poem of his which has approached popularity, and as showing the early influence of Wordsworth upon him. This influence could not make him a poet, but it made him a greater lover of nature and a better and wiser man. In 1830 appeared "The Tri-Color," a Byronic outpouring in honor of the Three Days of July. It is not surprising that an ardent Jeffersonian like Simms should have written on such a subject; even staid Charleston gave banquets in honor of French democracy; but it is a little strange that a London firm should have thought fit to issue the volume before the end of the year.

Meanwhile, South Carolina had entered upon a crisis which brought no little responsibility to every citizen, and especially to one who had assumed the rôle of public instructor. The era of peace was over, and throughout the country little was heard save the jangling of rival politicians and the hypo-

critical wailing of our perennial national bantling,
the Infant Industry. In South Carolina matters
were much worse. The protective features of the
tariffs of 1824 and 1828, the increasing appropri-
ations for internal improvements, and the general
feeling of uneasiness caused by the agitation of the
slavery question at the time of the Missouri Compromise, had greatly strengthened the hold of the
states-rights doctrine upon the people at large, and
had afforded ample opportunity for high and threatening talk to fiery and unbalanced politicians. As
early as 1822, the legislature had been so far carried away as to pass a manifestly unconstitutional
law infringing the rights of free citizens of color
of other States; and the famous anti-everything
resolutions [1] of Calhoun's rival, Judge William
Smith, were but a less extreme indication of the
spirit pervading the body. The crowning rashness
of the ordinance of nullification was not far off,
when so vehement a man as Judge Smith was de-
posed from the leadership of the states-rights party
because he was too mild.

During this exciting time of resolutions and pro-
tests, and harangues and banquets, Simms kept his
wits about him, and attached himself closely to the
party bearing a name which would have seemed
a contradiction in terms thirty years later, —
the union and states-rights party. As a patriotic
young citizen and the editor of an influential newspaper, he must have been thrown into something

---

[1] Anti-bank, anti-tariff, anti internal improvements.

like cordial relations with the chiefs of his party, Petigru, Legaré, Grimké, Poinsett, and others. It is at least certain that at the great Union celebration of the Fourth of July, 1831, he repeated "A National Ode," which was duly published along with the patriotic orations called forth by the occasion.

The cumbrous name of the party, in whose behalf he opened his columns to numerous letters signed by defunct Roman heroes, had the merit of describing accurately the political principles he held. He was a states-rights man, who still adhered to the Union. But so was Calhoun, whose zeal for the preservation of the Union was always as great as his exertions for its destruction. Simms, and most of those who thought and acted with him at this juncture, would have upheld as strenuously as Calhoun the ultimate right of a State to secede. No more than Calhoun did he favor protective tariffs and internal improvements. Where, then, was the difference between them? It lay in the fact that Simms's common sense refused to see that the time had yet come for the application of desperate remedies, or that Calhoun's scheme promised any remedy at all short of revolution. A consistent Jeffersonian, he refused to admit that the Kentucky and Virginia resolutions could be made, by any fair process of reasoning, to support the monstrous heresy of a separate state veto. He naturally distrusted a political cure-all unknown to the founders of the Republic,

and only discovered and brought forward by a
subtle theorist to meet a particular emergency.
And yet, thirty years later, when he was revising
his "History of South Carolina," he gave an account of this nullification movement that squinted
strongly in Calhoun's direction. But this turning,
although it may not be justified, will be satisfactorily explained, perhaps, as our narrative proceeds.

It would be out of place to enter here upon a
criticism of Calhoun's political doctrines or upon
an elaborate account of a crisis about which so
much has been written. Yet that crisis, coming
as it did at the beginning of his career, could not
have failed to exert some decided influence upon
the character of our young editor. He was compelled to choose his side and to stand by it, which
was an influence for good. He became involved
in pecuniary losses, and was thus thrown still more
upon his own resources. His responsibility as a
public man, his widened relations with his fellow-
citizens, his experience of anxiety and defeat,
strengthened all his powers and transformed him
from something of a dreamer to a man who never
afterwards lost his grasp upon affairs. On the
other hand, he was probably too young to resist all
the unfavorable influences that a period of excitement is likely to exert. To the day of his death he
was anxious to be recognized as an important factor in the politics of his section; for a long time it
was known by his friends that he would not disdain

to fill a respectable office.   Then again his nullification experiences taught him to look too lightly
upon great political movements; they accustomed
him to discuss the pros and cons of grave questions
which should have been approached with awe, if,
indeed, they should not rather have been shunned.
Finally, his awakening from his dreams must have
been a rough one; his ideals of human nature must
have been lowered, when he saw brother divided
against brother, and gentlemen ready to come to
blows on the streets of Charleston.

The times were indeed out of joint, and neither
the firmness of Jackson nor the compromises of
Clay were destined to straighten them.   Petigru
summed up the state of the case rather neatly when
he wrote: "I am devilishly puzzled to know
whether my friends are mad, or I beside myself.
Let us hope we shall make some discovery before
long, which will throw some light on the subject,
and give the people the satisfaction of knowing
whether they are in their right minds.   When
poor Judge W—— used to fancy himself a teapot,
people thought he was hypochondriac; but there
are in the present day very good heads filled with
notions that seem to me not less strange." [1]   Simms
was soon destined to experience in his own person
the truth of these remarks.

He had made himself quite conspicuous by his
Union editorials, and by the personal attacks he
had suffered to be printed in his columns.   He

[1] Grayson's *Memoir of Petigru*, pp. 118, 119.

had helped the Union men to carry the election for mayor, or rather for intendant, in July, 1830; and so he was no object of favor when, in their turn, the Nullifiers were victorious in the election for members of the legislature in September of the following year. Shortly after this latter victory the elated Calhounites determined to have a grand torch-light procession, the route of which lay in front of the office of the "Gazette," which then stood on the south side of Broad Street near East Bay. The scene which followed has been described by several bystanders, but no contemporary printed account of it has been discovered.

The "Gazette" office was brightly lighted, and Simms was standing in the front door alone, watching the procession. He was known to most of the crowd, some of whom took offense at what they regarded as his defiant attitude, and hissed. He looked scornfully at them, and muttered, "Cowards!" Those near enough to overhear him became excited and made a rush at the office. Simms stood his ground and defied them. The crowd, being in a good humor from their recent victory, admired the courage and audacity of the man, and were easily persuaded by some prudent friends of Duryea to pass by with a cheer for "nullification." So Simms's partner saved his printing presses, and Simms his body or, perhaps, his life.

Another eyewitness, as might have been expected, reports the occurrence somewhat differently. According to this authority the attack was made

by day and by an organized mob, composed, of
course, of the best citizens, rather than by a jolly
torch-light procession. Simms, too, appears in a
more formidable guise, for he is armed. But all
accounts bear testimony to the bravery of the man,
and to his success in overawing his assailants.[1]

Simms is described as having been at this period
a strikingly handsome and powerful man. All
traces of the weakness that marked his childhood
had disappeared. He was not far from six feet in
height, and as "erect as a poplar," with a fine head
set upon broad shoulders. Later in life he inclined
to corpulency, but now his figure suggested strength
and activity rather than heaviness. His brow was
superb, as any one that has seen J. Q. A. Ward's
bust of him, on the Charleston Battery, can readily
imagine. His bluish-gray eye, according to Paul
Hayne, flashed like a scimitar in moments of excitement. As he wore no beard in those days, the res-
oluteness and dogged determination of his heavy
jaws and chin must have told upon the crowd; and
the habitual curl of his full lips must have added
weight to his scornful words. There is a combination of the heavenly and the earthly in the face
which Ward has given us that finds its counterpart
in the life and character of the man; but fortunately the heavenly dominates the earthly.

---

[1] The authorities relied on are (1) A tribute to Mr. Simms by
Mr. A. P. Aldrich, delivered before the Court of Common Pleas
for Barnwell County, January term, 1871; (2) William L. King's
The Newspaper Press of Charleston, page 63 ; (3) A letter received
by myself from the late Mr. S. Y. Tupper of Charleston.

Personal danger was the least of the troubles in which Simms's editorship of the "Gazette" involved him. Even before the triumph of the Nullifiers he complained publicly of having lost some of his subscribers on account of his free expression of Union principles. After the successful election of Calhoun's candidates in September, the indignant editor felt bound to publish several letters that had passed between himself and gentlemen in the upper part of South Carolina and at the North. He had been accused of running his paper and asserting his Union principles for the pay and in the interest of wealthy Northern manufacturers. These charges he indignantly denied, and it was some consolation to be able to insert a letter from a correspondent, who spoke of the undoubted patriotism of the ancestors of the leading Union men, and alluded expressly to the fact that the grandfather of W. G. Simms was one of the hostages sent by the British to St. Augustine during the Revolution.[1]

But ancestral pride was of little avail in face of the fact that subscriptions were running short and debts being incurred to keep the paper going. To make matters worse Duryea died on the 25th of March, 1832, and on the 9th of April the "Gazette" appeared, with Simms as sole editor and pro-

[1] As the maternal grandfather of Mr. Simms was just of age in 1780 and as Doctor Ramsay's list of the hostages contains the name of Thomas, and not of John Singleton, it is reasonable to infer that the patriotic ancestor referred to was our editor's great-grandfather.

prietor. He struggled on for nearly two months;
then on June 7, it was announced that the paper
had been transferred to William Laurens Poole,
of Cheraw, who engaged to assume its politics, but
not its debts. With respect to these latter, creditors were politely informed that Simms could be
found for the present at the office of his friend Mr.
Charles R. Carroll. They doubtless found Simms,
but they found him, to use his own expression,
"over head and ears in debt," with every desire to
meet his obligations, but with little prospect of
doing so in the near future.

CHAPTER III.

A VOCATION FOUND.

PECUNIARY losses were by no means the only troubles Simms had had to contend with in recent years. True, his house at Summerville had been burned down, entailing the loss of all his furniture and of his few heirlooms, the most valuable of which was a picture of his mother. But this, even when taken in connection with his debts, would not have caused such an energetic man to despond for long. But when he found himself a widower and doubly an orphan, through the deaths of his father and grandmother; when he recollected that he had an infant daughter to provide for, and that his friends were both few in number and unpopular by reason of their political views, he began to despair in good earnest, and to wonder what new trials Providence had in store for him.

His father's death took place in Mississippi, March 28, 1830. There is reason to believe that Simms shortly after took a second journey to the Southwest, probably with the view of securing whatever property had been left him. The only known result of the journey is to be found in a few sweet verses published ten years later; but it cannot be doubted that he freshened and widened his knowledge of the primitive people among whom he sojourned, and that in this way he added to his intellectual capital, which was now all he had to draw upon. The exact date of Mrs. Gates's death has not been ascertained; it is known, however, that she lived to see the birth of her great-grandchild, and she could not long have survived the elder Simms. The "Gazette" of February 20, 1832, contained an invitation to the funeral of Mrs. Simms, which was to take place from her husband's residence on King-Street-Road, Charleston Neck. The cause of her death is not given; but the young widower alluded to his loss in more than one set of mournful stanzas. What disposition he made of his child is uncertain, beyond the general fact that she was intrusted to some member of her mother's family.

The disposition that Simms made of himself was a natural one. Everything that he had tried at Charleston had failed, and now that his political principles were in disrepute, there was still less chance for future success. On all sides disgusted Unionists were setting him the example of quitting the State; even Legaré was thinking of abandoning his literary dictatorship in Charleston for the position of *chargé d'affaires* at Brussels. Simms had fewer domestic ties than any of these men, and his State cared less for him. Why, then, should he stay only to be reminded more and more of his father's prophetic words? But he would

not go to the Southwest, as his father had advised.
He had already given up much that he might follow
his literary bent, and come what would he was
resolved to keep on as he had begun. But for a
literary aspirant the North and not the Southwest
was the proper field.

It is a pleasure to be able to record an obligation
to a gentleman whom every dabbler in American
literature, including the present writer, singles out
as a proper object for good-natured contempt or for
positive scorn. It is the Reverend Mr. Griswold
who informs us that, after traveling over the most
interesting portions of the North, Simms "paused
at the rural village of Hingham in Massachusetts,
and there prepared for the press his principal poetical work, 'Atalantis, a Story of the Sea,' which
was published at New York in the following winter." Griswold got his information in response to a
letter which he had addressed to Simms on the subject; it is therefore likely to be correct. How and
when the young poet got to Hingham is uncertain,
but he probably chose it as a good place for work
and one fairly safe from the ravages of the cholera.
As soon as that danger was nearly over (about the
second week in September) he hastened to New
York, where he had made, or was about to make,
several trusty friends. Chief of these was William
Cullen Bryant, who had temporarily removed to
Hoboken, in order to get away from the cholera
and to be near his friend Sands. Thither Simms
came in the afternoons, "and wandered with them

along the shores, at sunset, or strolled away, up
the heights of Weehawken, declaiming the graceful
verses of Halleck upon the scene." [1] The intimacy
thus begun with Sands was soon cut short by the
latter's premature death, but that with Bryant was
continued without interruption for thirty - eight
years. It was further cemented by subsequent
wanderings along Green River, and by visits to
Great Barrington, in Berkshire County, Massachusetts, where Bryant had once resided, and from
which the friends doubtless made frequent excursions to Stockbridge, to see that exemplary novelist, Miss Sedgwick.

Another life friend made at this period was
James Lawson, a pleasant Scotchman, seven years
older than Simms, but possessing kindred tastes
and aspirations in matters of literature and the
drama. Lawson was at this time editor of the
"Mercantile Advertiser," and was, therefore, in a
position to sympathize with the woes of the Southern ex-editor. His experience was also of service
in introducing Simms to the latter's first metropolitan publishers, the Harpers, and he kindly
consented to see the *magnum opus*, "Atalantis,"
through the press. As a bachelor it became him
to show the young widower the city, and to introduce him to his own friends of both sexes. If
we may judge from a letter of Simms's, written
a few weeks later, the Southerner was true to his
nature in paying delicate attentions to more than

[1] Simms, *Southward Ho*, Chapter II. fin.

one fair maiden of Gotham. He probably wrote
in their albums, and he certainly promised to send
them barrels of peanuts on his return home. An
æsthetically inclined biographer of the old school
might have been tempted to write "flowers" for
"peanuts," in the above sentence, but nowadays
one must go by the record.

But the theatre was the greatest source of attrac-
tion to both the friends. Lawson had already
had a tragedy, "Giordano," acted at the Park
Theatre, in 1828, and he was an intimate friend of
Edwin Forrest and of the less known George Holland. Simms and Forrest were thus brought together, though possibly at a later period, and a
close friendship was formed between them. He
saw and met Holland on this visit, and was one of
the enthusiastic crowd that applauded Miss Fanny
Kemble when she made her first bow to an American audience as Bianca, in Milman's "Fazio."

We do not know what other literary friends
Simms made on this first visit to New York. He
afterwards came so regularly that he became acquainted or intimate with nearly all the "literati"
that subsequently fell into Poe's clutches. Having little or nothing to do on these visits besides
correcting proofs, he spent his mornings in editorial offices and his evenings, when the theatre did
not attract him, at literary receptions and snug
little parties. Naturally he became a well-known
figure, and his easy manners and fund of anecdotes
gained him many friends. Indeed, he was for

some time so closely connected with New York that one is almost tempted to regard him as a Knickerbocker author. These facts being premised, his New York friends will be introduced into these pages without formality whenever the necessity shall arise.

On October 28, 1832, Simms addressed a letter to Lawson from Summerville. He had escaped quarantine, and three days after leaving New York was "at his own fireside, laughing at law and police, and bidding them defiance." The Nullifiers were triumphing around him, but he had great hopes of Old Hickory's firmness, and thought that the run-mad theorists would not know what to do with nullification now that they had got it. "Atalantis" was naturally a more important subject to him than politics, and he conjured Lawson to let him know how it was succeeding. His Charleston friends were in raptures over it. They were welcoming him back with parties every night, but he would settle down to steady work next week; in the meantime his gun looked inviting, and there were some doves to be seen from his window that were evidently waiting to be shot.

The only note of sadness in the letter appeared in the brief mention of the death of a young man with whom Simms had recently traveled, and to whom he had become much attached. This was Maynard D. Richardson, a very stanch opponent of nullification, who, had he lived, might have won some reputation both as a writer and as a politician.

Simms dedicated "Atalantis" to him, and the next
year (1833) wrote the memoir which was afterwards prefixed to a volume of his remains.
Whether Simms edited this volume is uncertain,
but he probably did; it is at least certain that
twelve years later he republished Richardson's best
verses in. "The Charleston Book." These productions show that Simms's friend was not the least
gifted of the *ignes minores* that lighted Charleston during the first quarter of this century.

Meanwhile, our hero had left the provinces, where
sooth to say he had been little of a star, and had
made his first bow on a metropolitan stage. In
plainer terms, he had published, in the "American
Quarterly Review" for September, 1832, a fairly
sensible, but hurriedly written critique of Mrs.
Trollope's "Domestic Manners of the Americans,"
and about two months later, at the somewhat reluctant hands of the Harpers, the ambitious poem
"Atalantis." Griswold tells us that the former
production "was reprinted, in several editions, in
this country and in England;" the latter seems to
have waited until 1848, when it made its second
appearance in a new but hardly improved form.

It is difficult for one who has grown fond of
Simms the man to criticise with impartiality this
pet creation of Simms the versifier. On the one
hand, the fact that posterity has consigned it to oblivion tempts one to ignore the zeal and traces of
power that are evident throughout its eighty pages;
on the other, the firm belief that Simms and some

of his contemporaries had in its greatness tempts
one to put on one's spectacles and look for beauties
and merits that do not exist.   But these temptations assail every biographer and critic; and in the
present case there is no great danger that serious
injustice will be done.

"Atalantis" is a story of a sea fairy who is per-
secuted with the love of a sea demon, but who finally
rescues herself, and marries a mortal lover.   The
scene shifts from the bottom of the sea to the top
of an enchanted island and the deck of a Spanish
barque.   There are good and bad spirits who sing
choruses of distinctly Byronic stamp.   In brief,
from one point of view, Timothy Flint was right
when he wrote, in the "Knickerbocker," that "Atalantis" was "an eccentric sort of water-witch
drama."   But from another point of view Campbell was partially right when he wrote of it as "a
well-written poem of a dramatic cast, the versifica-
tion of which is polished throughout, the characters
are sufficiently marked, and the machinery really
very beautiful." [1]   Flint judged the poem as a
whole; Campbell examined its parts, and saw that
its author had considerable literary power.   He did
not go far enough in his analysis to perceive that
this power was that of the prose writer rather than
of the poet.

The truth would seem to be that in "Atalantis"
Simms attempted a very difficult task.   Only a

---

[1] In the *Metropolitan* (London) for January, 1834, page 12.
The review is attributed to Campbell by Allibone.

poet like Milton or Shelley, possessing an imagination of the highest order, could possibly have
given life to the characters our rash young author
tried to set in motion; and Milton and Shelley
would have chosen better material for the exercise
of their powers. Most poets would simply have
rendered both themselves and their poem ridiculous.
It is to Simms's credit that he does not do this, possibly because of the sincerity which always characterized his work. However unformed and wooden
his characters, however vague and misty the action
of his poem, he, at least, had seen those characters
act their parts under the peaceful waters that surround Charleston's "palm-crowned isles." As a
lonely boy, lying on the sands or rowing about the
harbor, he had dreamed of fairies and sea nymphs
until he almost believed in them. Some of his
earliest prose essays took the form of delicately
framed fairy tales, and the spirit choruses, and
indeed other parts of "Atalantis," had been written for years. It was not his fault that he did not
recognize, until he had mixed long with the world,
that the day for such things had passed. He had
lived practically out of the world, among a primitive people; and his principal reading had lain
among the older poets and the mediævally inclined
romancists, whose day was just beginning to decline. Nor was it his fault that, like nearly all
Southern poets down to Sidney Lanier, he failed
to exercise proper control upon his imagination.
Self-control is essential to an artist, but there was

little in Southern life at that time that could teach a man how to control himself. In fact, a self-controlled man would have been looked upon with distrust in the South. They believed in inspiration and genius there, not in hard work; and so the list of Southern geniuses is a very small one. If this be not true, then it is certainly a curious fact that the two greatest Southern writers before 1861, Poe and Simms, were both men who were constantly brought under the sobering influences of the North.

The anonymity of "Atalantis" was not long preserved, and the fair success it enjoyed soon tempted its author away from South Carolina to the more literary North. Then, too, although the ferment of nullification had subsided, he felt as Legaré did, in Brussels, that it was a "scandalous *row*," and that it was very well to be out of it. Accordingly we find him, some time in 1833, settled peacefully at New Haven and meditating what literary work he should undertake besides his present task of writing short stories and poems for the magazines. At length it occurred to him that he had a bundle of manuscript that might be turned to some account. He had published in the "Southern Literary Gazette" a story, partly founded on facts, entitled "Confessions of a Murderer." While editing his daily newspaper, he had taken up this story and elaborated it. Now, in New Haven, he determined to make a book of it. Such is the genesis of his first prose work, "Martin Faber," for his knowledge of which and for many particulars to follow, the reader may consider himself indebted to certain "Personal and Literary Memorials," scribbled off by the young author on the fourth day of June, 1834, while he was smarting under the stupidity and malignity of some of his early critics.

When "Martin Faber" was finished, Simms contracted with Babcock, a New Haven publisher, to have a thousand copies printed at his own risk. When six or eight sheets had been printed, he inclosed them to the Harpers, saying that they might have the book "on their own terms, they assuming the cost of printing and all the risk and trouble of publication." This modest proposal was accepted, and the story was published at once, probably in September. It had a fine run. In four days, only one copy was left, which was reserved for the author, who likewise received one hundred dollars, greatly to his delight.

One might imagine that he continued, for a few days at least, to be fairly happy; but such was not the case, as his own words shall testify: —

"But, as I have said, the period of its publication was a period to me of bitter excitement. I had set out to produce an original book, and flattered myself to have succeeded; what, then, was my surprise to perceive, in several of the newspapers, notices, which, though in all respects highly favorable, yet charged the work with a glaring resemblance to ' Miserrimus,' [1] a work then only recently put forth in England, which, until after this

---

[1] By F. M Reynolds.

period, I had never read, and a few of the leaves
only of which I had glanced over in the bookstore
of Mr. Maltby at New Haven. The misfortune of
' Martin Faber ' consisted in being about the same
length with ' Miserrimus,' in being printed in similar form, with similar binding, and in comprising,
like the work to which it bore so unhappy a resemblance, the adventures of a bad man. There
was not a solitary incident, not a paragraph, alike
in the two productions; and a vital difference between the two was notorious enough in the fact
that the criminal in ' Miserrimus ' was such, without any obvious or reasonable cause, while ' Martin
Faber ' from the first sets out with an endeavor to
show how and why he became a criminal, and has
a reason for his offenses. ' Miserrimus,' on the
other hand, does his evil deeds wantonly, and simply because of a morbid perversity of mind, which
could only have its sanction in insanity. They all
praised, however, to a certain extent, some of them
evidently without reading it."

After this naive vindication of himself, Mr.
Simms mentions a favorable criticism by Charles
Fenno Hoffman, in the New York "American," and
a notice by Flint, in the "Knickerbocker," wherein
the hero was pronounced to be unnatural, and the
story to be horrible, though powerful. But here
the youthful author confounded his critic by pointing out that Flint himself, in the same number of
the magazine, had translated a French story, the
sub-title of which was "The Butcher of Girls."

But Simms could defend himself in less peaceable ways, as the following incident plainly shows.

On the Monday after "Martin Faber" was published, he called on the Harpers, who referred to the criticism in the "American," and asked if he knew Hoffman. Receiving a prompt negative, they showed some surprise, which they explained by stating that a Doctor Langtree had said that Simms and Hoffman were bosom friends, which accounted for the favorable nature of the latter's criticism. On this slight provocation our warm-blooded author grew angry, and, after getting further proofs, proceeded, in company with his friend Randell Hunt,[1] to call upon the talkative physician. Langtree (Samuel Daly Langtree, afterwards editor of the "Knickerbocker") rather evaded Simms's questions by answering that he had not read "Martin Faber." Whereupon Simms demanded a statement in writing of what had really been said. Langtree declining, the fiery author would have proceeded to violent measures, had not his friend Hunt interposed and induced Langtree to write his denial. When Langtree begged that the paper should be shown to the Harpers only, Simms declared that he would show it to anybody. He forthwith took it to Mr. Peabody, publisher of the "Knickerbocker," who had heard Langtree's remarks. Peabody, with an eye to business, advised him to publish the statement, as it would sell his

---

[1] An ardent anti-nullifier afterwards a successful lawyer in Louisiana.

book, to which Simms replied that he was a gentleman before he was an author.

This trivial incident has been recorded with minuteness because it is very characteristic of the man and of his section. He felt even then that he was among a people who did not understand him, and he made the mistake, so often made by his compatriots, of thinking that he must be aggressive in order to keep from being imposed upon. Naturally he was less understood than before; and with equal reason those who observed and criticised his action failed to see how thoroughly in keeping it was with the influences that had been brought to bear upon him since his birth. From just such trivial incidents Northerners and Southerners used to judge one another; and we cannot be too thankful for the fact that there are now forces at work which will enable the two sections to form their future judgments on far more reasonable and tenable grounds. The subject may be dismissed with the remark that when Doctor Langtree succeeded Flint in the editorship of the "Knickerbocker," he was able to pay off his score against Simms by some rather irritating criticisms.

Simms has now been heard on the subject of his first venture in prose fiction, has, in fact, been allowed to criticise himself. A modern reader would hardly agree with him in his estimate of his own work, in spite of the fact that Poe subsequently praised it. For, however original Simms may have thought himself, and however real the facts upon which his story was based, one has little difficulty in seeing that he was simply following, with hops and jumps, the devious, dark, and uncanny paths where Godwin had once walked with a stately tread. It is true that he not infrequently takes a leap that would be impossible to a man not endowed with strength and activity, but one's admiration of his agility is not sufficient to make one follow him willingly. But one does follow him, willy-nilly, and therefore those critics were right who, while observing his indebtedness to Godwin, and while expostulating against his jerky style and his extravagances of character and action, nevertheless saw in him promise of future power and usefulness. Simms, as we have seen, felt no great love toward these critics, and when "Martin Faber" was reissued in 1834, he wrote a preface which, from its lengthy animadversions upon his reviewers, was enough to make his readers fear that a second Cooper, as unamiable as the first and certainly less able, had been added to American literature. But he felt their strictures sufficiently to omit "Martin Faber" from the revised edition of his works, issued twenty years later.

There is no need at this late day to criticise minutely the story of a criminal who out-fathoms Count Fathom, and throws Jonathan Wild in the shade. Poe was doubtless attracted by its gruesomeness, and by the way in which Simms developed some circumstantial evidence. A modern

lover of Mr. Browning might still find some pleasure in contrasting the crude horror of Faber's last
hours in prison with the great poet's more artistic
presentation of the last moments of Count Guido.
But most readers of the present day would turn
with loathing from the book; and few would read
far enough to note the early appearance of a fault
which was to mar all of Simms's future work, —
careless inattention to details, consequent upon hurried writing. What is one to say of an author who
describes a brilliant and fashionable wedding as
occurring in a stagnated village of some sixty families? or of one who gives the same village an art
gallery, where exhibitions are held yearly with a
hundred pictures lining the wall?

Shortly after the publication of "Martin Faber,"
Simms seems to have taken a trip to Philadelphia,
in company with Timothy Flint, and there to have
made arrangements for the speedy appearance of
another book, a collection of short tales entitled
"The Book of My Lady." These stories, most of
which had previously seen the light in magazines,
deserve only one brief comment. Some of them
show that Simms was master at times of a prose
style which, if not charming, might nevertheless
have been made with a little pains distinctly graceful. Unfortunately as the years went by, and as
the temptation to do hurried work became less easy
to resist, his style lost these early traces of pleasing
qualities, and was never more than a serviceable
style with some strength, but with a constant ten-

dency to become slipshod. It may also be mentioned that many of the tales in this collection were subsequently republished in various forms; for Simms, like Poe, was a great believer in the ability of the public to swallow any amount of rehashed work.

The year 1834 probably found Simms again in New York, for his first elaborate romance, "Guy Rivers," demanded his presence as proof-reader. Charleston, meanwhile, had not treated him much more kindly, for some time in 1833 he had attempted to start there a new publication somewhat after the order of "Salmagundi," and had dismally failed. This was "The Cosmopolitan: an Occasional," which seems not to have got beyond its first number. In his "début" Simms professed to be one of a club of three, whose lucubrations were intended to furnish material for the new magazine. But in all probability he was the sole writer of the stories and chit-chat criticism which made up the contents of what might have been called more properly "The Provincial."

"Guy Rivers" was published toward the last of July, 1834, and immediately enjoyed a great run. A London reprint, in three volumes, appeared the next year. Magazines and newspapers vied with each other in extravagant praise of the new Southern author. The "Mirror" declared that at last America had produced a writer whose women characters were not mere sticks, like those of Cooper and Brockden Brown. The "American Monthly" made the astounding and somewhat enigmatical discovery that, while Cooper and Scott were mere novelists of matter, Simms was a novelist of mind. The "Knickerbocker" and the "New England Magazine" followed suit, and it was not until December of the same year that the dull "American Quarterly" found courage enough to point out with some severity the obvious and great faults of a book over which so many people had been raving. But this voice of dissent did not prevent the work from passing through three editions in little over a year; and Simms went back to Charleston to begin a new novel, with the comfortable feeling that his bank account had been increased by several hundred dollars. But in Charleston he still found himself a nobody, and he bitterly contrasted the warmth of the North with the coldness of the South, regardless of the fact that in the case of prophets the laws of temperature do not hold. But one old Charleston merchant thought enough of "Guy Rivers" and its author to offer to send the young man to Europe for study and travel, — an offer which Simms's sturdy independence forced him to decline, although a visit to Europe had naturally been one of his dearest dreams. He doubtless thought then that he would one day be able to gratify his desire, but the day never came.

Returning now to "Guy Rivers," it may be noted that Simms does not seem to have been without a high opinion of his own importance at this period. Having been disgusted by some of the criticisms

which Harpers' reader had bestowed on "Martin
Faber," he made it a condition to the publication
of his new romance that it should pass through no
reader's hands. It is a pity that it did not. If it
had, Simms would have had fewer alterations to
make in his revised edition of twenty years later,
and his besetting sin of hurried writing would have
been brought forcibly to his mind at a very important juncture. As it was, the popular favor which
could be commanded by a crude performance
tempted him to the rapid publication of much
equally crude and often more feeble work.

No one called "Guy Rivers " feeble. In spite
of its stilted style and its wooden characters, there
was a bustle and movement about it that interested
an uncritical public. Even now one feels a desire
to know what new adventures the rather priggish
young hero will fall into and what new villainies
Guy Rivers, the outlaw, will commit. It mattered
little to a public which was soon to go into raptures
over "Norman Leslie " whether Simms's aristocratic hero and heroine really represented the upper classes of his native State. That hero fell into
all sorts of traps set by his villain enemy, barely
escaped being unjustly hanged for murder, and
wound up by marrying his sweetheart and nearly
breaking the heart of the young girl of low origin
who had saved his life and fallen in love with him.
Surely here was enough to interest a public which
had grown rather tired of Cooper's Indians and of
the thin humor of Paulding's pleasant but unexcit-

ing tales. Even Dr. Bird's "Calavar," orthodox
and slightly dull romance though it was, could be
read with pleasure for a change, Flint's "Francis
Berrian" being long since forgotten. But was not
Georgia at the time of the gold fever a more *Amer-*
ican subject than Mexico even at the time of a higher
gold fever? Undiluted Americanism was what
many readers were crying for, and they got it in
"Guy Rivers;" excitement, sentimentality, bom-
bast were what others were crying for, and they got
all three in "Guy Rivers." What wonder, then,
that the book was popular? Would any of these
readers smile over such a sentence as "her lips
quivered convulsively, and an unbidden but not
painful suffusion overspread the warm brilliance of
her soft fair cheeks"? or would they care a straw
whether Simms quoted Garrick's lines on Quin
correctly or incorrectly? It is even doubtful
whether they were disgusted when Colleton, the
hero, insisted that Lucy Munro, the poor girl who
loved him with a devotion which constitutes the
single element of charm in the book, should come
to live with him and her successful rival, — a proposition, by the way, which had been made in a still
more startling fashion by Shelley to his first wife
Harriet.

But, as has been said, these uncritical readers
were right in holding that the author of "Guy
Rivers" was a man of ability. They were right in
saying that he knew how to tell a story without al-
lowing its interest to flag. They felt, moreover,

that he had opened a new world to them, — a
world lying near their very doors in that year of
our Lord eighteen hundred and thirty-four; not
an old world separated from them by thousands of
miles of ocean and by centuries of time. They
preferred a South Carolina aristocrat and slave-
owner to a worn-out English lord ; and an outlaw
fighting the Georgia militia in true backwoods
fashion to a robber baron of the Middle Ages.
They had no objection to the author's building up
his new-world romance out of the stock materials
of the old-world romancer. They took the solitary
horseman, the desperate villain, the impeccable
hero, the haughty highborn maiden, as a matter of
course, but they saw something new in the rough
proceedings of the regulators with the Yankee peddler, in the conflict of the squatters with the militia,
in the primitive forms which backwoods justice
and religion had taken on. They had found an
author, too, who could describe in a lively way the
wild and picturesque scenery of a virgin country, and
who was quite successful in his delineation of striking and original characters drawn from the humbler walks of life. That he painted with broad
strokes was a matter of no concern to people who
had not become accustomed to minute and almost
photographic studies of the life of a narrow region.

Little more need be said of this unequal production. It was destined to form the first of a series
of romances generally known as Simms's "border
romances," a series which has been reprinted sev-

eral times, and which is still read. The same merits and faults which are to be found in "Guy Rivers" are to be found in them all, and they will therefore require hereafter little more than a mere mention in the order of their publication. All are successful in representing striking phases of backwoods life; and they give one a better idea of that curious stage of existence, viewed as a whole, than the contemporary stories of Judge James Hall, or of the pseudonymous Sealsfield [1] (Karl Postel). Sealsfield, indeed, gives the humorous side of the life he is describing better than Simms does, but the latter's work is less sketchy and more comprehensive. Again, all these romances are more or less readable on account of their rapid movement. No matter whether we like the characters or not, we cannot resist being carried along by the action. There is not enough moralizing or prosy description to stop us, for we are not too conscientious to skip. On the other hand, it cannot be denied that these "border romances," the scenes of which are laid in nearly all the Southwestern States, are sometimes as rough in their construction as the people described were in their manners and customs. All are marred by a slipshod style, by a repetition of incidents, and by the introduction of an unnecessary amount of the horrible and the revolting. Some of Simms's critics used to object to the lavish

---

[1] Sealsfield is said to have copied whole pages from *Guy Rivers* in one of his stories. This is an exaggeration. Cf. *The Courtship of Ralph Doughby, Esquire*, chap. i., with *Guy Rivers*, chap. vi.

oaths put in the mouths of his characters, to which
he was wont to reply that he could not change for
the better a backwoodsman's vocabulary. But he
might have avoided, at least, introducing brutal
murders not necessary to the action of the story,
and he might have remembered that a good artist
is not called upon to exercise his powers upon subjects not proper to his art, simply because such subjects belong to the realm of the real and the natural. He might have remembered that nobility is
that quality of a romance which is essential to its
permanence; and that the fact that he was describing accurately the life of a people whom he
thoroughly understood would not alone preserve
his work for the general reader. When all is said,
one is forced to wish that Simms had written fewer
or none of these stories, and that he had spent the
time thus saved in polishing the really excellent
historical romances which will be discussed presently. But he had to make a living, and the public
liked sensational tales, so there is great excuse for
him.

The "Mirror" for August 2, 1834, announced to
its readers that Mr. Simms, encouraged by the
brilliant success of "Guy Rivers," had "already
commenced the plot of another American novel."
He was not a man to let the grass grow under his
feet, and by the spring of the next year he was
back in New York with the completed or nearly
completed manuscript of what was destined to be
the most widely read of all of his romances. We

have already seen how the early history of Carolina
had laid hold on his imagination; it was only natural, therefore, that having used up most of the materials furnished by his juvenile essays in story-
writing (for "Guy Rivers," like "Martin Faber,"
was but the elaboration of a tale begun in his youth),
he should be tempted to give up the rôle of acting
interpreter to murderers and outlaws, and to undertake the higher rôle of revealing to the world,
through the pages of an historical romance, the
wealth of beauty and charm hidden away in the
chronicles and traditions of his native State. But
of these chronicles and traditions none were more
interesting than those that told of that great uprising of the Yemassee Indians that went so near destroying the infant colony. Already, as a youthful
poet, he had sung the dirge of the last of these brave
people; now, ripened in years and in historical
knowledge, and flushed with recent success, he determined to do justice to the heroism of this well-
nigh forgotten tribe and to the bravery and reso-
lution of the early Carolinians, in a romance which
could have no more fitting title than the name
which had once struck terror into many a heart,
but which was now vanished from the earth.

With a rapid writer like Simms seven months
was ample time in which to finish a work of ordinary length. The stores of information on which
he could draw were unusually large for a man of
his age. He had not only read deeply in the
printed and manuscript sources of his State's his-

tory, but he had collected from oral sources a fund
of legends and anecdotes which were carefully
noted down in a commonplace book. He had also
familiarized himself with the physical aspects of
the country in which the scene of his romance was
to lie; and he had never omitted an opportunity
for studying Indian character, whether by means
of books, or of personal observation. From the day
when he saw scores of drunken and naked Creeks
lying about the streets of Mobile, he was thoroughly alive to all their vices; but from the time
of his sojourns in both Creek and Cherokee "Nations," he had also been fully conscious of their
many undeniable virtues. He was not likely,
therefore, to make the mistake Dr. Bird afterwards made in "Nick of the Woods," of dwelling
exclusively on the darker side of their character;
nor was he likely to err with Cooper, if indeed that
can be considered an error which has given us such
characters as Uncas and Chingachgook, in exag-
gerating their good qualities. In short, he was ad-
mirably equipped for the work he had undertaken
save in one respect, — his lack of an artist's power
of self-control.

"The Yemassee" was issued in the mid-spring of
1835. The first edition, although twice as large as
usual, was exhausted in three days. Before the
end of the year it had caught up with "Guy Rivers," and was in its third American and first English edition. Like the latter romance it was much
bepraised, but a few editors thought it necessary to

be critical enough to let the young writer see that
his work was by no means perfect. The "American Quarterly," in particular, though not going to
the lengths it had gone in the case of "Guy Rivers," gave the author some very wholesome advice
which he could well have afforded to follow.

In his new romance Simms was, of course, following, afar off, in the footsteps of Scott and
Cooper. Inasmuch as there are considerable differences between these writers, his work squints
two ways. In his description of the brave and
handsome Governor Craven, who mingles in disguise among the doughty frontiersmen, and, as
Captain Gabriel Harrison, foils Indians and pi-
rates, and wins the love of the fair Bess Matthews,
daughter of the strict old Puritan preacher, he is
undoubtedly following Scott. In his description
of the noble Sanutee, the well-beloved of the Yemassees, and of his wife Matiwan and their son
Occonestoga; in his animated account of the attack
on the block-house, and of Harrison's adventures
in the Indian village, he is as undoubtedly following Cooper. In his description of trackless swamp
and sluggish river, of the deadly serpent lurking
in the centre of luxuriant groves, of the faithful slave
who will not accept his freedom, he strikes out for
himself, and proves that he has a right to a distinct
place among American men of letters. But when
he wearies his readers with hairbreadth escapes,
with tedious love-scenes, and with the affected humor of very lack-humorous characters; when he

is careless in his grammar and pompous in his diction, one confesses with a sigh that it is his own fault that his position as a writer is not more secure. Yet it might be more true to say that he owes the place he has to the fact that he was a patriotic Southerner, with a keen eye for the charm and beauty of Southern life and character; and that he owes the fact that he never rose to the front rank, even of his own country's writers, to the limitations imposed upon him by his Southern birth.

It would be tedious to detail the main features of the plot of a story which can be had in a cheap form, and which ought to be read by all conscientious students of American literature, as well as by those thousands of readers who are daily devouring much worse novels. It is sufficient to say that the action is fairly sustained in spite of certain tedious prosings on the part of the minor characters, and that in the three chief Indian personages, Sanutee, who is the soul of the uprising of his people, and who dies with them in their defeat, Matiwan, his wife, the loveliest and purest Indian woman that I have met with in fiction, and Occonestoga, their unfortunate son, Simms shows a power of characterization which his earlier work did not warrant his readers in expecting, and which his subsequent work scarcely maintained. One scene, indeed, between these characters seems to call for special mention. I refer to the twenty-fifth chapter, in which Occonestoga is saved from the evil demon of his tribe by the desperate devotion of Matiwan, his mother. There is a concentration of power conspicuous in this entire chapter which is hardly to be found in the pages of the two American romancers who are in most respects Simms's superiors, — Cooper and Brockden Brown. None of Simms's work was destined to display the sustained energy that characterizes "The Last of the Mohicans," or the weird intensity of power that makes "Wieland" memorable. But in this one scene he showed what he could do in spite of the defects of his Southern qualities. · Yet, although the defense of the block-house and the charming of Bess Matthews by the rattlesnake have been made fairly familiar by school readers and volumes of selections, this admirable scene has been passed over in almost complete silence.

The success of "The Yemassee" naturally prompted Simms to attempt another historical romance, and the example of Kennedy's "Horse-Shoe Robinson," besides his own interest in the period, was enough to determine him to lay the scene of his next volume in the troublous times of the Revolution. Accordingly, "The Southern Literary Messenger" for August, 1835, announced that he would soon be delivered of a new romance, and late in the same year The "Partisan" was published. But as "The Partisan" was intended to form the first number of a trilogy, and as this chapter is getting rather long, it will be as well to postpone for a space the discussion of its merits.

Simms's vocation has now been found, but it

will not be well to close this chapter without alluding to his second marriage. It can be seen from
a notice prefixed to "The Partisan," that on July
1, 1835, its author was at Barnwell, South Carolina. Now not many miles distant from that
place was a plantation called "Woodlands,"
whereat resided a certain Mr. Nash Roach and his
only daughter Chevillette. It is to be shrewdly
suspected that Mr. Simms had some other business
at Barnwell than writing romances; for on November 18th of the following year, he wrote to his
friend Lawson that he was once more happily married, and to this very Miss Chevillette Roach. A
description of this lady and her father, and of the
life Simms was destined to lead at their pleasant
plantation, will form a fitting introduction to a
new chapter.

CHAPTER IV.

A PROLIFIC ROMANCER.

MR. NASH ROACH, the father of Simms's second wife, was a well-to-do gentleman of English extraction. His father had emigrated from Bristol to Charleston, and had laid the foundations of a considerable fortune, which the son had probably increased, for Woodlands was not his only plantation. Mr. Roach was about forty-four at the time of his daughter's marriage, and a widower. His wife is said to have been the child of a Colonel Chevillette, one of Frederick the Great's soldiers; certainly it was Mrs. Simms's pride to show to her visitors letters from that monarch to her grandfather, strongly encouraging the culture of the grape in South Carolina. Of Mrs. Simms herself little can be learned, save that she was an admirable mother and stepmother, and that all who knew her were fond of her. She was doubtless an excellent example of that charming type of the affectionate and domestic woman which it has been the good fortune of the South to produce in all periods of its existence.

Those of Simms's numerous visitors at Woodlands, who have recorded their impressions, have

said little of Mr. Roach and his daughter, but
enough of the house and of its quasi owner — for
Mr. Roach gave Simms *carte blanche* in the matter
of entertaining, and grew to depend upon him in all
things as the years went by — to enable us to form
a fair conception of the conditions under which most
of our author's future work was done. Of these
visitors the most conspicuous were William Cullen
Bryant, G. P. R. James, John R. Thompson, and
Paul Hayne. But though this list is small, the
number of visitors was large, for hardly any Northern gentleman who could get an introduction, or
of whose coming South Simms could hear, failed
to stop at Woodlands, to pay his respects. The
plantation was within easy walking distance — but
what expected guest would be allowed to walk even
a hundred yards to a Southerner's house? — of
Midway, a station which, as its name implied, was
the half-way stop between Charleston and Augusta.
Hence visitors found it accessible, and as Simms
was known far and wide for his hospitality,
Woodlands was seldom without a guest.

The house itself was a large and comfortable
brick building, with an odd-looking portico in front
spacious enough to allow Simms to promenade in
bad weather. One of the largest rooms on the lower
floor was reserved for the library and study, and
here most of the romances to be mentioned in this
chapter were written. The library was well chosen,
and at the time of the war numbered about ten
thousand volumes, — a very large library for the

South. Simms was a born reader and a book fancier, but many of his books came from publishers who desired to secure a notice from his pen. The dining room, that very important part of a Southerner's house, was in close proximity to the study, and thither Simms and his guests were wont to repair before the early dinner, in order to mix a toddy. The toddy disposed of, they sat down to a table loaded with good things, most of which came from the plantation or from the neighboring river, the Edisto. Over this table Simms presided with a hearty hospitality. He let his guests eat while he himself told anecdote after anecdote, taking off "the peculiar dialect and tones of the various characters introduced, whether sandlapper, backwoodsman, half - breed, or negro." Sometimes he declaimed his own poetry or that of others; sometimes he discoursed on topics of literature or art with a vehemence and insistence which left his guests little room to get in a word. Some afterwards revenged themselves by saying that Simms could declaim only, not converse; but his friends excused him, and compared him to Dr. Johnson.

Dinner over, cigars were produced, although Simms himself did not begin to smoke until after he was forty. He had promised his father not to use tobacco, and he began its use only in order to counteract a tendency to corpulency. Smoking being ended, guests were at liberty to take a nap, or to drive, ride, or walk through the picturesque

neighborhood. The Northerners generally went
first to the quarters, to satisfy their curiosity with
regard to the South's peculiar institution. They
found about sixty or seventy slaves living by families in comfortable cabins, each with a plot of
ground on which the occupants could raise poultry
and vegetables. These productions were afterwards sold to Simms or Mr. Roach for prices which
seem to have astonished one frugal visitor (Lawson). This same guest saw one negro man who
had just returned from consulting a physician in
Charleston, Simms, of course, having paid the cost
of the trip. If it happened to be Christmas time,
the guest was likely to be awakened early by the
sound of sweet singing, blended with tones from
numerous banjos; and if he had arisen he would
have seen Simms, though the latter, being a late
worker, was no early riser, standing in the porch
distributing all sorts of presents to all sorts and
conditions of grinning and grateful darkies. And
unless he were a thinker not easily misled by
appearances, he might have gone back to bed
with the conviction that slavery was after all not
such a bad institution. So, at least, declared
one Northern visitor in a letter that has been
preserved. But although slavery at Woodlands
was as harmless as it could be anywhere, a
thoughtful man like Bryant, though fully recognizing the kindly treatment his friend's slaves
received, could find no reason to change his anti-
slavery principles.

The quarters having been visited, the guest could take a ride through majestic forests of oaks or pines along bridle paths of hard white sand. He would pass by fields of cotton or maize, or by swamps filled with cypresses, at whose roots the alligator reposed. If he knew anything of his host's poetry he would recall "The Edge of the Swamp," and think that Simms had described the uncanny place with some little power. A boat horn might remind him that this was the season when the lumbermen went down the Edisto on their rafts, and he might ride on to see them pass by; or, if he were a fisherman, he might go to select a proper spot for angling, on the morrow, for the famous Edisto "cat." In short, there was much for a horseman to explore, and he would not, in all probability, have thought of the loneliness of the neighborhood.

If, however, the guest were, like his host, not much inclined to take exercise, he could find plenty to interest him in the grounds immediately surrounding the house. He could admire Simms's taste as a landscape gardener, or he could take his book and go out for a seat in the grape-vine swing, which his host had celebrated in a song. A wonderful swing he would have found it, for the vine had drooped its festoons, one below another, in such a way that half a dozen persons (so says an apparently veracious traveler) could find a comfortable seat, and yet not one of them be sitting on a level with his neighbor, nay, could not only sit, but could hold a book in one hand and reach ripe grapes with the other.

But enough for the present of the charms of Woodlands during the fall and winter months. In summer the place was untenantable, but that was the very time that Simms liked to visit Charleston and the North. At Woodlands he could live with safety from October to May, and there he could write his books and see his friends. Not being primarily a planter, he could sit up late in his study and then take his time about rising. But when he did rise, he went straight to work at his desk, and wrote with unceasing rapidity until dinner time. Visitors were told to scour the country, go hunting or fishing, or else pass the time with a book or a cigar; Simms himself must finish thirty pages of manuscript in the morning, or else make it up at night, in addition to his heavy correspondence. If the visitor sat quiet, as Paul Hayne was wont to do, watching the rapid pen move over the sheets until Simms exclaimed, "Near dinner time, old boy, — what say you to a glass of sherry and bitters?" then it was likely that the study would be abandoned for the rest of the day, and that after supper would come a rubber of whist, or a long conversation on the portico about literature or metaphysics, — a subject in which Simms liked to dabble, with how much success no one will now determine. But this life, however charming, was not Simms's whole life, and it must be left for other things.

In our eagerness to get Mr. Simms married before finishing our last chapter, we were compelled to pass over a space of fourteen months of considerable literary activity. Now that we have him quietly settled at Woodlands, it will be well to retrace our steps and recover the lost trail of the author. It has been stated that after the great success of "The Yemassee" Simms went to work with redoubled energy on another historical romance, "The Partisan," which was published in the fall of 1835. A year later he was again in New York with another revolutionary romance, the second in his proposed series of three, entitled "Mellichampe: a Legend of the Santee." After revising the proof sheets of this last production, he went to South Carolina, and was married.

In addition to this work he became the chief contributor to a new publication that aspired to represent the literary talent of Charleston. This was the "Southern Literary Journal," a small monthly magazine which was begun in September, 1835, under the editorship of a certain Daniel K. Whitaker, a New Englander by birth, but connected with the South by a long, though inconspicuous literary career. Simms does not seem to have liked Whitaker personally, an unusual fact in his case, but this could not keep him from aiding an enterprise that promised to develop Southern literature. But Charleston was destined to be a graveyard for magazines, and Simms alone could not keep one going, or counteract the deadly effects of the sentimental poetry showered upon Whitaker by local scribblers. Sooth to say, his own contributions seem to have been the offscourings of his desk, and in many respects worthy of the company they had to keep. It is not surprising, therefore, to learn that by the spring of 1839 the "Southern Literary Journal" had ceased to exist.

There was another reason for its demise. The South could not possibly support more than one respectable magazine, and that one had already been begun at Richmond by Thomas W. White, in August, 1834. At the very time Whitaker began his publication, the "Southern Literary Messenger" was being edited by the ablest man of letters of whom the South, with not an absolutely perfect claim, could boast, Edgar Allan Poe. Poe soon gave his journal a position which enabled it to drag on a weary existence long after he himself and White, the founder, had relinquished all interest in it, the one on account of his bad habits, the other on account of death. Under John R. Thompson and with the support of men like Simms, the two Cookes (Philip Pendleton, the author of "Florence Vane," and John Esten, the novelist) Paul Hayne, and others, the "Messenger" was destined to occupy for a few short years a position, not indeed equal to that which it occupied under Poe's editorship, but still a respectable position. Thompson had a faculty of singling out young writers of promise, and Donald G. Mitchell and Thomas Bailey Aldrich are two living authors, some of whose youthful effusions first saw the light in the "Messenger." But except for these two short periods it cannot be said that the Richmond monthly did a great deal for Southern literature. It is true that in some respects it stands a fair comparison with Northern publications like the "Knickerbocker" and "Graham's," all being on the whole respectably dull; but there is more of the appearance of a struggle for even a dull existence visible in the Southern magazine. The poetry is as a rule deadly. The prose fiction is scarcely better, except for some passable tales by that engaging personage the elder Cooke, and there is constant evidence of padding in the frequent appearance of lectures delivered by professors to their classes and of orations spoken at the commencement exercises of young ladies' seminaries. It could not have been otherwise. The Southern people were not great readers, and when they did read they preferred Northern publications. The editors of these could pay for contributions, and even patriotic Southerners like Simms sent their best work to them, — for authors cannot live on patriotism alone. Northern prices for work were by no means high, but Thompson recognized the fact that he could not give as much, and he therefore considerately forebore to press Simms for contributions, although gratefully accepting what could not well be published elsewhere. Perhaps a careful study of the thirty odd volumes of this often praised journal will give one as fair an idea of the thin quality of ante-bellum Southern literature as can be got from any one source. During the former half of its existence it does not compare as unfavorably with Northern magazines as during the latter half, which is precisely what we should expect when we remember that freedom elevates, while slavery either keeps at one level, or lowers. It was fitting that it should perish during the throes of the war that finally destroyed slavery; and it remains an admirable source of information for the laborious student of Southern life and manners.

But Simms in 1835 could not foresee all this, and he cordially lent his support to the "Messenger." He not only sent poems, some new and some old, but he paid his five-dollar subscription and had his name printed in the roll of honor on the cover of the magazine. After Poe resigned his editorship, another notice appeared on the cover announcing that Mr. William Gilmore Simms was *not* the editor. Northern readers knowing of only two Southern writers, naturally supposed that when Poe resigned, Simms had to step in.

But enough has been said of these attempts to create a sectional literature and of their failure; let us turn to the works in which Simms did lay a foundation for Southern literature by following out the universal, not sectional, principle of literary art which requires that a man should write spontaneously and simply about those things he is fullest of and best understands. In the case of most men this means that they must write of what lies near their very doors, and so a literature may be produced which is in this sense, sectional. But no nation or section will ever get a literature by shrieking for the "national" and the "sectional" and not praying for the true and the beautiful. That Simms did not pray enough for the true and the beautiful while writing "The Partisan" is evident from the bald passages in which he forgets that he is a romancer and fancies himself an historian of the Revolution in Carolina, — notably from the passage preliminary to his description of the battle of Camden, in which he gives *in extenso* Gates's special orders to the army. But on the whole it is easy to see that he wrote "The Partisan" because his mind was full of Marion and his ragged troopers, of brave deeds done by lowly men, of midnight sallies from camps hidden in the depths of a swamp, of Tarleton and his ruthless dragoons, — in short, of war in all its picturesqueness and all its horror. He had studied the chronicles of that stirring time, had read Marion's own letters, had conversed with old men who had served under "the Swamp Fox," and had walked or ridden over all the spots that their bravery had consecrated. It was because he tried to charm his readers with a true picture of men and times that had charmed himself that he succeeded in spite of his many shortcomings in making "The Partisan" a delightful romance.

The scene of "The Partisan" is laid in and around the once prosperous, but in 1835 utterly

decayed town of Dorchester. Simms, as he tells
us in the preface to his revised edition, had spent
part of a summer (perhaps that of 1834) in its
neighborhood, and had taken occasion to revisit its
ruins. As a boy he had frequently rambled over
the spot, and had listened to its traditions from the
lips of some old inhabitant whose name has not
been recorded. Now as he wandered about, looking at dismantled fort and neglected church and
vacant sites of once happy dwellings, these traditions came back to him. In his imagination he
peopled the streets once more. The British flag
was again flying over the fort, the blare of the
bugle was heard, and Marion's men emerged from
a neighboring swamp and came thundering through
the village up to the gates of the stronghold. Here
was material enough for a story; but as he re-
volved the matter in his mind, he became convinced
that more than one romance would be required if
he proposed to give the world a fairly complete picture of Carolina during the times of partisan warfare. Whether he knew that another Southern
author was preparing to publish a romance on a
similar theme cannot be absolutely determined, but,
at any rate, he must have felt that it would be his
own fault if he did not prove himself to be a fair
rival for Kennedy. When he read "Horse-Shoe
Robinson," he probably concluded that even if it
contained fewer faults of style than "The Partisan," it was much too leisurely a book for the exciting period in which its scene was laid, and that,

in spite of all the critics could urge against the inequalities of "The Partisan," that romance gave a better insight into the character of the Revolution in the South than the more elaborate and orthodox production of the elder and not to the manor born romancer.

He was convinced, then, that "The Partisan" and "Horse-Shoe Robinson" did not exhaust the subject, and more than this he was so pleased with the characters he had called to life to people the streets of old Dorchester that he could not bear to kill them off or get them happily married within the compass of one romance. He accordingly formed the plan of writing a trilogy, each member of which should, however, form a fairly complete story. He did not succeed in this, for "Mellichampe," as he himself afterwards confessed, has only an episodical connection with "The Partisan," and with the real sequel of that romance, "Katharine Walton." Perhaps this was the reason that made him wait thirteen years before writing the last mentioned book. But whether he succeeded in his elaborate plan or not, he did not cease to write revolutionary romances, or to continue the adventures of his favorite characters from book to book, and the reader is perhaps just as well satisfied with the result. For although his plots are always interesting and full of action, Simms displayed no great art in the construction of his romances, and his deficiencies in this regard would have been more striking if he had really attempted to construct a series of romances that should form an organic whole.

Space is wanting to describe "The Partisan" in detail. None of the characters can be called fascinating unless it be Lieutenant Porgy, whom most critics, including Poe, have regarded as a vulgar copy of Falstaff. To this verdict I do not subscribe. Simms said that Porgy was a transcript from real life, and I have it on good authority that he intended Porgy to be a reproduction of himself in certain moods. Porgy is in many respects a typical Southerner, brave, high talking, careless in money matters and as generous as careless, fond of good living, and last, but not least, too frequently inclined to take his own commonplaces as the utterances of inspired wisdom. It cannot be denied that Simms at times overdraws this favorite character, who is introduced in many succeeding volumes. But he is better drawn than most of the high-born gentlemen that figure in Simms's romances. Simms always succeeded best in his characters drawn from the humbler walks of life, because he had studied their ways too thoroughly in his border journeys not to be able to make them live in his pages. With his better-born characters he failed, partly because such characters do not easily permit themselves to be studied, partly because in drawing them he was naturally influenced by his recollection of similar characters in the numerous romances he had read.

The charm of "The Partisan" lies in its action

and in its descriptions. Few of its readers are likely to forget the terrible storm that overtook Major Singleton, the hero, in the forest; fewer still will forget the rescue of Colonel Walton by Marion's gallant troopers. Being from beginning to end a story of adventure, it is naturally a boy's book, but there is sufficient charm and power displayed to interest an older reader. It is true that for the sake of these merits many faults must be pardoned, of which careless grammar and unnecessary moralizing are unfortunately not the least. As in the case of the border romances, there are murders which either should not have been committed, or else should have been described in a less horrible way. There is an absurd lugging in of historical details and an unfortunate proneness to paint every Englishman and Tory in the darkest colors; there is an unnecessary amount of pompous diction and of stilted conversation, — but when all is said, "The Partisan" remains a striking romance, not indeed worthy to be placed on a level with "The Spy," but certainly superior to most of the early efforts of American romancers.

But how could a story written as "The Partisan" and too many of Simms's other works were written, escape being full of faults? When he went to New York to arrange with his publishers, he had completed only part of his manuscript. The printers were set to work immediately, and soon caught up with him. But the young man wanted a holiday, and went to inform the Harpers

that he would be out of town for a week. "But,"
said Mr. James Harper, "we are out of copy, and
unless you can furnish more, we shall have to sus-
pend work on your novel until you return." "That
will never do," replied the author, "give me pen,
ink, and paper, and I 'll go upstairs and find a
place to write." In less than half an hour he came
down again with more manuscript than would be
required during his absence. This sounds marvelous, or else New York printers in 1835 were not
rapid workers, but such was the story which Mr.
James Harper told in after years to a great admirer of Simms. He added, and we must perforce
agree with him, that Simms had the most remarkable talent for writing he had ever known. But
could any talent neutralize the effects of such
methods of composition?

A very few words will suffice for "Mellichampe,"
the romance that followed "The Partisan." In
some respects it is a more even production than its
predecessor, but it does not leave as distinct an impression upon the reader. It is redeemed only by
the character of the scout who follows Mellichampe,
the priggish young hero, like a faithful hound, and
finally dies for him. Witherspoon, or "Thumb-
screw" as his companions call him, is a character
worthy of Cooper. He is not, perhaps, as remarkable a scout as some that Simms afterwards
drew, — the peculiar features of the "low country"
of South Carolina make Simms's scouts a distinct
variety, — but he is what is better, a noble man.

The chapter that describes his death shows that Simms for once in his life was able to be genuinely pathetic.

After his honeymoon was over, our now popular author had abundant leisure to lay his plans for new literary work. Although his latest romances had been quite successful in the North, his Carolina friends could not bring themselves to believe that an author of his powers should waste his time on such trivial subjects as the legends and traditions of a country not two hundred years old. They urged him to try a more ancient and foreign and, therefore, more dignified theme. Their advice was seconded by his own restlessness, and so "Katharine Walton" was dismissed for the nonce, and "Pelayo; a Story of the Goth" was rapidly ground out. Simms had always been fascinated by the romantic history of Spain, and the casual discovery of the manuscript of his youthful play on the fortunes of Roderick was sufficient incitement to carry him through the two volumes of "Pelayo" and well on to the completion of its sequel, "Count Julian." Perhaps another reason for his choice of a foreign theme was a desire to succeed where his great forerunner, Cooper, had confessedly failed.

But, as if to show him that he had made a mistake, bad fortune attended both his new ventures. Owing to the general depression of business, the Harpers did not publish "Pelayo" until the autumn of 1838; and the first five books of "Count Julian" which were sent on, probably to the same publish-

ers, went astray through the carelessness of the
person that had charge of them, and did not turn
up again for two years. By this last incident we
are reminded of one of the chief difficulties Southern authors had to encounter. Unless they could
carry their manuscripts in person to their publishers, they ran constant risk of having them lost, and
proof-reading at home was almost an impossibility.
Even as late as 1850, articles addressed to Simms
as editor of the "Southern Quarterly Review" were
continually being lost; and when our South Carolinian author wished to compliment a brother man of
letters in Virginia (Beverley Tucker) with a set of
his works, he was compelled to send the books to
Richmond via Baltimore, — a proceeding which
resulted in their detention in the latter city for
several weeks. Simms, as we have seen, generally
managed to get to New York once a year to superintend the publication of his own books, — one is
forced to wish that he had not gone so often, — but
most Southern aspirants for literary fame were
poor, and were easily tempted to give up after they
learned of the difficulties that lay before them.
Sometimes they tried local publishers, and were
made to say fearful and wonderful things by the
printers; but as a rule they contented themselves
with writing to Simms, and asking him, as the
representative Southern man of letters, with, of
course, plenty of time to spare, to get them publishers for their lucubrations. After a kindly answer from Simms, telling them that they must help

themselves, they went to their graves as so many "mute, inglorious Miltons" had gone before. It must be added that Simms's kindly, genial nature never shone forth more clearly than in his treatment of these well-meaning but pestering correspondents.

But whatever hopes our author may have had of his Spanish romances were destined to be disappointed. "Pelayo" did not make a hit, and when in 1845 "Count Julian" was finished and published, Simms confessed, in his dedication to Kennedy, that he had made a mistake in abandoning the rich field his State and section had afforded him. With this mature judgment of the author himself we may well rest content. Both romances are readable, when one is in a charitable mood, and each has an occasional passage or scene of some power. But there was no excuse for their publication, except the perennial one, *il faut vivre.*

This same plea must probably be urged for the frequent appearance, in the magazines and annuals of this period, of slight poems and sketches "by the author of 'Atalantis,' 'Guy Rivers,' etc." A by no means exhaustive search has shown that, in 1837, he appeared as a contributor twenty-two times in three magazines. The contributions vary in length from a single sonnet to six or eight double-column pages of dull blank verse; and from a short sketch of some wandering minstrels to an elaborate review of Miss Martineau's "Society in America." White, the proprietor of the "Southern Literary

Messenger," thought this critique good enough to deserve publication as a separate pamphlet, and we shall find ourselves obliged to resort to it in a future chapter as the first authoritative expression of Simms's views on the subject of slavery.

If our prolific author could have been content to let these effusions die with the magazines that contained them, it would have been better for his fame; but he could not do this, and, in 1838, he added to his previous unsuccessful collections of tales a third, entitled "Carl Werner," after the principal story. What object he had in view, except to show that he had been reading translations from the German of late, is hard to conceive. Yet there is still to be found among his papers a volume, evidently designed for publication, made up of clippings from these long-forgotten collections. He died hard in everything, this indefatigable writer of the old South; and if he could only have imparted some of his indefatigability to his compatriots, he would not have collected his tales in vain. But this was not to be, and we are left to regret that he should never have been able to discriminate between his worthless and his worthy work.

But Spanish romances and weird tales after the German were not enough to content the author of "Guy Rivers." The success of that romance necessitated the production of others like it, and as Alabama lay next to Georgia, "Richard Hurdis: a Tale of Alabama," was a proper story with which to continue the series of border romances. It was published anonymously; for Simms, being something of an experimenter, wished to ascertain whether his books sold on their own merits, or because the popular author of "Guy Rivers" had written them. He soon discovered that it was the sensational character of his stories that made them sell; for "Richard Hurdis" was at once successful, and the public was assured that a new author had been discovered fully equal to the Carolina novelist. But the true parentage of the blood-curdling romance was soon an open secret; certainly after it was furnished with a sequel, "Border Beagles: a Tale of Mississippi," which appeared in 1840. This last production was followed by "Beauchampe, or the Kentucky Tragedy," in 1842.

These three stories need little criticism after what has been said of "Guy Rivers." They are less stilted in diction than that romance and more power is shown in their construction; but then years of practice will naturally affect for the better even a prolific writer of sensational stories. The Alabama and Mississippi tales were based upon the history of the famous Murrell gang of "land-pirates," who in the early thirties made life no very enviable thing in the Southwest. Simms had had many conversations with Virgil A. Stewart, the captor of Murrell; besides, he had Stewart's own narrative of his adventures to rely on. He stuck closely to his authorities and gave a vivid picture of backwoods lawlessness and an amusing, if sad, description of backwoods justice. The fictitious

characters and events introduced are not specially
interesting; but there would seem to be no reason
why the modern reader of sensational stories
should not be able to while away an hour with
these. Simms certainly managed to transfer no
little of his own vim and energy to his exciting
pages.[1]

"Beauchampe," the third of this series, demands
a few words to itself. It is an almost literal account of the killing of Colonel Sharpe by Colonel
Beauchamp, which took place in Kentucky in
1828. Sharpe had been the seducer of Beauchamp's wife before the latter married her. Beauchamp took summary vengeance as soon as he
learned the fact, and *mirabile dictu*, a Kentucky
jury was found that could bring in a verdict of
guilty of murder in the first degree. The details
of the wretched affair can be found in any newspaper of the time, and they certainly are not
needed here; but one cannot help smiling at the
laxness shown by jailers who could admit the criminal's wife to his cell on the night before his execution, and then be surprised that the precious
pair should attempt to commit suicide.

But Simms gives these details with relentless
accuracy. Even Poe, whose morbid taste was
tickled by the border stories, had to remonstrate
with the author for his unwillingness to trust his

---

[1] The reader who desires a soberer account of the Murrell gang
can consult an article on "The Uses and Abuses of Lynch Law"
in the *Whig Review* for December, 1850.

imagination in a single particular. Simms really
seems to have thought that he was doing the cause of
public morality a service by exposing the just and
terrible fate that fell upon these offenders; but it
was a strange error for a man of his sense to make.
Fourteen years later he actually took up the subject
again, and in "Charlemont: the Pride of the Village," gave a detailed and often salacious account
of the steps by which Sharpe succeeded in seducing
the ambitious village beauty, Margaret Cooper.
Here, too, he thought that he was doing public
morality a service: but he was no George Eliot, and
Margaret Cooper is, therefore, no Hetty Sorrel.
"Beauchampe" and "Charlemont" were largely
sold in Kentucky, and it is to be hoped that at
least they put some money in the pocket of their
honest and deserving, if sadly mistaken writer.

This is a gloomy subject, but it ought not to be
dismissed until its humorous side is shown, for it
has one. In that exemplary periodical, "Godey's
Lady's Book," for May, 1842, after a very favorable notice of "Beauchampe," the editor, Mrs.
Susan J. Hale, addressed her readers as follows:
" It is a curious fact that simultaneously with
the publication of the novel, we actually received
a communication, signed by a number of our
respected friends and subscribers in Missouri, requesting us to obtain the necessary materials relating to this famous Kentucky tragedy, and work
them up into a tale for the Lady's Book. . . . The
daughters of the West will now see the seducer and

slanderer of female innocence consigned to that
immortality of infamy which he has so richly deserved." Encouragement from so unexpected a
quarter must have greatly delighted Simms and
those of his fellow-craftsmen who worked up this
choice scandal, for Simms was by no means alone
in the predilection he showed for the tragedy.
Isaac Starr Classon wrote a poem on it, which
has fortunately been lost, and Charles Fenno
Hoffman gave a diluted version of it in his over-
rated romance, "Greyslaer."

Meanwhile Simms had published another volume
of miscellaneous verse, the title of which, "Southern Passages and Pictures," is more quotable than
any of the pieces it contained. The prefatory note,
written by the author while on a visit to New York
in the fall of 1838, makes one regret that little can
be said in favor of these collected results of six
years' labor in verse making. While correcting the
proof sheets Simms had heard of the death of his
first child by his second wife, a daughter, Virginia
Singleton, who lived only eleven months.

But before long there was a prospect that
Woodlands would again be cheered by the sight
of a baby's face, so the disconsolate father settled
down to the production of another romance in order
to lay by something for the support of the new-
comer. This time he thought he would combine
Spain and America instead of separating them;
and he was doubtless urged thereto by the success
of Bird's two romances and of the romantic histo-

ries of Irving. He accordingly rushed through
what Poe with some truth pronounced to be the
worst of his romances, "The Damsel of Darien"
(1839), — a story founded upon the adventures of
Balboa. There was really little excuse for this production, for nothing of any consequence was added
to Irving's pleasant narrative, and certainly the
dilution of Irving's matter did not make up for the
loss of Irving's charm of style.

The year 1840 is not an especially marked year
in Simms's calendar. Besides "Border Beagles,"
he continued publishing, in the "Southern Literary
Messenger," a series of scattered poems under the
title "Early Lays," which must not be confounded
with the juvenile volume already criticised, and he
prepared for the use of school children a short and
fairly interesting history of South Carolina. His
daughter Augusta was now thirteen, and her father
thought it necessary that she should know more
about the history of her native State than most
girls, or indeed boys, knew then, or, it may be
added, know now. Especially was this necessary,
if she was to be educated at a Northern school,
and he had doubtless already formed a plan to
send her to Great Barrington, where she could
be with one of Bryant's daughters.

In 1841, our untiring writer published two romances of the usual length in addition to his accustomed quota of short stories and poems. The first
of the romances was "The Kinsmen, or the Black
Riders of the Congaree," issued in the spring of

that year by Lea and Blanchard of Philadelphia,
which city was to be in the future as much his
publishing Mecca as New York. This story was
afterwards rechristened, and now appears as "The
Scout." Both names are appropriate; for if the
admirable woodsman, John Bannister, is the re-
deeming feature of the book, certainly the unnatural and horrible relations existing between the
heroes, the half-brothers Conway, are enough both
to give it a title and to furnish a ground for its con-
demnation. It is true that Simms had now returned
to his proper field and given his readers a tale of
South Carolina in the Revolution; but the bad
company he had kept while writing "Richard Hurdis" and "Border Beagles" had not been without
its effects. Woodlands was quiet and domestic
enough, but whenever he shut himself up in his
study he fell to talking with thieves and outlaws
and brothers eager to kill one another, so it is no
wonder that in this new romance he dwelt almost
exclusively on the darker side of Carolina's revolutionary history. There were enough Tories riding
over the State in those days to furnish him with any
number of villains: and so, with a partisan half-
brother, who is as brave and noble as a lion; and a
Tory half-brother, who is equally brave, but decidedly ignoble; and a high-bred damsel, who is loved
by both; together with a contemptible British
dandy, and scouts of all shades of loyalty and
skill, a romance was evolved which occupies a mean
position between "Richard Hurdis" and "Border

Beagles," and is warranted not to put a reader asleep.

This cannot be said of the second of the romances of this year, "Confession ; or, the Blind Heart." Here Simms, by his own acknowledgment, went back to Godwin again, and, as in the case of "Martin Faber," worked up an old theme that had long been cast aside. We have seen how his rummaging among his papers led to the useless inditing of "Pelayo" and "Count Julian;" now another long-lost manuscript leads to a greater failure. The *motif* of "Confession" seems to have been a desire on Simms's part to rival Shakespeare in his greatest play. He had too much sense to attempt to create a second Falstaff in Porgy; but his dabbling in morbid psychology rendered him blind to the real nature of Shakespeare's triumph in "Othello." Simms declared that Othello was not truly jealous, because he had been practiced upon by Iago, and he therefore resolved to write a romance in which the hero should be moved by the inward workings of jealousy alone. But here he unconsciously placed himself between Scylla and Charybdis. On the one hand, he ran the risk of making his hero a repulsive and unlovable character, if not a villain; on the other, of making him a fool or a madman. But to make one's hero a villain or a fool or a madman is but to write a repulsive novel. Shakespeare was too great an artist to make such a mistake. The fact that Othello has been practiced upon by

Iago excites our sympathy for him and sustains it even to the horrible catastrophe. Othello is still human, still a noble man, though wrecked; Edward Clifford, the hero of "Confession," excites our loathing and contempt. Indeed, there is not a single strong or wholesome character in the book, which may fairly be described as made up of exaggerations and absurdities. It is worse than "Martin Faber," to which it bears many striking resemblances; and so the reader may be spared the steps by which Clifford is worked up to killing his by no means Desdemona-like wife. That refined and sensible man, Paul Hayne, used to praise this story, for what reason it is hard to discover; the present writer can see in it only a striking proof of the futility of attempting to write a novel in order to illustrate a pet theory, whether of psychology, or social science, or theology. It was because Simms's head had gone astray and not his heart, that he was tempted to write, within a year of each other, two such repulsive and uncalled-for stories as "Confession" and "Beauchampe."

But psychological speculations were not the only ones occupying Simms's mind at this time. The political future of the South was just as often the subject of his meditations, and the only two pages worth remembering in the romance criticised above are those in which one of the characters gives his reasons for emigrating to Texas. To Simms's vivid imagination the conquest of Canada was certain to come in a very few years, and the North would

then be increased by "six ponderous States," which
would be "New England all over," in policy and
character.   To balance this the South would have
Florida, of which two feeble States could be made.
But war with England for Canada would necessi-
tate our taking possession of Cuba, "after a civil
apology to Spain;" and the British West Indies,
"which should of right be ours," would of course
be ours in fact.   But this would not be enough.
Texas would soon be settled sufficiently with Southern men to render the conquest of Mexico natural
and easy, and "the brave old English tongue"
would "arouse the best echoes in the city of Mon-
tezuma!"   Then with Texas, Mexico, Cuba, and
the West Indies, the South could feel fairly safe
with regard to Canada; whether the national conscience would be at rest was a point on which the
glowing prophet did not see fit to dwell.   Ingenuous dreamer!   As one reads his swelling periods
in the light of cold facts, and endeavors to realize
the state of mind that could produce such visions,
that wonderful line of Herrick's rises unbidden to
one's mind: —

> " In this world, *the Isle of Dreams,*"

and, the sad years of war and suffering in store for
these dreamers being recalled, the stanza naturally
completes itself: —

> "While we sit by Sorrow's streams,
> Tears and terrors are our themes."

CHAPTER V.

ONLY one romance of any length was published by
Simms between "Beauchampe" (1842) and "Katharine Walton" (1850). This was "Count Julian,"
which has been mentioned already. But if during
this period he made his bow as a romancer less frequently to the American public, he certainly did
not slight the English public. For "Guy Rivers"
had been reissued in a cheap form by a London
house, in 1841, and "The Kinsmen," "Beauchampe," and others had speedily followed, some
very shortly after their publication in America.
The English publishers seem to have been satisfied
with the success of their reprints, and they entered
into an arrangement with Simms by which they
were allowed to issue "Count Julian" simultaneously with its appearance in America. But they
thought it necessary to prefix a note combating the
opinion that had been advanced by a reviewer in
the "Spectator," that the author of "The Yemassee" had not the strength, comprehension, and flex-
ibility necessary for a romance. Surely this reviewer will be confounded by the present romance,
added the ingenuous publishers. Whether he was

or not is doubtful, but Simms was read, and one
publisher found it to his interest to announce that
the American romancer was present in London superintending the issue of his own works, and editing
a "Library of Trans-Atlantic Romance."
But although he is now gaining readers in England, and although his best works are soon to be
translated into German, we suddenly find him
practically giving up romance writing for eight
years. He does write a few short stories and
novelettes, and he increases his poetical output; but
these seem to be mere asides, mere holiday tasks
compared with the main business of his life, which
appears to consist in endeavoring to thrust as
many irons as possible into the fire. In these
eight years he edits two magazines, begins to edit
a third, is his own chief contributor, and favors his
New York, Philadelphia, and Richmond confrères
with a perennial supply of manuscript. He is
equally dexterous in dashing off satires and in delivering Fourth of July and Commencement orations. He turns biographer, and with apparently
little effort writes the lives of three American heroes, and then adventurously tries his hand on the
romantic career of Bayard. He continues his in-
vestigations into the history of his native State, and
publishes a geography of the same. He assumes
the rôle of critic, fills his magazines with reviews
long and short, and collects the best in two volumes. He edits apocryphal plays, and serves two
years in the legislature. And in the midst of it all

he finds time for an annual visit to the North, for
jauntings through the South and Southwest, for
balls and parties in Charleston, and for the duties
of a planter at Woodlands.

Now, although the quantity of this work is not
surprising to those who have followed Simms in his
early career as a romancer, it is somewhat remarkable that he should have ceased so completely to
hobnob with outlaws, or to accompany partisans on
their midnight sallies, or to stand silent with Spanish discoverers upon their peaks in Darien (Keats
has made Cortez stand on one, so there is no reason
why they should not all be made to do the same).
Perhaps, however, a little reflection will tend to
lessen this surprise.

In the first place, it is doubtful whether the public were running after his later romances with the
eagerness they had shown when "Guy Rivers" and
"The Yemassee" appeared. American competitors
were becoming more numerous, and there were already signs that the romantic school was beginning
to lose its hold upon the world. Simms may, therefore, have thought, or else it may have been a mere
feeling with him, that it was time for him to be
turning to something new. Besides, he had always
valued his poetry more than his romances, although
he held the romancer's function in high esteem, and
he might have thought that if he could make more
money by other means, it would give him greater
opportunities for developing his poetic talents.
Then, too, he had always had a hankering for the

editor's desk and for a greater share in the conduct
of affairs than can usually fall to the lot of a romancer, weaving his far-off plots in the seclusion of
a retired country house. His mind, moreover, was
naturally a restless one; he liked to move rapidly
from one subject to another, he was fond of airing
his theories whether of politics, or art, or metaphysics. Thus the rôle of critic came easily to him;
and in a State which venerated the states-rights doctrine equally with Christianity, it was no undesir-
able thing to be elected a member of the legislature.
This state pride might also be expected to increase
his penchant for studies connected with his State's
geography and history; and from these studies he
might easily be led into the flowery paths, as they
were then, when minute or unpleasant details were
not required, of biography, especially when the subjects of his eulogy were more or less connected with
his State. In short, reasons are not wanting to explain what at first sight seems a curious step; but
the chief reason, perhaps, has not been stated.

We have seen what exclusive people the South
Carolinians *par excellence* were, and we have seen
how natural it was that a man born outside the
pale of the aristocracy should have desired to have
his talents recognized by that aristocracy. Not
that Simms had any fawning characteristics about
him. No man had less false shame than he, or had
less desire to push himself where he was not wanted;
no man saw so clearly the narrowness and unfruit-
fulness of the life led by wealthy and high-born

Southerners, and no man had less desire to lead it, or less disposition to undervalue his own self-achieved reputation. Nevertheless he did desire that the people among whom he had cast his lot should recognize the value of his work, and accord to him the honor and position that are due to great talents however displayed. In this he was right; and yet the fact was forced upon his notice every day that the upper classes of his native State did not recognize him as a credit to the State. Doubtless he chuckled,— but it was a grim chuckle,— when he heard how Lord Morpeth had silenced the Charlestonians who, when they were asked by the traveler as to the whereabouts of Simms, replied that they did not know, and intimated that he was not considered such a great man in Charleston. "Simms not a great man!" replied the astonished visitor; "then for God's sake, who is your great man?" Still, although he could chuckle sometimes, and at other times denounce this treatment in his declamatory way, or insert into his writings a few well-pointed sneers at the vapid pride of your born aristocrat, he was hurt to the heart by the indifference with which his labors were received. But could this state of things be altered? Certainly not, if he continued to write romances, for the best South Carolinians disdained to read such things. Yet were not clouds looming up over the South, was not every intellect that she could call her own needed in the war that she must wage in defense of her institutions? Would not the recognition denied to the mere romancer be gladly given to the man who, as editor, defended the South against all enemies and proved that she had a host of capable writers in all departments; who, as critic, pierced the armor of her captious assailants and carried the war into Africa by pointing out the weak places in this proud modern civilization, so called? It would certainly seem that to do less would savor of the rankest ingratitude. "Then good-by to romances, and welcome to any work that will foster my section's interest and win my countrymen's regard." So, doubtless, thought Simms the romancer, and he forthwith set about his new tasks; or, rather, he never thought anything of the kind, and drifted into his new work impelled by influences similar to those outlined above, but by no means so plainly defined. It is not often that a man in real life ponders over the propriety of taking some important step in exactly the fashion his biographer points out; but the latter, although he gives shape and coherence to influences that are really shapeless and incoherent, not infrequently gives us a true insight into his hero's character and actions.

It is obvious from the brief sketch that has already been given of Simms's varied labors during the period of eight years which this chapter is intended to cover, that many achievements and events which seemed very important   our author at the time of their accomplishment or occurrence must be passed over at the present day in comparative silence. The literary value of work done under such circumstances is naturally slight; and our main object must be to get a fair idea of Simms's remarkable versatility, and of his relations to contemporary Southern life and thought. This can best be done by grouping his labors under several convenient heads. And first of his work as editor and critic.

After the failure of the "Southern Literary Journal," in 1839, its place was supplied by a small magazine called the "Southron," which speedily went under. Simms certainly contributed one article to it, and probably more. In 1841, a Mr. P. C. Pendleton, of Savannah, who had been publishing a Southern rival to "Godey's Lady's Book," changed its name to the "Magnolia, or Southern Monthly," and in some way or other, hardly by large payments, induced Simms to become first its main contributor, then its associate editor, and finally, after the publication office had been moved to Charleston, in June, 1842, its editor in chief. Simms labored heroically, and secured contributions from the best Southern writers, such as Carruthers, Longstreet, Meek, and Charleston's mild poetess of the L. E. L. type, Miss Mary E. Lee. But a year of that climate, so fatal to literary journals, withered the promising bud, and the "Magnolia" was decently buried in June, 1843. Simms had got it talked about, however, by publishing in its columns a story entitled "The Loves of the Driver," which described in rather too suggestive a manner the amours of a negro Adonis. While critics were doubtless right in assailing this story, Simms had at least avoided a fault only too common with some modern delineators of negro manners. He had neither described the negro as an ideal being, the possessor of virtues that are seldom seen even in representatives of higher races, nor had he painted him as an absolute brute, destitute of all human traits. This ability to hold the balance even, when he is describing characters of an humble type, is to be noted in all of Simms's work.

In the meantime Mr. Whitaker, of the defunct "Literary Journal," had begun to edit a successor to the old "Southern Review" of Elliott and Legaré. This was the "Southern Quarterly Review," the first number of which appeared in January, 1842, at New Orleans, but which was shortly after published at Charleston. Whitaker soon took as associate editor Mr. J. D. B. De Bow, afterwards founder of the review that bore his name, and matters continued in this state until a number of Charleston gentlemen, who were dissatisfied with the editorship of a man not born a Southerner, bought the review and intrusted its conduct to Mr. J. Milton Clapp. This was some time about February, 1847. But Clapp was no great improvement upon Whitaker, and in March, 1849, Simms was induced to take the editorial chair. He had previously been a voluminous contributor, but he had not equaled the gentleman who wrote an article one hundred and two pages long on the French Revolution. Under his management the review improved, as we shall see in the next chapter, but he could never induce his contributors to shorten their articles or to make them more interesting. The padding to be discovered in his own papers may be excused, from the fact that even long-winded contributors were scarce.

Charleston was, however, to have the pleasure of supporting, or rather of not supporting, two other magazines. Mr. William C. Richards, an Englishman by birth, for some years connected with Southern periodical literature, and afterwards a Baptist minister at Providence, R. I., had been publishing at Penfield, Georgia, a small magazine rejoicing in the meaningless title of the "Orion." But the "Orion" outgrew Penfield, and at the solicitation of Simms and others it was transferred to Charleston. In that unwholesome atmosphere it lived a year, possibly two; nor did it die for lack of aid from Simms. He wrote articles and poems without number for it, and he edited it during the very oppressive months of July and August, 1844, when Richards was taking a holiday. How he was paid, except by the belief that he was doing his duty by his section and by his friend, is hard to determine. Still he kept the numerous books sent to him for review, and he certainly utilized his carefully prepared articles on "The Moral Character of Hamlet," as materials for a future lecture.

But contributing to the "Orion," "Godey's," "Graham's," the "Democratic Review," and the "Southern Quarterly," was not like editing a magazine of his own; so in January, 1845, the "Southern and Western Monthly Magazine and Review," often known as "Simms's Magazine," made its appearance. Whether it was its ambitious name, or the fact that Simms for the most part filled its pages with his own productions, or the air of Charleston that killed it, is uncertain. Possibly all these causes were effective; at least it is clear that after surviving twelve months it was absorbed in the "Southern Literary Messenger," that magazine becoming, in January, 1846, the "Southern and Western Literary Messenger and Review," which most ponderous title it soon dropped.

"Simms's Magazine" was not a bad one as magazines, especially Southern magazines, went then. Its editor was conscientious enough, and he persuaded a few of his Northern friends, like Evert Duyckinck and Headley, to help him out with an occasional contribution. He also relied on Meek, Albert Pike, W. C. Richards, Mrs. Caroline Lee Hentz (afterwards a prolific novelist), A. J. Requier, and a young Carolinian poet and protégé, J. M. Legaré. But his main dependence was himself and his double self, "Adrian Beaufain," whose name was appended to many lyrics. It is easy to count up over twenty-five long articles and tales of his own composition, some of which had never been published before, but which were certainly made to do good service afterwards. A glance at the bibliographical appendix will show that this editorial

work constituted only a small part of Simms's
labors for the year 1845. Certainly if ever a man
strove to make the outside world believe that his
section had a literature, Simms was that man.
·There is no need to speak here of the quality of
his work; for as he himself subsequently collected
the best of it for publication in a more permanent
form, there will be occasion shortly to be sufficiently critical.

A somewhat different piece of editorial work,
and of later date, is found in "A Supplement to the
Plays of William Shakespeare," a volume which
Simms had long planned, and which he finally succeeded in having published, in April, 1848. Seven
only of the apocryphal plays were given, and the
editor's own work was slight both in quantity and
in quality. The only play annotated with any fullness was "The Two Noble Kinsmen," and the
notes and introduction to this were mainly derived
from Charles Knight. Indeed, a cursory examination of the volume would lead to the conclusion that
it was but a piece of hack work, and therefore
scarcely worthy of mention. Such a conclusion
would be highly unjust to Simms. He really undertook the task as a labor of love, and his own
editorial and critical deficiencies were due to his
lack of education and to his Southern environment.
Ever since the days of his boyhood he had been devoted to the old drama. He had discoursed wisely
on Shakespeare in the "Southern Literary Gazette,"
and more lately in the "Orion," and he had never

tired of jotting down his supposed textual emenda-
tions. He had a fancy for digging out quotations
from little-read plays, and setting them at the heads
of his chapters, and he not infrequently put them
into the mouths of his characters, regardless of the
proprieties of time and place. His library was
doubtless better supplied with works relating to the
drama than that of any private gentleman in the
South; and he was constantly advising his friends
and readers to take up his favorite study.

But though Simms had become an enthusiastic
student of what is, perhaps, the greatest body of
literature the world has ever seen, he could not
make himself a scholarly student. His early
training and associations, nay, his life-long environment, were against this. The vicissitudes of his
youth had deprived his mind of that quality of re-
pose which is essential for scholarly work. Simms
was restless and aggressive. The scorn the Carolina literati had bestowed upon him had created in
him a spirit of defiance and of self-reliance almost
amounting to conceit. Such a man could display
great energy, but no great patience; could be good
at dashing off outlines, but not at filling in. It is
no wonder, then, that as a critic he is often discovered to be shallow where he thought himself profound, that he is never subtle or penetrating, and
that he is at his best when he forgets his theories
and his second-hand erudition, and talks simply
about things he has seen and heard and done.

We are now prepared to conclude our survey of

Simms's critical work by a brief examination of the two volumes entitled "Views and Reviews in American Literature, History, and Fiction" (1846). Under this somewhat grandiloquent title were collected the best of his contributions to his own and other magazines. It is true that he continued to do critical work to the day of his death, but he never surpassed the essays here collected, and except for an occasional reference there will be little necessity for further comment in this connection. Of the eleven essays thus republished, three deserve favorable mention. These are "Daniel Boone," an unpretending sketch of a character Simms could fully appreciate; "The Writings of James Fenimore Cooper," a sound critical essay with no trace of unworthy rivalry on Simms's part; and "Weems, the Biographer and Historian," a gossipy article, which would almost bear republication to-day. In 1852, Bryant wrote of the paper on Cooper as "a critical essay of great depth and discrimination, to which I am not sure that anything hitherto written on the same subject is fully equal."

The most elaborate essay is styled, "The Epochs and Events of American History, as suited to the Purposes of Art in Fiction." This was the final form Simms gave to two lectures previously delivered before the Georgia Historical Society, and here he allowed his theories to run away with him. In consequence the crudities of the production attract more attention than the vigor of thought which

is occasionally visible. For example, when he attempts to show how a future dramatist can use the
story of Arnold's treason (he tried it himself), and
tells us of Washington that, "while his sword
achieves the death of the foreign emissary (André),
his stern voice, rising preëminent over all the sounds
of battle, shall send the traitor (Arnold), hell in
his heart and curses on his lips, to the inglorious
scaffold, which the audience does not see," he is
simply amusing, without in the least intending to be
so. One can perceive, however, that constant writing has simplified Simms's style, and one concludes, therefore, that he has not crystallized.

From the point of view of his contemporaries the
most important work done by Simms during these
crowded years is, perhaps, to be found in his four
biographies of Marion (1844), Captain John Smith
(1846), the Chevalier Bayard (1848), and General
Greene (1849). Even now the books have some
value as popular and uncritical accounts of the romantic heroes with whom they are concerned, and
the wide circulation of the two first mentioned is a
proof that Simms must have done some good by fa-
miliarizing his countrymen with the noble deeds of
noble men. Of these four works the one that enjoyed most popular favor would seem to be the least
interesting. "The Life of Marion" went through
three editions in three months, and is known to
have reached as many as ten; yet, if it is not posi-
tively dull, it fails to charm one as a life of such a
fascinating character ought to do. But perhaps

this judgment comes from a comparison of the Marion of the revolutionary romances with the Marion of the biography, which is hardly a fair procedure. The life of the magniloquent founder of the Virginia Colony was a more interesting and scarcely less popular production; but the biography on which Simms took most pains and which he fancied most was very little read. It is not often that one can agree with an author in his estimate of his own work; but it is not difficult to share with Simms his liking for "The Life of the Chevalier Bayard." True, there is no great research visible in its pages; but then a general reader does not usually care for great research when a romantic character is in question. It suffices that this book reads smoothly, that it treats of interesting men and times in an easy and acceptable way, that it makes no pretense of being a work of erudition. If Simms had always used such simple English as is to be found here, he would have to-day a much higher rank as a writer.

"The Life of Nathanael Greene" deserves a special paragraph only from the fact that it purports to be edited by Simms. There is, however, no reason to believe that he did not write it. He speaks, it is true, of "revising for the publishers the manuscript of the present work;" but Simms's ear-marks are visible through the whole of it, and he had had such a biography in contemplation for years. Be this as it may, the book is an orthodox and decorous biography and, on the whole, well written. Of course no one would now think of consulting it as an authority, but Professor Channing is right when he tells us that it "has at least the merit of being interesting."[1] The reader will probably conclude from all that has been said that if Simms did not add permanently to his reputation by these biographies, he nevertheless enabled the public to get much useful information in a pleasant way, and also added to an income which was by no means too large for an ever-growing family.

This income could not have been much increased by the lectures and orations and political harangues which occupied what might be called spare hours, if Simms could be conceived as having had any such luxuries. They helped, however, to spread his reputation, and doubtless made him think that before long he would be recognized as a political leader. Several of them were published, but none needs any special notice. One delivered at the University of Alabama, in December, 1843, seems to have been followed by the degree of Doctor of Laws, the honorable abbreviation for which was afterwards tacked on to his name on all occasions by his admirers, and gave those who did not like him an opportunity for indulging in a little sarcasm. Simms himself modestly wished that the degree had not been conferred upon him, for in his soberer moments he did not fail to remember and regret his lack of thorough scholarship.

Some of his orations were political in character,

---

[1] In Winsor's "Narrative and Critical History," etc., vi. 512.

and the one delivered at Aikin, South Carolina, on
the 4th of July, 1844, was certainly bold enough
in its utterances to convince all classes of South
Carolinians that Simms would lend his support to
any scheme of Southern aggrandizement that the
more violent leaders of the aristocracy might counsel. It was probably as a reward for this boldness
that he found himself elected a member of the
state legislature from Barnwell County for the session of 1844–46. Although his career in the lower
house of that body does not seem to have done
much to advance his political interests, he soon became noted as a forcible speaker and a stanch upholder of the cause of his section. For drafting
resolutions against the protective system, the
schemes of abolitionists, and the opposition to the
annexation of Texas, the pen of so ready a writer
was naturally in demand. He never needed preparation, but could always be relied on for a telling
speech against lukewarm members who thought
that their State was speeding too fast along its
eccentric path. His talents commanded respect,
and his hearty manners and his fund of good stories won him many friends. Some of these were in
the habit of writing to him in after years, and wishing that he were still in the House to thunder out
his patriotic speeches as in the days of yore. But
they did more than remember him when he was absent; for, as a reward for his honorable services,
it was proposed to give him a strictly honorable
office, that of lieutenant-governor. According to

the Columbia correspondent of the "Courier," it
was believed up to the day of the election that
Simms would receive the office; but on December
8, 1846, the aforesaid correspondent wrote to his
paper as follows: "The Hon. David Johnson was
elected governor to-day, without opposition, and
the Hon. W. M. Cain, of Pineville, lieutenant-
governor, by a majority of one vote over William
Gilmore Simms, Esq."

What happened in the one day that intervened
between these announcements can only be left to
conjecture. Perhaps Simms had made enemies as
well as friends by his boldness; perhaps there was
some secret log-rolling. It is certain, however, that
he never afterwards came so near to getting an
office, and his political aspirations, if not crushed,
must have received a great check. But his influence upon the policy of his State and section was to
be none the less felt, and it is not certain that his
happiness or his usefulness or his income would
have been increased by his election. He did not,
however, give up public speaking because his voice
was no longer to be heard in legislative halls.
Paul Hayne tells us how, when in the midsummer
of 1847 he was an interested boy listener at a public meeting in Charleston, a cry arose for "Simms,
Gilmore Simms." He describes how the author
whose romances had time and again thrilled him
with delight "came forward with a slow, stately
step under the full blaze of the chandeliers, a man
in the prime of life, tall, vigorous, and symmetri-

cally formed." He gives an animated account of
the effect produced upon him by the noble head
with its "conspicuously high forehead, finely developed in the regions of ideality," by the frequent,
unrestrained gesticulation of the speaker as with
almost grotesque emphasis of voice and manner he
denounced certain editors that had aroused his ire
by their treatment of exciting topics connected with
the Mexican war.

Having now passed in rapid review the labors of
the editor and critic, the biographer, the orator
and politician, we are left to consider the short
stories and poetry that saw the light during these
busy years. The volumes that fall under these
categories would be considered numerous for any
other man than Simms; but though numerous, they
can be easily grouped, and only two will require
special notice. And as poetry rightfully has the
place of honor over prose, we may consider Simms's
poetry first, in spite of the fact that it is only by
courtesy that we can apply the term "poetry" at all
in his case.

Seven volumes of serious verse and one lengthy
satire of local interest are certainly a sufficient
tribute for one man to pay to his muse in eight
years. It is true that some of these productions do
not extend to a hundred pages, but they amount in
the aggregate to a formidable quantity of printed
matter. First in order of time was "Donna Florida" (1843), an avowed imitation of Byron, in
which Ponce de Leon takes the place of Don Juan.

This youthful production had been left unfinished, and Simms's long preface gave no sufficient reason for its subsequent publication, especially in an incomplete form. Next came a series of sonnets entitled "Grouped Thoughts and Scattered Fancies" (1845), which may be left for fuller consideration. This small volume was followed by a larger one, called "Areytos, or Songs of the South" (1846). Simms had borrowed the word "Areyto" from the native language of Cuba, and he did his best to introduce it into English, being ignorant, perhaps, of the fact that Sir Philip Sidney, in the "Defence of Poesy," had forestalled him by nearly three hundred years. The collection graced by this pretty name consisted in the main of juvenile love lyrics. It was followed by "Lays of the Palmetto" (1848), a patriotic tribute to the valor of the Carolina regiment of that name in the Mexican war, and by the cumbrously named volume "Atalantis: a Story of the Sea; With the Eye and the Wing — Poems chiefly Imaginative." In the latter publication he included a revised edition of "Atalantis," and a collection of such of his poems as seemed to have their source in the imagination rather than in the fancy. This Wordsworthian experiment was hardly successful, except for a very spirited paraphrase of Isaiah xxi., entitled "The Burden of the Desert." The long list of his poetical ventures is concluded by "The Cassique of Accabee" (1849) — a pathetic Indian tale which is even now not unreadable — and by "Sabbath

Lyrics " (1849), a collection of biblical paraphrases
more remarkable for their pious than for their
poetical qualities. An unpublished work of this
period is an adaptation of Shakespeare's "Timon
of Athens" for the stage, made at the request of
Edwin Forrest. For some reason or other the
manuscript was left on Simms's hands, and it now
lies among the numerous literary effects bequeathed
by our author to his heirs.

In considering the volume of sonnets ambitiously
entitled "Grouped Thoughts and Scattered Fancies," it is only fair to say at the outset that they
will be used as a text to point some remarks on
the chief characteristics of Southern poetry in general. Their intrinsic value is slight; nevertheless
Simms thought fit to publish them twice, once serially in the "Southern Literary Messenger," and
shortly afterwards in a tiny volume. There are
eighty-four of these quatorzains, — for with a few
exceptions they cannot be called sonnets, — most of
them evidently modeled upon Wordsworth's least
meritorious efforts of a similar nature. Occasionally a legitimate sonnet of the Shakespearean type
occurs, — since Mr. Theodore Watts's discussion
of the sonnet in "The Encyclopædia Britannica"
one is warranted in writing thus, — and then the
poet is evidently at his best. The wonder is that
he did not see that the stricter his form, the better
his poetry became. But neither he nor any other
ante-bellum Southern poet seems to have seen this
fundamental truth of poetic art. The Southern

poet was too easy-going to succeed in any form of
verse that required patience and skill. He preferred a less hampering stanza than the sonnet in
which to display his genius, and so, as might have
been expected, he seldom displayed any genius at
all. Mr. Stedman was right when he said "that
a collection of the earlier Southern poetry worth
keeping would be a brief anthology;" but he was
wrong when he spoke of Wilde and Pinkney singing " their Lovelace lyrics," unless indeed he had
reference to those careless, slipshod poems that
make one wonder how they could ever have been
written by the author of "To Althea from Prison."
It is almost an insult to the memory of the real
Lovelace to speak of his perfect work in connection with even the best of the early Southern lyrics.
For although Pinkney's "A Health" and Wilde's
"My Life is like a Summer Rose" and Cooke's
"Florence Vane" are poems of decided merit, they
nevertheless fall far short of that perfection which
is characteristic of the best Caroline lyrics. The
present writer will not be suspected of denying that
in many respects these Southern cavaliers, who
sang of love and wine and sunny skies, were like
their dashing gallant prototypes, who sang of their
lady-loves and fought for King Charles. They
were alike in many particulars and they took much
the same easy view of their art, but — and the difference is immense — the Southern poet never by
any chance sang one pure and perfect strain; while
Montrose and Lovelace and Suckling are names

that can never be dissociated from the memory of perfect songs. To take but one example, there is little doubt that more than one Southern gentleman with a taste for pleasant rhyming loved his section as well and fought for her cause as nobly as that ill-fated but glorious soldier and poet, James, Marquis of Montrose; and yet, though volumes have been filled with the verses written by these gallant men in behalf of the cause for which they fought, though such lyrics as Randall's "My Maryland" and Timrod's "Charleston" are enshrined in our memories, all their volumes and all their poems would not compensate us for the loss of those eight lines beginning "Great, good, and just," wherein Montrose mourned the death of his unfortunate sovereign.

Now while it may be difficult to explain why the Cavaliers of England should, with their known indifference with regard to a purely literary reputation, have written such perfect songs, it is not so difficult to see why the cavalier poets of the South failed to equal them in their flights. The influence of the age of Elizabeth had not yet died from the England of Charles the First. There was little that was commonplace about the life that Lovelace and Suckling led. But life in the South, in spite of its picturesqueness in certain directions, was largely commonplace with respect to the things of the mind. A Southerner had to think in certain grooves, or else have his opinions smiled at as harmless eccentricities. His imagination was dwarfed because his mind was never really free, also because his love of ease rarely permitted him to exercise the faculty. He had no incitement to high poetic achievement from the influence shed upon him by great poets of a generation just passed. The models before him were those of statesmen and men of action, and he lost his chances for distinction if he proposed to himself any others. Besides, he had no critics, no audience whose applause was worth having. His easy verses were received with a smile by his friends or with extravagant praise by an editor only too glad to fill his columns. When praise was so readily obtained, he naturally took the easiest way to obtain it.

A study of Southern sonnets will prove the truth of these remarks. The number of regular and commendable sonnets written in the South before the war might, one may venture to say without having read all the quatorzains published, be numbered on the fingers of two hands. Even Hayne, by far the best of Southern sonneteers, wrote such of his sonnets as are really worthy of preservation after the war had taught him the necessity of patience and labor. Timrod, who had a greater poetic genius than any of his contemporaries, failed conspicuously in his sonnets; and this, not because he had nothing to say, but because he did not see the necessity of choosing a proper metrical form. It is not proposed to claim that there are only three forms that the sonnet can assume, but to maintain that poets who use other forms must make good

their choice by the success of their experiments.
And if a poet goes on writing in forms that are
obviously not successful, it is a sign that he does
not appreciate the first principles of his art. But
this is precisely what Simms and the galaxy of
small poets that surrounded him did for years.
Hence, nearly all their poetic work, especially their
sonnets, must be considered as having failed.
They could occasionally produce a good verse or
two, they not infrequently had something to say;
but their poems rarely approximated perfection, and
so perished. Then, too, these poets lacked self-
control in other respects. They let their emotions
run away with them, and were forever gushing.
They could not stop to think whether the subjects
they had chosen were capable of poetic treatment.
Simms wrote twelve sonnets on "Progress in
America," and an equal number on the Oregon
question, and one is thankful that he did not see
fit to furnish Wordsworth's "Sonnets upon the
Punishment of Death," with a companion series
upon "The Benefits of Lynch Law." They were
also more attracted by poetry of a rhetorical kind
than by purer and simpler styles; but then a fond-
ness for gorgeous rhetoric was a common Southern
weakness. These remarks may be brought to a
close with the observation that while the faults that
have been mentioned are more or less characteristic of all early American poets, they are preëminently characteristic of Southern poets, Poe alone
excepted. For Poe was an artist, whatever one

may think of the subjects on which he exercised his art.

During these busy years Simms published little in his proper department of prose fiction that need occupy our attention. In the latter part of 1844 appeared a ghost story entitled "Castle Dismal." Poe praised this story highly, and as its theme lay in Poe's own province, his opinion is entitled to carry much weight; a modern reader, however, might be inclined to set less store by the supernatural portions of the story than by the description of the old homestead from which it took its name. Poe also praised, but less highly, another novelette published shortly afterwards and entitled "Helen Halsey." This was a "border" story, but it was honorably distinguished from "Richard Hurdis" and its class by being shorter and by having a smaller complement of crimes and casualties.

But the year 1845 saw the publication of a book which seems to have marked for his contemporaries the culminating point of Simms's reputation as a writer of fiction. This was the first series of the collected tales known as "The Wigwam and Cabin." A second series appeared in February of the next year. These volumes contained thirteen of the best short stories that Simms had contributed to the various magazines and annuals. As the name imported, they were concerned with pioneer and Indian life; and they had two obvious advantages over the romances he had previously published on similar subjects. They were shorter, and so gave little room for the diffuseness which had so constantly characterized his more elaborate works; and, depending as they did on a single dramatic incident, they furnished no opportunity for the development of a plot in which virtuous heroes should fall into all sorts of diabolical traps set for them by professional villains. Not that the villain does not appear in these tales; he does most decidedly, but he is precluded from running through a long course of crimes which must be described with a painful accuracy. It is one thing to be present at a crime that is quickly over; it is another thing to be forced to take cognizance of every revolting circumstance connected with a crime.

The first tale in the collection was entitled "Grayling, or ' Murder will out.' " Upon its first publication in "The Gift," for 1842, the London "Examiner " had said: "This is an American ghost story, and without exception the best one we ever read. The *rationale* of the whole matter of such appearances is given with fine philosophy and masterly interest. We never read anything more perfect or more consummately told."[1] Now in 1845 Poe said in his "Broadway Journal: " "We have no hesitation in calling it the best ghost story we ever read. It is full of the richest and most vigorous imagination, is forcibly conceived, and detailed throughout with a degree of artistic skill which has had no parallel among American story-tellers since the epoch of Brockden Brown."[2]

[1] Quoted in the *Knickerbocker* for November, 1841.
[2] The *Broadway Journal* for October 4, 1845.

This testimony to the merits of "Grayling" cannot be regarded lightly; but it would seem to be a little extravagant. The tale is certainly well told; but Poe or Hawthorne would have told it much better. They would have paid more attention to details, and thus have provided a more artistic setting; in other words, they would have thrown an air of glamour over the various events described, and so have strengthened the spell that the successful narrator of a ghost story must cast over his hearers or readers. Simms, on the contrary, pays little attention to details, and tells the story just as we may imagine his grandmother told it to him. Of course it required no little power to do this, but by adopting this simpler method of narration he to some extent lost his hold over such of his readers as were prone to disbelief in the supernatural. And he marred the symmetry of his work when he appended the four or five pages in which his father was represented as giving a rationalistic explanation of the mysterious events that had just been related. Simms's readers could easily have supplied this explanation for themselves; and it is hard to see how the critic in the "Examiner," who may have been Albany Fonblanque, could have seen a "fine philosophy" in a process of rationalizing so perfectly simple and obvious. But "Grayling" is easily accessible, and the reader who is sufficiently interested in the matter can judge for himself as to the merits of the story.[1]

[1] It is given in Griswold's *Prose Writers.*

As a whole "The Wigwam and Cabin" was a readable collection of tales which deserved a fair portion of the praise it got. It was certainly better than any of the similar volumes Simms had previously published, and it surpassed most of the collections of short stories with which American authors had hitherto favored their readers. Poe and Hawthorne are of course excepted from this category, for they were artists; and Irving, in spite of "Rip Van Winkle," can hardly lay claim to the title of story-writer. The book with which it was most frequently compared at the time of its publication was Judge Hall's "Legends of the West;" but to this it was manifestly superior. The press at large joined with Poe in its praise, and even the sleepy "North American Review" thought Simms worthy of an article. Up to this time it had studiously ignored him, while lauding much inferior romancers; now, through the pen of Professor Felton, it snubbed his more elaborate works, whether of fiction or criticism, but condescended to say a few pleasant things of "The Wigwam and Cabin." Simms had had no great love for New England and her writers for some time, and this article did not increase his affection. It was some compensation, however, to find that in less than a year his tales had been translated into German, and that soon after this an Aberdeen firm had introduced them in the mother country.

This chapter may be closed with a brief account of Simms's social life during these laborious years.

It would seem at first thought that he must have
been a mere writing machine, but this was by no
means the case; for he never sunk the man in the
author, and never forgot that there were other people in the world besides himself. There was, of
course, little to occupy him at Woodlands besides
writing, and the years were marked for the household by the birth of a child or the advent of a less
permanent visitor like Bryant. But death and
birth are inseparable, and Woodlands was often
in mourning. Of the six children born between
1839 and 1848, three died in infancy. But the
fourth child was a son who was destined to live and
to transmit his father's name. Two daughters also
lived, one named Mary Lawson in honor of
Simms's old friend, the other Chevillette Eliza,
after her mother.

In his adopted county Simms was a marked
and well liked man. At Barnwell Court-house he
had a great admirer in Mr. A. P. Aldrich, an
able member of the bar; and a mile from Woodlands lived Gen. David Jamison, another friend,
afterwards president of the convention that took
South Carolina out of the Union. With these two
gentlemen Simms used to exchange frequent visits;
and many were the glasses of hot whiskey punch
consumed, and many were the political discussions
started, as hot and intoxicating as the punch, but
by no means as harmless. Another warm friend
was James H. Hammond, governor in 1842 and
afterwards United States senator. Simms and

Jamison used often to ride over to Hammond's plantation, "Silver Bluff," on the Savannah River; and there more punch was consumed and more political scheming indulged in. Hammond was already looked up to as one not unlikely to take Calhoun's place when that great man should be gathered to his fathers. His orations and pamphlets were destined to have considerable effect on the public mind, but few of them ever saw the light until they had been submitted to Simms for revision.

About the 15th of May, the family were accustomed to migrate to Charleston, where Simms owned a house. Here he found more congenial society and a less monotonous life. Among his special friends were Dr. Samuel Gilman, the pastor of the Unitarian Church, and his better known wife, Mrs. Caroline Gilman, whose "Recollections of a Southern Matron" still retains its value as an interesting and old-fashioned description of a very old-fashioned society. To this lady's exemplary little journal, "The Southern Rose," Simms had long ago been a contributor. Other friends were J. Milton Clapp, a man of some scholarship; Dr. Samuel Henry Dickson, one of the most cultivated physicians of the city; the Rev. James W. Miles, a remarkable instance of a Southern clergyman steeped in German metaphysics; William Porcher Miles, his brother, mayor of the city in 1849, and afterwards member of Congress; and finally the witty Richard Yeadon, a veteran journalist and

leader of the bar. There were, of course, other
men of note with whom he was on terms of more
or less friendly intimacy: Petigru, William J.
Grayson, Mitchell King, the eccentric lawyer, and
Col. A. H. Brisbane, professor of belles-lettres at
the Citadel Academy. But with none of these men
was Simms on such terms of intimacy as he afterwards was with a coterie of bright young spirits
which shall be described in good time. He was
too much inclined to play the leader to suit the
tastes of men of his own age, and nowhere is this
Johnsonian tendency of his better shown than in
a little volume entitled "Father Abbot," which appeared in 1849. This consisted of a series of letters originally contributed to the " Mercury," and
published in book form only to oblige a firm of impecunious printers. In it Simms appeared as a
Charlestonian Christopher North, — Bryant used
to compare him to Wilson both in temperament and
in personal appearance, — the burden of whose
monologue was that Charlestonians should not race
North in search of health and scenery when they
could obtain all they wanted nearer home, on
Sullivan's Island, where the officers stationed at
Fort Moultrie were good hands at drawing a cork.
It should be mentioned, perhaps, that Simms
was prevented from going North the summer that
"Father Abbot" was written, through fear of the
cholera.[1]

[1] One of the most interesting citizens of Charleston at this
period was Charles Fraser the painter, who, like his friend All-

Of these visits North, which he so much deprecated in others, and against which he wrote a violent article in the "Southern Quarterly" that
attracted hostile criticism, we have only a few
fleeting memorials in the shape of a letter or two
received from Duyckinck after his return, or of a
stray personal notice in a magazine or newspaper.
It is known, however, that he was a familiar figure
at literary receptions, and that he was more or less
acquainted with all the prominent Knickerbocker
authors. With Halleck and Irving and Cooper
his relations were friendly, but he was probably
never intimate with them. He was frequently
thrown, however, with Tuckerman, Cornelius Mat-

ston, not infrequently wrote some sweet verses. It is not known
that Simms was at all intimate with Fraser, but they had a brief
correspondence on a subject which is of some interest to students
of Southern life and manners. It illustrates very strikingly the
growing feeling of hostility in Carolina to anything hailing from
New England. In one way or another it had been intimated to
Simms that Richard Henry Dana the elder would like to deliver
in Charleston some of his lectures on Shakespeare. Simms was
at Woodlands at the time, but he entered enthusiastically into
the project, and wrote at once to Fraser as a prominent citizen of
Charleston, that steps ought to be taken immediately to invite
Mr. Dana to the city. Fraser wrote a very chilling reply, on December 20, 1849, saying that Dana's whole object was to levy a
contribution on the South " in pursuance of a system in which the
scholar and the mechanic of New England are always alike happy
to exert their best efforts." He continued that if Mr. Dana came
he (Fraser) might be induced to go to hear him, but he declined to
take any part in inviting him. This unworthy treatment of one
man of culture by another is a sad proof of the evil effects being
wrought by slavery, and it is all the more curious when we remember that Dana was Washington Allston's brother-in-law.

thews, William A. Jones, then a prominent contributor to the "Democratic" and other reviews, Prosper M. Wetmore, F. O. C. Darley, C. F. Briggs, and the latter's sometime partner Edgar Allan Poe. Of the fair authoresses whom Poe so much affected, we hear little; but Duyckinck does occasionally remind him of Mrs. Kirkland and Mrs. Ellet. In New York, too, he was accustomed to meet some of his Southern literary friends like Gayarré and Wilde, and possibly Meek.

There is no need to waste space conjecturing how he spent his time while on these trips. They were not all holiday, for he invariably had proofs to correct. Parke Godwin tells us that he used often to drop into Bryant's office, and there endeavor to convince all who would listen to him that slavery was a much slandered institution. He also made New York a centre from which to make excursions to Nahant and Rockaway; to Great Barrington, where his eldest daughter was at school; and to Poughkeepsie, where he visited William Wilson the poet-publisher, whose son, General James Grant Wilson, has pleasantly described a drive which he took with Simms and Duyckinck to visit the retired Paulding at "Placentia." [1]

But perhaps the relations of Simms with the only Southern man of letters who was his superior will be of more interest than his relations with the

[1] This visit took place in 1854, but the date is of little consequence. See Appleton's *Cycl. Am. Biog.* art. Paulding.

Knickerbocker writers, and they are certainly more fully recorded. After a stinging review of "The Partisan," Poe seems to have paid little attention to Simms until, as editor of "Graham's," in 1841, he wrote or else allowed to be published a very favorable notice of "The Kinsmen," in which that romance was proclaimed to be the best that had been published in America since "The Pathfinder." In 1844, he devoted a few sentences to Simms in the scrappy "Marginalia" he was publishing in the "Democratic Review." Simms had evidently risen greatly in his estimation, for he wrote: "Mr. Simms has abundant faults — or had; among which inaccurate English, a proneness to revolting images, and pet phrases are the most noticeable. Nevertheless, leaving out of the question Brockden Brown and Hawthorne (who are each a *genus*), he is immeasurably the best writer of fiction in America. He has more vigor, more imagination, more movement, and more general capacity than all our novelists (save Cooper) combined." [1] Poe has sometimes been accused of unduly favoring Southern writers; but there can be little question that he really believed what he said of Simms.

In 1845 [2] Poe appeared as a still more zealous champion of our romancer. He was now editing the "Broadway Journal" on his own responsibil-

---

[1] I follow the reprint in Poe's *Works* (N. Y. 1871), vol. iii. p. 510.

[2] About this time Poe must have met Simms frequently at the house of their common friend, Lawson.

ity, Briggs having withdrawn, and he was very
anxious to secure contributors and subscribers.
He evidently recognized Simms's influence, especially in the South, and made a dead set to capture
him. Every time he could decently do so he wrote
an enthusiastic notice of "Simms's Magazine,"
carefully selecting for praise articles which he
must have shrewdly suspected to have been written
by Simms. He did not stop here. William A.
Jones had written a paper for the "Democratic"
on "American Humor," in which he spoke dispar-
agingly of Simms's romantic and poetic efforts.
Poe replied to him in one of those stinging pieces
of personal criticism which he alone could write.
Then "The Wigwam and Cabin" appeared, and
he seized the opportunity to write a long and appreciative review of Simms's work in general, announcing at the same time, in more than one number, that Simms would be a regular contributor to
the "Journal." But an unknown writer in the
"Mirror" dared to criticise Poe for his attempt
to make out that Simms was a better writer than
Cooper or Brockden Brown (which, in the case of
the latter at least, he had not done), and Poe again
took up the cudgels, evaded the main issue, and
went off in a tirade against Fay's "Norman Leslie," and the smallness of the Mr. Asterisk who
had dared to criticise him in the "Mirror." In
the mean time the subject of all this praise was re-
paying his upholder by publishing in the "Journal" some of the trashiest of his shorter poems.

Up to the last issue of the paper, Poe continued his praise and Simms his sonnets and epigrams. It is almost impossible not to believe that Poe was trying by every means in his power to secure Simms's friendship. What he expected to get in return, except poor sonnets and small patronage, is doubtful; but it is at least certain that Simms was never so continuously puffed in his life as in the two volumes of the "Broadway Journal" for the year 1845. Poe subsequently republished in "Godey" [1] his review of "The Wigwam and Cabin," and he doubtless, to the day of his death, stood by his protégé, Simms on his part retaining warm memories of his able and eccentric critic.

[1] See also Poe's *Works*, vol. iii. pp. 272–5.

CHAPTER VI.

ROMANTIC DREAMS AND POLITICAL NIGHTMARES.

DURING the twelve years from 1850 to 1861 in-
clusive, Simms lived in two very different worlds.
In both he dreamed dreams and saw visions, the
difference between which has been briefly indicated
in the heading of this chapter. He went back to
his old trade of romance writing, and added sub-
stantially to the reputation he had already acquired; he went forward with the rasher spirits
of his section, and floundered about in the bogs of
doctrinaire politics, in the most horrible world
of political nightmares that had lured a brave people on to their destruction, since the days of the
French Revolution. It will be necessary, therefore, for his biographer to pass and repass between
these different worlds; and if he must regret the
time that has to be spent in the world of nightmares, he will at least be able to derive some satisfaction — and he trusts that the same will be the
case with his readers — from his sojourn, temporary
and fleeting though it be, in the world of romance.
But as a bad beginning makes a good ending, it
may be as well to begin with the nightmares; and
if the reader wonders how any good can come out

of nightmares, he is requested to preserve his patience for a while.

When, in the early months of 1849, Simms allowed the gentlemen proprietors of the "Southern Quarterly Review" to engage his services as editor, at the small salary of one thousand dollars, he knew very well that he was making a rash experiment, but he also knew very well what he proposed to do. He knew that as his salary was guaranteed by the publisher only, a man in wretched health and notoriously impecunious, it was not likely that he would see a penny of his money; he knew also that he would have infinite difficulty in securing contributors and subscribers, and that all the shortcomings of the review would be fathered upon him. But he still felt sure that the cause of the South, which he believed in with all the intensity of his nature, needed a weighty organ, and he felt in himself an indomitable energy that would overcome many obstacles. In all this he judged wisely. The publisher did die in a year heavily in his debt. Contributors and subscribers were hard to get, and they showered letters upon him complaining of typographical mistakes in their uninteresting articles, of the fact that their copies were lost in the mails, or never sent from Charleston, and of a thousand other small matters for which Simms was not responsible. If the publishers neglected to answer a letter (and they did things in a slipshod way in the printing offices of slow-going Charleston), Simms was immediately attacked for it, although at the time he was far away at Woodlands, cudgeling his brains for the four or five articles he needed to make up the contents of a review that seldom contained more than ten.

And yet, in spite of all these difficulties, he achieved something like success, certainly greater success than would have attended the labors of any other man in the South. He took the review when it had reached a condition of worthlessness not easily to be conceived. In two years he had made it a very respectable publication, comparing not unfavorably with its Boston contemporary, the "North American." From paying nothing to his contributors, he advanced to the almost unheard-of extravagance of paying the best of them a dollar a page. It is true that the new publishers often dishonored the drafts drawn on them by eager contributors, — a proceeding which drew down on Simms's head vials of wrath, — but still some payments were made, and the quality of the articles improved accordingly. He himself got part of his salary in money and part in the free printing of his books and pamphlets. And all the while he managed, if not to satisfy, at least not to alienate the thirty-six gentlemen proprietors.

His first proceeding was to obtain contributors; and in this undertaking his large acquaintance with the leading men of all sections stood him in good stead. His main dependence was, of course, on South Carolina. From that State he got promises of assistance from ex-Governor Hammond and his brother, M. C. M. Hammond (a major in the Mexican war, whose articles upon the noted battles of that unjust struggle were a chief feature of the review), from Poinsett, Mitchell King, Lieber, Grayson, De Bow, Jamison, Colonel and Mrs. D. J. McCord, Father P. N. Lynch (a well-known and cultivated Charleston priest and afterwards bishop), Rev. James W. and William Porcher Miles, William H. Trescot, B. F. Perry, Professor Fred A. Porcher, Dr. R. W. Gibbes, the antiquarian, and others of less note. Most of these gentlemen kept their promises and some were voluminous contributors. From Alabama came John A. Campbell, afterwards associate justice of the Supreme Court of the United States, Chancellor J. W. Lesesne, A. B. Meek, journalist and poet, B. F. Porter, and Dr. Nott, the ethnologist. Georgia furnished Henry R. Jackson; Florida, William H. Simmons; Mississippi, Dr. J. W. Cartwright; Missouri, W. G. Minor; and Virginia, her great apostle of secession, Beverley Tucker. A few better known names, and not confined to the South, were those of M. F. Maury, Brantz Mayer, Professor George Frederick Holmes, Henry T. Tuckerman, and William A. Jones.

As most of the articles that appeared in the "Southern Quarterly" were unsigned, it is impossible to say whether all these gentlemen were actual contributors; but from stray information gleaned from Simms's correspondence, it is certain that most of them were. It will be observed that Bev-

erley Tucker's is almost the only name that is
thoroughly identified with the cause of secession;
but the teachings of the review were none the less
directed towards this end. Simms did not, indeed, go as far as Tucker tried to push him, but
he went far enough. The absence of Calhoun's
name is no matter of surprise, for his race was
soon to be run; and if it appears to be singular
that neither Yancey, nor Toombs, nor Stephens,
nor Davis, nor R. M. T. Hunter is known to have
written for so pronounced a Southern organ, it
must be remembered that some of these gentlemen
were by no means eager for secession at any time,
certainly not at this, and also that they very probably had the politician's fear of the pitfalls that
await the unwary rusher into print. Hunter, indeed, promised Calhoun to write for the review,
but he does not appear to have kept his promise.
The great leader could make no such promise, but
he interested himself in getting other contributors, and he wrote Simms a very complimentary
letter upon the latter's assumption of his editorial
duties. Simms, it may be remarked here, had all
a South Carolinian's veneration for Calhoun, although he thought that the senator's great genius
had overshadowed and blighted the individual promise of some of the younger public men of the State.
On one occasion at least he was favored with a sight
of one of those mysterious letters which Calhoun
was in the habit of inditing to his political followers. This letter came through Colonel Brisbane,

who commented upon it as follows: "Of course you will be discreet, as he requests, with his name, but do study the matter. It will never do to be treated of in print, but *we* should know the worst, who have to guide and calm [sic] particularly the public mind. Truly, the world is deranged. The poor Pope, the poor French, the poor everybody, but worst [sic] than all, the poor Americans. Are we to fall asunder? Do return these epistles."

But how had the Union editor of 1832 become the disunion editor of 1849? The answer can be given in one word, slavery. Simms, like nearly all the rest of his party, had held in 1832 that secession was an ultimate right belonging to every State, but one to be used in dire emergencies only. He had not thought the "tariff of abominations" a sufficient cause for secession, or even for nullification; but now he thought that slavery was doomed in the Union, and that it must be preserved as a peculiar institution of the South, therefore the obvious inference was that a dire emergency had come, and that the Southern States must secede. That secession was wrong in itself was a fact that could find no lodgment in his brain or in that of any other typical Southerner. The reason for this inability to see clearly what is so obvious now to any tyro in the theory of politics, is to be found in the fact that the South was inhabited by a primitive people. The right of secession would have been disputed by few leaders of opinion in 1789; it had been alluded to by Izard in the first session of the first Congress; it had been appealed to by States north, east, and west, during the first years of the government. It would have been marvelous if the states-rights doctrine had not been firmly held during the days when the advantages of union were little known, when the States had a mutual distrust of one another, and when there was practically no national feeling except against foreigners. Besides, the states-rights doctrine was in many respects but another name for the doctrine of strict construction, — a doctrine sure to be preached by whatever party happened to be out of power. But a doctrine that could be naturally held by a Southerner in 1789 could be naturally held by a Southerner in 1850. It was merely an instance of a "survival," not of the fittest. The fact has been frequently pointed out that Southern men could think only along certain grooves, and that hence their opinions were liable to change only with respect to the intensity of conviction of those who held them. Therefore the Southerner of 1850 not only clung to the states-rights doctrine, but believed in it with a greater degree of conviction than his ancestor of 1789.

On the other hand the particularistic tendencies of the Northern States had been more or less counteracted by frequent intercourse with one another, due to the extension of commerce and public highways. Whatever was done for the moral, mental, and material progress of one State was practically done for them all. The New Englander, too, became an emigrant to what was then the West, and he carried with him a stock of religious and political ideas that acted as a leaven to public opinion wherever he took up his abode. North of Mason and Dixon's line, then, there was such a thing as a national feeling, and hence the Northerner of 1850 thought very differently on political subjects from his ancestor of 1789.

In the South there was only one thing that knit the several States together, and that was slavery. Virginia, indeed, helped to populate some of her more southerly sisters, and was therefore somewhat venerated by them; and the best families in each State knew one another, and sometimes intermarried. Still, as a rule, each State cared for itself and thought no great deal of its neighbor. Even now there are abundant traces of this insular feeling to be discovered, although it does not often get into print. Yet States knit together by slavery could not develop a true national feeling; for that there must be a consciousness of progress, a desire to share in and further a common civilization. But progress and slavery are natural enemies, and the South had no great desire to progress except in her own way, which was really retrogression. True, Southern statesmen had done much to found the Union, and even Calhoun himself was always a Union man. Nevertheless, they wanted a Union in which they could be masters, or in which they would be allowed to preserve their own customs and institutions. In other words, they wanted a hegemony or an anarchic confederacy, not a nation. Geographical and racial and other considerations demanded, however, that we should become a nation, — to say nothing of the *Zeitgeist*, — and a nation we became accordingly.

All this is trite enough, but it has to be insisted on in order that we may understand how natural it was that Simms should be able to call himself at one time a Union and states-rights man and at another time a states-rights man anxious to get out of the Union.[1] The Union was not a nation to him, and from the nature of things it could not be. It had been founded on a compact, and he could not see how it could have grown into a nation. Even Webster himself had not been clear on this point, and had argued in the teeth of history against the theory of compact, because he could not shut his eyes to the fact that in the North, East, and West we really were a nation. What puzzled Webster was certainly enough to puzzle Simms; and because we of the present day understand our constitutional history better than they did, is no reason for our concluding that either could have judged more wisely with the light he had. They lived in a transition time, and Webster had his eyes toward the future, while Simms looked back at the past. Both were products of their time and section, and if we do praise the one, we should think twice before we blame the other.

---

[1] That it was the slavery question which in a few years turned anti-nullifiers into violent secessionists will be plain to any one who makes a careful study of Legaré's letters and speeches.

Now if it was natural for Simms to believe in the right of secession, it was equally natural for him to believe that the South could not exist without slavery; and, as he saw plainly that slavery was doomed in the Union, he had a logical reason for urging instant secession. His belief in the necessity of preserving slavery was as erroneous as his belief in the right of secession; but he should not be blamed for the one any more than for the other. It has been shown in a previous chapter that the advanced views of the great Virginian statesmen on the evils of slavery could not have exerted any profound influence upon their section.[1] Those views had never been largely shared by the politicians of the more southerly States; and now when Virginia was in her decadence, it was only natural that a fiery little State, which had never liked her lack of importance in the Union, should come forward proclaiming in trumpet tones that wrong was right, and that if the rest of the world did not like the proposition, South Carolina was ready to fight for it.

Of course what was wrong to the great Virginian leaders and to the States of the North and the nations of Europe was right to South Carolina. Slavery was an institution coeval with the commonwealth itself. There were more slaves than freemen, and some little experience had been had of slave insurrections. The negro had thriven in South Carolina, and it was evident that he was

[1] The opposition to slavery in the Virginia Convention in 1829–30, came chiefly from what is now West Virginia.

there to stay; but if the schemes of the abolitionists were carried out what was to become of him?
He could not be received as the equal of his former
master; and if left to himself, he would speedily
sink into barbarism, or become dependent on the
State for his support. So argued the South Carolinian, and the more he read abolition tracts the
angrier he got. But Washington and Jefferson
had argued that slavery was morally wrong. If
that were so, then the South ought to liberate
her slaves instantly. She was not prepared to do
this, therefore slavery must be right. This was a
horrible perversion of logic, and if all men were
wont at all times to argue thus, this earth would
soon be a hell; but there were certainly many
things that conspired to blind these advocates of the
divine origin of slavery, and now that slavery is
a thing of the past, we can afford not to be too
severe in our strictures.

Perhaps it will be as well. however, to let Simms
speak for himself on some of these points. He
had made up his own mind as to the course to be
pursued with reference to slavery ever since the
publication of his review of Miss Martineau in
1837. In that publication he had agreed with
many of the English traveler's remarks on the
low tone of morals occasioned by slavery, and had
expressed his regret at the passage of laws by
South Carolina against the freeing of slaves. Yet
while he was willing to see the institution of slavery
amended, he could not for a moment contemplate

its abolition. The South must calmly and courteously explain to the North how the case stood, and perhaps all would be well. It was to be regretted, however, that the slave-trade had been forbidden instead of being regulated. The idea that it was wrong to hold a human being in bondage had gained no entrance into his mind.

A few years later we find him a little more anxious about his favorite institution; but he dreams of a perpetual series of balances between North and South by means of the wild conquests that have already been described, and he contents himself with an occasional threat of disunion if these precious schemes are not carried out. Now after the squabbles over the territory acquired from Mexico, he resigns his schemes for the preservation of the Union, and boldly challenges the rest of the world to admire and fear the South. Disunion is inevitable, but before the step is taken, the South must vindicate herself at every point. Accordingly he writes in the "Southern Quarterly" for January, 1852: —

"We beg, once for all, to say to our Northern readers, writers, and publishers, that, in the South, we hold slavery to be an especially and wisely devised institution of heaven; devised for the benefit, the improvement, and safety, morally, socially, and physically, of a barbarous and inferior race, who would otherwise perish by famine or by filth, by the sword, by disease, by waste, and destinies forever gnawing, consuming, and finally destroying."

A year later he writes in the same periodical: —

"If it be admitted that the institution of negro slavery is a wrong done to the negro, the question is at an end. No people can be justified for continuance in error and injustice. Once admit that there is a wrong and a crime, and it must be followed by expiation and atonement. In the South we think otherwise. We hold the African under moral and just titles, founded upon his characteristics, his nature, his necessities and our own; and our accountability is to the God of both races. We, alone, are in possession of the facts in the case, and our consciences are in no way troubled in relation to our rights to hold the negro in bondage. Perhaps our consciences are a thought too easy; but we believe ourselves quite equal to the argument whenever we appear before the proper tribunal. But we are a people, a nation, with arms in our hands, and in sufficient numbers to compel the respect of other nations; and we shall never submit the case to the judgment of another people, until they show themselves of superior virtue and intellect."

All this is nightmarish enough, but it seems tame compared with a few other utterances which are appended in order to show that Simms was not the only or the most extreme instance of a Southerner tortured by nightmares. In January, 1853, he allowed one of his regular contributors, Mrs. D. J. McCord, perhaps the ablest woman of her day in the South, to review "Uncle Tom's Cabin" for the "Southern Quarterly." He himself had been requested by a Philadelphia firm to write a romance of Southern life which should serve as an answer to that great book; but he had shown his good sense by declining to give any such opportunity to the world at large to indulge in invidious comparisons. He preferred the seemingly poetic justice of having the Northern woman answered by a Southern woman; but how could he help feeling the weakness of an answer which ended with such a statement as the following? "Christian slavery, in its full development, free from the fretting annoyance and galling bitterness of abolition interference, is the brightest sunbeam which Omniscience has destined for his [i. e. the negro's] existence."

The next quotation is a poetical one, taken from Mr. William J. Grayson's "The Hireling and the Slave," a work which should be studied by all those who are interested in determining what is the greatest extent of aberration allowed to a sane and cultivated mind. It is fair to say that the italics are my own.

" Hence is the negro brought by God's command
　For wiser teaching, to a foreign land ;
　If they who brought him were by Mammon driven,
　Still have they served, blind instruments of heaven ;
　And though the way be rough, the agent stern,
　No better mode, can human wits discern,
　No happier system, wealth or virtue find,
　To tame and elevate the negro mind :
　Thus mortal purposes — whate'er their mood,
　Are only means with Heaven for working good ;

And wisest they who labor to fulfil
With zeal and hope, the all directing Will."

But if Mrs. McCord thought highly of the negro's lot, the author of the following sentence was
equally satisfied with the condition of the master:
"I venture to affirm that there are no men, at any
point upon the surface of this earth, so favored in
their lot, so elevated in their natures, so just in
their duties, so up to the emergencies and so ready
for the trials of their lives, as are the six million
masters in the Southern States."

It will hardly surprise the reader to learn that
this description of a new Utopia, lying to the south
of Mason and Dixon's line, was inserted in a speech
delivered by a gentleman of Charleston, before the
South Carolina legislature, on the propriety of re-
opening the foreign slave trade.

But these quotations from printed sources are by
no means so interesting or so valuable as some ex-
cerpts that may be given from a correspondence
that has never yet been published. Among the
first persons to whom Simms applied for contributions for his review was Beverley Tucker, of Virginia. Tucker was then (1849) sixty-five years old,
and within two years of his death. The half-brother of John Randolph, of Roanoke, he displayed
many of the qualities of that eccentric genius and
came largely under his influence. After practicing
law and serving as circuit judge in Missouri, he
returned to Virginia, and was in 1834 elected to
the chair of law in William and Mary College, a

position which he held for the rest of his life, and in which he exercised great influence on the rising generation. His Missouri experiences furnished him with material for his first novel, "George Balcombe," a work which Poe and Simms praised highly, and which with a little more care might have been made a success. His remarkable and almost prophetic "Partisan Leader" is too well known to require comment. But his chief influence on his generation was exerted by means of his lectures and by his correspondence with public men. In his extreme and able advocacy of states-rights doctrines his career parallels to some extent that of Judge William Smith, of South Carolina, to whom reference was made in a former chapter.

Simms had no personal knowledge of Tucker, but he admired the latter's novels, and he felt that the old professor would sympathize with the political objects of the "Quarterly." He did not mistake his man; for Tucker was until his death the ablest supporter the review had, and moreover he became one of Simms's warmest friends.

Many letters passed between them, most of which have been preserved. They met only once, in the summer of 1851, at Richmond; but they poured out their hopes and fears in their letters as though they had known each other for years. Both were fluent and characteristic letter writers, and it is to be hoped that some day the portion of their correspondence which survives may be given to the public. The scope of this work precludes anything but extracts.

On January 30, 1850, Simms wrote from Woodlands, whither he had just returned from a visit, with Jamison, to Hammond. After describing how they had drunk Tucker's health, he went on as follows: —

"We greatly wished for your presence, and concluded with the congratulatory thought that the formation of the new republic would bring us wonderfully nearer to one another. The idea grows upon us rapidly, and we are pleased to think upon the Southern people. I have long since regarded the separation as a now inevitable necessity. The Union depends wholly upon the sympathies of the contracting parties, and these are lost entirely. I have no hope and no faith in compromises of any kind; and am not willing to be gulled by them any longer. Any compromise now, the parties knowing thoroughly the temper of each, must originate in cowardice and a mean spirit of evasion on the part of the South, and in a spirit of fraud and deliberately purposed wrong on that of the North. Yet you will see that Cass and Clay, still having the flesh-pots in their eye[s], will equally aim at some miserable paltering to stave off the difficulty, and be called a compromise, upon which they are [to] found their new claims to the presidency. These scoundrelly professional politicians are at the bottom of all our troubles."

He then goes on to say how these matters are being discussed all over the South, and alludes to the proposed Nashville convention, at which Ham-

mond hoped to meet Tucker. Simms himself had
been proposed as a delegate, but had discouraged
the use of his name. In this connection he remarked, "I regard the Southern convention as in
fact a Southern confederacy. To become the one
it seems to me very certain is to become the other."
A fortnight later, he writes with dampened ardor,
fearing that the convention will do nothing, and the
South drift on. Soon after, we learn that he is
going to see Hammond again in order to talk politics. During his visit he hears that Virginia is
going to submit, through the influence of politicians
like Rives and Ritchie, and concludes that there is
no hope for the South unless things are taken out
of the hands of the professional politicians and
given to the people. He and Tucker and men of
their stamp must take the stump and yet refuse
office. Late in May he addresses Tucker, at Nashville, expressing his doubts whether Tennessee,
North Carolina, Georgia, and Kentucky will come
up to the scratch.

When Tucker returned from Nashville he passed
through Charleston, where Simms, who had gone
to celebrate the Fourth at Orangeburg, to the regret of both missed him. Then a brisk correspondence ensued between them relative to Tucker's
proposed life of John Randolph. Simms got estimates from his Charleston publishers as to the cost
of getting out the work, and urged Tucker to write
it. For a time politics are mentioned only in brief
sentences, but after the Georgia elections of 1850,

in which the hopes of the violent secessionists were dismally crushed, he broke forth as follows: — "Were I to trust my feelings, I should say to South Carolina, Secede at once. Let our State move *per se*. But here's the danger: none of the Southern States stood to the rack in 1833, when South Carolina threw herself into the breach, and owing to the same cause, — the faithlessness and selfishness of trading politicians. Were South Carolina to secede, her ports would be blocked up, her trade would pass to Georgia, and the appeal to Georgia cupidity, filled as that State is with Yankee traders, would be fatal to her patriotism. It would be irresistible in keeping her in her position. The next consequence would be that South Carolina would lose a large portion of her planting population. It would give a new impulse to emigration. They would abandon their lands and pass to Georgia and the West. Those who remained, goaded by privation, distress, loss of trade, profit, and perhaps property, would rise up and rend their leaders to pieces. We must at all hazards goad Georgia to extremities and give her no encouragement in her submission. With South Carolina and Georgia moving for secession the effect would be conclusive upon all the South. British assistance could not be expected unless they were shut out from *all* the cotton ports. Leave the majority of these open, and they will encounter no contest with the United States for the trade of one or more of our Southern cities. Patience, and

shuffle the cards! Our emissaries must be at work.
If we are to incur the imputation of rebellion, we
must use all the arts of conspiracy. We must
enter the field with the United States, and hold out
all the proper lures to buy able politicians. We
must show them that a confederacy of thirteen
Southern States must have the same foreign and
domestic establishment now maintained by the
thirty-one States, and thus be able to *bid* more
highly for their support. We must select our men,
and give them their price. Meanwhile, events
must favor us. The Abolitionists *will* go on.
Quos Deus vult perdere, prius dementat. The
South has but a single interest, and when it is no
longer possible for her people to doubt in respect
to its danger, there will be no longer difficulty in
inciting them to its defense. They may well continue to doubt, while Virginia, the mother of
States, and as deeply interested as any, shows herself so perfectly quiescent. *Our* legislature is in
session, — a very feeble body, but full of spirit.
They will probably call a convention of the people."

To this letter, which was written from Woodlands on the 27th of November, 1850, Tucker replied from Williamsburg, on the 5th of December.
He complained of not getting enough letters from
Simms, and showed something of the state of his
mind by hazarding the extravagant conjecture that
the government was intercepting letters, as it certainly had done in 1833. Apropos of Georgia he

quoted what James Gunn[1] had said forty-seven
years before: "The State of Georgia is a damned
rascal. I bought her and sold her, and will buy
her and sell her again when I please." And he
added, "For terms: apply to Messrs. Toombs and
Stevens [sic] auctioneers. N. B. Texas scrip taken
in payment."

The first letters of 1851 are taken up with allusions to the article Tucker was preparing for the
"Quarterly," on Garland's "Life of John Randolph," an article which eventually appeared and
which was horribly scathing. On March 2, Simms
wrote from Woodlands, reporting illness in his
family and the advent of a visitor in the person of
John R. Thompson, editor of the "Southern Literary Messenger." Thompson was not inclined
to Simms's views of politics, and the latter urged
him to make the "Messenger" a "proper vehicle
for the true political opinion of Virginia;" but
Thompson could not "rise to the necessity of the
case."[2]

On March 12, Simms wrote that South Carolina
had called her convention, and must now do or die;
but he added that, Calhoun being dead, she had no
pilot to enable her to weather the storm. Cheves
ranked next to Calhoun, but he was too much removed from the public view, and was "said to
shrink from the issue which Rhett and the violents"

---

[1] Probably the first Senator from Georgia, who died, however,
in 1801.

[2] The *Messenger* soon became pronounced enough in its politics.

had precipitated. Hammond was unpopular, and hostile to the bank, then a considerable factor in local politics. Rhett and his followers taught that if South Carolina chose to secede, she would be allowed to do so quietly. On which Simms remarked, "I regard this assumption as quite absurd; and the question with us is, how shall we force the blockade — how force a fight." It was true that if the other Southern States would agree to send out no cotton, the fight would be won, but then there was no spirit of combination in the South.

To these epistles Tucker sent prompt replies, so that we have no reason to suspect that the government was watching him very closely. On February 14, he indulged in reminiscences of Calhoun, and recalled how John Randolph had sent him (Tucker) in 1833 to talk with the arch-nullifier, warn him of Clay and his compromises, and bid him not let South Carolina back down. He (Tucker) saw that the Union was a curse in 1820. "I vowed then, and I have repeated the vow, *de die in diem*, that I will never give rest to my eyes nor slumber to my eyelids until it is shattered into fragments. I strove for it in '33; I strove for it in '50, and I will strive for it while I live, and leave the accomplishment to my boys. Time was when I might have been less desperate, because I could have sought refuge under some emperor or king. But all such refuges are broken up, and there is now no escape from the many-headed despotism of numbers, but by a strong and bold stand on the banks of the Potomac. . . . If we will not *have* slaves, we must *be* slaves." On the 30th of March he continued this strain. He had no country now, but if South Carolina would but stand her ground he would have a country. "If not, so help me God, as, if I were twenty years younger, I would go to Russia and claim the protection of the Emperor Nicholas as the very last man in his dominions who would ever think of changing the dominion of a single despot, Porphyrogenitus, for the multitudinous tyrannies of a mob."

But a few days previous to this last remarkable twinge of nightmare, he had written a letter which deserves insertion almost entire. However wild it may seem in many respects, it shows that Tucker had a clear enough head to perceive that out of the anarchic confederacy which he and Simms were proposing, and which was attempted in 1861, a dictator, and finally a perpetual despot, would have been sure to arise.

WILLIAMSBURG, *March* 17, 1851.

MY DEAR SIMMS, — . . . I have just mailed two long letters to Hammond and Governor Means,[1] and all because I cannot get your affairs out of my head. The providence of God has placed the destiny of the South, and of large portions of two sections of the human race, in your hands. He has put it into your hearts to assume this high responsi-

---

[1] John Hugh Means (1812–1862), then Governor of South Carolina and an ardent secessionist.

bility. Do you distrust Him, or do you distrust
the righteousness of your cause? If the latter,
pause and reconsider. But if not, take Davy
Crockett's maxim: "Be sure you are right, and
go ahead." The time to redress a wrong is in the
moment it is felt to be a wrong. We have felt
this for thirty years. Have we gained or lost
strength by delay? Has our enemy? Are we
more or less united? Are the principles of the
Constitution more or less understood? Had the
move been made, as it should have been, in 1820,
would any one have doubted the right of a State
to secede? When before this would any man have
ventured to question it in a Virginia convention?
Are our public men becoming more or less corrupt? Are the flesh-pots of Washington becoming
more or less seductive? Is the number of those
who propose to themselves politics *as a trade* increasing or diminishing? Is power in our state
constitutions passing *to* or *from* the hands of that
class who "feel a stain to honor like a wound;"
who can detect a future mischief in a specious doctrine; who have the sagacity and the boldness to
anticipate a coming blow, instead of letting the
enemy choose his time for attack? Is your wily
adversary eager to precipitate this trial, or is he
trying to keep all things quiet, until the old organ-
ization of parties, to which we have been the victims,
can be fully restored? Now! Now!! Now!!! is
the accepted time. Now is your day of salvation.

You may have discovered that this is my opinion

from something in my last. But to make this course of action wise, it should be *determined* on *promptly* and *executed deliberately.* This is in general not the true rule, but the reverse of it. But it is true here, because there is no doubt what *should* be done. Moreover, the case demands preparation before the final step; of which the most important is an understanding with others. Not Virginia. She is sunk in the slough of democracy, which has no sense of honor, no foresight, and is never valiant but against its own instruments. Not Georgia. She has been bought, and her price is in the pockets of those she trusted. Wait for neither, for neither will act until they hear their brother's blood crying from the ground. The scent of blood has a mighty power, and it is the only thing that can rouse the mass of any people who have shaken themselves loose from the influence of high and enlightened minds. No rabble ever shook off foreign yoke unless provoked by violence and bloodshed. The peasants of Dalecarlia would have worked in the mines to this day, had not Gustavus come among them. When mobs aim at no more than rapine they may make it necessary to use violence to put them down, and as soon as blood flows they become fierce and desperate, and the *émeute* becomes a revolution. The wise rulers of England were aware of this on the 10th of April, 1848,[1] and the demonstration ended as all demonstrations of mobs do, when it is left to

[1] He refers to the Chartist meeting on Kennington Common.

them to strike the first blow. And what are our democracies but mobs? South Carolina alone can act, because she is the only State in which the gentleman retains his place and influence, and in which the statesman has not been degraded from his post. You are fast coming to that hopeless and irreclaimable condition; and then all hope of action is gone. Work now. "Work while it is yet called to-day, for the night cometh when no man can work." The twilight is already upon you, and hence I fear you will not act even *now*. And if not now — never, never, never!

I like your notion of a permanent convention. It chimes in with mine of deliberate action. It will admit of the exercise, in emergency, of such powers as ought not to be committed to any organized government. It admits of the appointment of a dictator, if necessary. Unlimited power is often necessary to call forth and concentrate all the resources of a people, and the only way to make it safe is to limit its existence to the duration of the emergency. To do this effectually it must be extra-constitutional. In the struggle which may be before you, no government meant to be permanent can be efficient under the constitutional restraints which are indispensable. What you want is a convention commissioned to see "*quod nullum detrimentum capiat respublica.*" The first use this many-headed dictator should make of this power, in case of war, should be to delegate it to a dictator with one head. If I could be sure you would do this, I should be almost wicked enough to wish you a little brush. Such things call out the men worthy to rule, and show the people their value, so that the evil day of democracy may be indefinitely postponed.

Meantime, are you taking no measures to understand what may be expected from foreign powers, especially England? If any thing of the sort be done, I know it must be done secretly, and therefore I hope it is done.[1] Let England be made to understand the quarrel, and her interest in it, and your enemy will be checkmated at the first move. Let her keep the port of Charleston open, and Georgia will presently join you; you form the nucleus of a Southern confederacy, and we all fall in, one by one. Then if we can but steer clear of the treacherous syrtis of democracy, we may flourish and be free and happy for the full time of the natural life of a republic. That I take to be about three generations. What befalls our great-grandchildren we rarely care. A life or lives in being, and twenty-one years after, is as long as the wise old common law allows any man to control his own property. What folly, then, for any generation of men to think itself called to establish political institutions in perpetuity. Our Constitution, just sixty years old, is an example. What has become of it ? Except as an engine of power it has no existence. . . .

[1] The letters to Hammond and Governor Means suggested the sending of an accredited agent by the governor. .

We have now seen how these old Southerners
talked politics over their toddies and plotted to
destroy the Union of their fathers, with the thorough conviction that they were doing their duty in
that state of life to which it had pleased God to
call them. That they were doing what some might
think wrong they knew very well; but when they
questioned their own consciences, their consciences,
and they had them, approved their actions. It
may be hard for a modern reader, especially one
not Southern born, to believe this; but no historical truth is more capable of verification. And
in face of this truth we must refrain from blam-
ing them even when we think of the desolation
and ruin that followed upon the adoption of their
counsels. "Blind leaders of the blind" we may
well call them; but we must remember that at
least they marched bravely and cheerily into the
mire, and that their march and their plight are
not subjects for laughter or for frowns, but for
tears.

Many other letters of this period treating of politics have fallen under my eyes, some of them very
interesting, especially those which Simms received
from his friend Major Hammond, the brother of
the ex-governor. In all of them secession is more
or less preached, and one is enabled to see how
thoroughly the people were being educated to the
idea of a new confederacy. One also sees how
well informed the private gentlemen in the South
always were on political subjects. Men who knew

nothing of the steps Richelieu had taken to centralize France could tell you every step that had been taken in that direction in America since the formation of the Union. Nor was this at all remarkable. In the North a man had his business to attend to, and he naturally fell into the habit of letting his politicians manage his politics for him, just as his clergyman attended to his religion. In the South few men had any absorbing business to look after, and hunting and fishing and smoking and drinking and dancing could not occupy all their time and thoughts. They had to read sometimes, and tradition and the fact that as aristocrats they were born leaders of men, naturally turned their reading to political lines. They never failed to read the political leaders in their favorite newspaper, or to hear a political speech if one were delivered within twenty miles of them. They read law, especially Blackstone, without the slightest intention of practicing it, merely in order to train their minds for politics. They read constitutional history for the same reason, but to very little purpose, if one may judge from Calhoun's praise of the constitution of Poland. Hence, one is not surprised to find that the best articles in the "Southern Quarterly" are those that treat of politics, or that Simms, literary man though he was, was often more at home in criticising works like Guizot's "Democracy in France," than he was in criticising contemporary novels and poetry. But perhaps we have tarried long enough in the world of nightmares.

During the eight years treated of in the last chapter, it was not infrequently announced that Simms had in hand a new historical romance. He probably began several, as was his wont, and then cast them aside. This may have been the case with "Katharine Walton," the concluding volume of his Revolutionary trilogy, which began to appear in "Godey's Lady's Book" in January, 1850. Like too many of his works it was written piece-meal, in answer to the printer's cry for copy.

In one respect at least the romance had not lost by its thirteen years of waiting. During that period even Simms's friends, who had formerly advised him to avoid writing on home subjects, had been forced to confess that South Carolina was a "very storehouse for romance." He therefore had some hope that his story would find more readers at home than his former romances had done, and he knew besides that his knowledge of the period he intended to treat had greatly increased. A study of his letters of this date shows how conscientiously Simms always labored in gathering materials for his work. He filled commonplace books with information culled from all quarters. He was constantly in correspondence with local antiquarians like General Jamison, asking such minute questions as where the Orangeburg tavern was standing in 1780, and what was the tavern keeper's name. Nothing was too trivial to require investigation. Now this thoroughness is an admirable characteristic, and a somewhat remarkable one in a South-

ern author, but its results are not always satis-
factory. "Katharine Walton" is a much more
conscientious piece of work than "The Partisan,"
but it is not so interesting a romance. It reads,
in fact, too much like a carefully prepared social
history.

Simms indeed tells us, in a preface, that he has
been thoroughly accurate in his descriptions of
life in Charleston during the British occupation,
for "Katharine Walton" presents us with the chief
characters of "The Partisan," cooped up for the
most part within the walls of the stately old city.
He even vouches for the historical character of the
bits of repartee assigned to his various personages.
But this is a claim to be advanced by an historian,
not by a romancer; and if Poe had lived to read
"Katharine Walton," he would probably have
said of it, as he did of "Beauchampe," that its author did not rely sufficiently on his own imagination. It may be remarked that in one exciting
scene, — in which a young British officer, "Mad
Archy Campbell," drives off with an American
beauty and terrifies her into marrying him, —
Simms seems to have drawn on the imagination
of some one else when he thought he was retailing
veritable history. One of the descendants of the
pair has recently published a denial of the whole
romantic episode.

The chief element, then, that is lacking to the
book is that indefinable something called charm
which is found in "The Partisan." Simms, in

spite of his historical knowledge, in spite of the
fact that he was a Charlestonian born, did not
move as freely in the city as in the swamp, or
among haughty gentlemen and ladies as among
plain-speaking troopers and scouts. Hence, although his romance keeps us moving through exciting and interesting scenes; although we take an
interest in the fortunes of its heroine; although we
feel that we have made acquaintances among some of
its characters, — we nevertheless lay it down with
the conviction that it would have been a greater
success had it come from a writer more in sympathy with the company he was keeping, and possessed of an innate understanding of their modes of
life and thought. Charleston under British rule,
with its patriotic citizens scarce daring to speak
above a whisper, and its sycophantic adherents to
the royal cause basking in short-lived sunshine,
was almost, if not quite, as suitable a theme for
the romancer as courtly Williamsburg at the time
of the advent of "The Virginia Comedians." Yet
John Esten Cooke, although only twenty-four, and
with no such store of historical information, or
indeed with such native powers to draw on, as
Simms, succeeded, in his romance bearing the
above title, in transferring far more of the charm
of that old-time life to his pages than our veteran
romancer did in this work of his prime.

Cooke, it is true, did not fulfill the promise of his
youth; but this was less his own fault than the unfortunate result of the years of strife through which

he was destined to pass. He is one of the saddest
examples in all Southern history of a man of
marked ability wrecked in the turmoil of the
times in which his lot was cast. When he came
out of the war, the school of fiction in which he
had been trained (he always called Simms his master) had seen its best days. He could not change
the style of his work to suit the changed tastes of
his public, and in his extremity he turned to his varied war experiences to eke out his literary capital.
His "Surrey" and his "Mohun" were, however,
huge failures, which should stand as grave warnings
to all writers who shall hereafter turn to a period
that must sooner or later furnish abundant materials to future writers of fiction. If he had only
contented himself with writing with soldierly sim-
plicity his own memoirs, he would have secured for
himself an immortality.[1] As it is, he is easily the
second Southern romancer after Simms, and perhaps, had he been born twenty years earlier, he
might have made the South Carolinian look to his
laurels. Those laurels, indeed, Cooke never disputed, and to the day of his death Simms had no
warmer friend than the pure-hearted Virginian.

But Simms did not always fail in his descriptions of the social life of the Carolina aristocracy.
He failed when sympathy and an innate understanding were required, but not when he undertook
to satirize the peculiarities and unlovable qualities
of that life. The reason for this is obvious. The

[1] *Wearing of the Gray* is hardly such a book.

indifference always manifested for his work and for himself by the upper classes naturally provoked him and sharpened his eyes to the obvious faults of his critics. Hence in his novelette, "The Golden Christmas; a Chronicle of St. John's Berkeley" (1852), he gives a very amusing description of some of the oddities produced by six generations of intermarriages between first cousins. His Madame Agnes-Theresa Girardin, gaunt, colorless embodiment of family pride, walking down King Street like a social barometer, rising and falling, stiffening and unbending, according to the blueness of the blood of the persons she meets, is a really successful creation, even if she is described in broader strokes than our modern story tellers use.

This Madame Girardin, who cannot see a woman with a fresh complexion without suspecting that her blood is no better than it should be, and Major Bulmer, descendant of one of Locke's palatines, who still drives his old family coach, swears by the English and hates the French, even the Huguenot Carolinians, make what would be otherwise merely a thin love story rather entertaining reading. It is true that, as has been remarked above, Simms is by no means as careful in his sketches as a modern writer would be. He does not indulge in any nice character shading, he gives us nothing approaching a photograph; and he never by any possibility charms us by his style. But the conditions under which he wrote were very different from those which surround the modern writer. He

was primarily a romancer, and he did his genre
work as a pioneer. His public were not educated
to the merits of the short story as a work of art,
and he did something to make them see, had they
cared to open their eyes, that there was a great future in store for that form of fiction. Were he alive
and writing now, his immense energy, his keen
appreciation of local differences of tone and color,
his ability to keep his characters, whether puppets
or not, always in motion, would make him a formidable rival to the many younger writers of
promise who have to a large extent crowded him
off the stage.

The year 1850 saw, besides "Katharine Walton"
and a rather creditable poem delivered at the consecration of Magnolia Cemetery in Charleston,
another book bearing Simms's name on the title-
page. This was "The Lily and the Totem," a
volume modeled upon the once popular series of
works known as "The Romance of History."
Coligny's colonies in North America formed the
subject of Simms's new publication, and one is certain that the prolific author did more credit to himself and to his subject by writing in prose than he
would have done had he stuck to his original intention of writing in verse. "The Lily and the
Totem" seems to be the only one of Simms's books
that has been republished at the South since his
death.

It would not be right to pass to another year
without alluding to the large quantity of work

done by Simms for his review within this twelve-
month. He wrote exactly ten articles, few of
them under forty pages, and four "critical notices," in which upwards of one hundred and fifty
books were passed in review. Of course many of
these were skimmed, but some, it can be perceived,
were carefully read. The quality of the criticisms
is by no means as bad as would be expected from
the quantity. One is never sure of entirely sane
criticism from Simms, he was much too full of
crotchets; but certainly the man who could write
thus of Browning forty-one years ago is entitled to
some regard : —

"Browning is no common verse maker. He is
a writer of thought and genius, of peculiar and
curious powers as an artist; subtle, spiritual, and
singularly fanciful, and, though as yet unacknow-
ledged, is one of the master minds of living European song. . . . He will grow slowly in public
esteem, and finally, when his peculiar phraseology
shall become familiar to the ear, it will compel an
admiration which is very far from general now.
. . . His claim to the regards of those who require
a deep and earnest thought in verse, as well as
music and fancy, is beyond question. All such persons must take him to their studies, if not to their
hearts." [1]

When American authors were in question,
Simms was loyal to his Knickerbocker friends over
the rising influence of New England. In 1845, he

[1] *Southern Quarterly Review*, Sept. 1850, pp. 256-7.

had a few pleasant words for Longfellow and Emerson, and more for Lowell, but when he came, in 1850, to review "A Fable for Critics," which he was loath to attribute to Lowell, he seems to have made up his mind that no abolitionist was worthy of any manner of praise. Emerson is now little more than an idiot, Lowell, if he wrote the poem under review, is a base-hearted slanderer, whose publishers are warned to cease disseminating his abominable opinions on the subject of slavery. Alcott is a silly pilferer from Plato, fit only for ridicule, which he gets, by the way, from Simms in no measured quantity. Still, as the abolitionists, taken by and large, did in spite of their sincerity lack sweetness and light to a certain extent, at least from a Southern standpoint, our critic's aberrations may be pardoned even when he is unjust to so large-hearted a man as Emerson. It is a little curious, however, to find him writing, in 1849, that there is no imaginative faculty in New England, and proving it by the fact that most of the earlier American romancers owed their genius to a friendlier climate where, indeed, they were not puffed as New England's literary sons were wont to be. One recollects that Hawthorne had written some tales worthy of being called imaginative, and that "The Scarlet Letter" was already in his mind; and that Judd had written "Margaret" some four years before. But Massachusetts and Carolina were not on easy terms in 1849, and the "North American" had once upon a time been needlessly severe on Simms.

The year 1851 calls for little special notice. Simms produced as usual a large quantity of manuscript, but the only thing of any consequence that was published was his "Norman Maurice; an American Drama," which appeared in the "Southern Literary Messenger," and was shortly after issued in pamphlet form. This was a bold, if unsuccessful undertaking. Simms grappled with a problem which has yet to be solved, and thought he had solved it by combining a strictly American plot with a method of presentation taken at second hand from his favorite Elizabethans. He has no difficulty in making a Philadelphia lawyer and a Missouri politician talk in blank verse which is sometimes so bald that it seems a very appropriate medium of expression for the absurd political theories advanced by the latter. As a matter of course the reader is at one moment breathless at the author's audacity, and at the next moment laughing at his crudities of thought and expression. How could it be otherwise, and who shall say that Simms did not have the courage of his convictions when he could write such lines as these?

> "Another action,
> The insurance case of Fergusson and Brooks,
> Secures him handsome profits."

There is certainly no lack of melodramatic effect. The villain commits a forgery and accuses the hero of the crime; he likewise threatens the virtue of the hero's wife, and that Roman dame stabs herself and her would-be ravisher, and ends

the play just at the time her husband is elected
United States senator from Missouri.   There is
plenty of swagger, a duel, long speeches in high-
sounding verse, enough in all conscience to keep
reader or spectator awake.   Yet the world was no
nearer having a good modern drama than it had
been before Simms made his heroic experiment.

"Norman Maurice" was praised highly in certain quarters, — for example, by the "International Magazine" and by G. P. R. James, — and
it went through four editions.   In 1854 an aspiring
actor, Mr. George K. Dickinson, put it in rehearsal at Nashville, Tennessee, and wrote Simms an
exuberant letter about the triumph to be expected
for it at St. Louis.   But although Dickinson filled
an engagement at St. Louis during the Christmas holidays of 1854, and although the "Missouri
Republican" contained a glowing notice of Mr.
Simms's new American play, which would shortly
be produced at the People's Theatre, the performance did not come off, and Dickinson's letters
suddenly ceased.

The year 1852 was more prolific in publications than 1851 had been.   Not satisfied with his
novelette, "The Golden Christmas," Simms gave
it a companion tale of Georgia life, entitled "As
Good as a Comedy."   This was issued anonymously, and the story was put in the mouth of a
Tennessean, with a dialect somewhat familiar to
modern readers.   The book rather belied its name,
for the humor is not as abundant as the critic in

the "Lady's Book," who thought that Simms excelled Dickens in many respects, would have had his readers believe; but it has the merit of describing certain phases of Georgia life very well, and the account given of an ante-bellum Southern racecourse has lost none of its interest with the lapse of years. A third novelette was "Marie de Berniere: a Tale of the Crescent City," originally contributed to T. S. Arthur's "Home Gazette," and afterwards published in a volume along with other tales. The reader who thinks that Mr. Cable is here forestalled is decidedly mistaken. The local color introduced is of very thin quality, and the only thing French about the story is a not entirely unsuccessful attempt to make a stalwart Tennessean play the part of a Vidocq. Had Simms so chosen he could have won a fair reputation in a school of fiction best represented, perhaps, by the name of M. Fortuné du Boisgobey.

We must not linger, however, over these stories which Simms dashed off with such astonishing ease, nor can we pause to consider his second and only acted play, "Michael Bonham," for that will occupy us hereafter. Our attention must be confined to what is certainly the most humorous, and in many respects the best sustained, of all our author's works, "The Sword and the Distaff," which now appears under the revised but hardly improved title of "Woodcraft." This romance is the fourth in the connected series of Revolutionary romances, but from the time of its action it should properly have been the sixth and last.

Its hero is Lieutenant Porgy, who, upon the advent of peace, has left the swamp camps of Marion, and is returning full of honors and debts to his dismantled plantation. Just before reaching it he manages to rescue a fair widow neighbor of his from a band of ruffians, who are trying to kidnap a train of slaves she is bringing home. A boy reader would take intense delight in the exciting description Simms gives of the swamp fight that took place at this juncture. An older reader would feel that he was getting an admirable description of the wild and lawless condition of Carolina just after the Revolution. As the story progresses the desolation that has fallen upon plantation and planter alike is described in a graphic way; and the evil effects that a period of strife is likely to exert upon weak or vicious natures are forcibly exemplified in some of the leading characters. One of these, Bostwick the squatter, typifies most accurately the Southern poor white at his very worst. Both for its interest and for its faithfulness to the truth of history, the romance deserves to be read.

The humor which, for a wonder, Simms succeeded in putting into "The Sword and the Distaff" is not of a high order, but it is humor nevertheless. It emerges from the situations in which the characters find themselves, rather than from anything they say. Porgy is urged by his one-armed Sancho Panza, Sergeant Millhouse, who is also a reminiscence of Corporal Trim, and of other worthy followers of romantic heroes, to better his

fortunes by marrying the rich widow he has res-
cued. He half consents, and is led into all sorts of
blunders which make him vow to live and die a
bachelor. Although it is obvious that Simms is
only following Smollett afar off, and although his
most amusing scene is taken bodily from an Elizabethan play, he certainly succeeded in writing an
entertaining book; and one is disposed to regret
that its proposed sequel, "The Humors of Glen
Eberley," was not written and handed over to the
Georgia publisher who applied for it.

Passing now for a moment from romance to politics, I may remark that during this period Simms
did not cease to indulge his dreams of public office.
It is true that he refused to allow his friends to
push him forward as a candidate for Congress from
the Charleston district; but it was otherwise with
diplomatic sinecures, and he did not discourage the
applications made to President Taylor by Major
Hammond through the former's **private secretary,**
Bliss. A mission to one of the minor courts would
have pleased our author greatly, but the overtures
of his friends seem to have been received in silence.
Then Hammond, who was a capital fellow if one
may judge from his letters, began to urge the
claims of "Father Abbot," as he delighted to call
Simms, to the presidency of the South Carolina
College, which had just been resigned by ex-Sen-
ator William C. Preston. But although Simms
would not have disliked this position,—no sinecure,

by the way, — he knew too well the prejudices existing against him to hope for such an appointment.   He accordingly contented himself with
helping to spread the doctrine of the divine origin
of slavery by contributing to a volume that rejoiced
in the contradictory title of "The Pro-Slavery Argument." His fellow-contributors were Chancellor Harper, one of the most prolific and forcible of
all these apologists, ex-Governor Hammond, and
Professor Dew.

Soon after, he gave this volume a companion by
reissuing, under the title "South Carolina in the
Revolutionary War," two articles that had attracted some attention on their first publication in
the "Southern Quarterly Review" for 1848. The
name of the volume would suggest that Simms had
again taken up the role of historian; but such was
not primarily the case. The essays, indeed, possessed some little interest to historical students, but
they were first and foremost the work of a heated
controversialist.   Lorenzo Sabine had just (1847)
published his "American Loyalists," and had therein taken occasion to make some reflections upon
the support South Carolina had given to the cause
of the Revolution. His remarks had been by no
means violent, and not entirely ill founded. But
that South Carolina should be criticised at all,
much less by a New Englander, was more than
Simms could stand. He rushed at Sabine, and all
loyal Southerners proclaimed that the Yankee had
been demolished. As far as I can gather, Simms

did succeed in convicting Sabine of one gross error, which the latter at once acknowledged in his correspondence, and subsequently corrected in the second edition of his laborious and honest work. He also opposed to Sabine's charges many facts which went far towards explaining South Carolina's alleged apathy in the great struggle for freedom. Here he was on his own ground, and although Sabine, after mature consideration, did not retract his charges, those charges should be read only in connection with Simms's vindication of his native State. When, however, our hot-blooded Southerner proceeded to carry the war into Africa by retorting against New England very much the same charges that had been made against South Carolina, he was betrayed into gross indiscretions, and injured his own cause. Sabine had been dignified, however malicious his criticism in the eyes of a loyal Southerner; but Simms was decidedly undignified in his coarse strictures on the memories of New England patriots like Stark and Putnam. One can only contrast his petulance and want of courtesy with the quiet tone in which Sabine alluded in his second edition to the attacks that had been made upon himself. Still, as this petulance and want of courtesy subsequently put Simms into one of the most trying positions of his life, and as many excuses are to be made for a man who was living in the heated atmosphere of South Carolina in those days of agitation, it will be as well to dismiss, for the present, the unpleasant subject.

It is certainly a great step from these controversial tracts to the first collected edition of our author's poems. Simms and many of his friends had long been wishing for such a consummation; now, in 1853, there appeared two thick volumes with the following sufficient title : "Poems Descriptive, Dramatic, Legendary, and Contemplative." Surely the public had now an ample opportunity to form its judgment upon Simms's merits as a poet. But that judgment had been practically formed already, and there was nothing in these volumes to change it. On the score of quantity Simms had had nothing to fear for a long time; on the score of quality he was neither better nor worse off than before, his youthful "Atalantis" still remaining his most considerable work. The mildest judgment that can be passed is that the volumes were needless, — a judgment which is equally applicable to another publication of this year, "Egeria," a collection of what Simms regarded as the best passages or "gems" to be found in his multifarious prose writings.

In the early part of 1854, Simms made a short but successful lecturing tour to Washington, Richmond, Petersburg, and perhaps other places; then he settled down to the routine work of editing his review, which was beginning to drag, and relieved the tedium, we may imagine, by observing what the critics had to say of a certain romance he had just published under the pseudonym of "Frank Cooper." This was "Vasconselos: a Romance of the New

World," which had been begun several years before, and cast aside for pleasanter or more profitable work. The wanderings of De Soto had affected Simms's imagination ever since his own southwestern excursions in company with his father; and he had already pointed out in print what a great romance could be constructed out of the materials furnished by the adventures of the ill-fated discoverer. He was now to try his own hand on the theme, and to endeavor to atone for his unsuccessful "Damsel of Darien." Hitherto the fascinating period of Spanish discovery and conquest had been more fortunate in its historians like Irving and Prescott than in its romancers like Bird or Simms. But could not something be done to raise the romancer's end of the balance? Simms resolved to try, and, in order not to be handicapped by his previous failure, to try under an assumed name. Redfield, his publisher, suggested "Frank Cooper" as a good *nom de plume*, and so that gentleman's romance appeared, and was duly read and praised. It was dedicated to that typical old New Yorker, Dr. John W. Francis, whose burly, honest friendship and hospitality Simms had long enjoyed.

If our author desired merely to surpass his own youthful efforts and those of Dr. Bird, he had his wish; but if he also expected to write a great romance, he failed of his purpose, and the cause of his failure lay mainly in himself. "Vasconselos" showed much power and no little audacity. De Soto's preparations for his departure from Cuba,

his tournaments and fêtes, are described in a way to
make one read on, which is a sign of some success
on the part of a romancer writing more than twenty
years after Scott's death. The long and perilous
marches of the Spaniard, his encounters with hostile tribes, his gradual disillusionment, and finally
the pathetic catastrophe of his death on the banks of
the great river he discovered, are all graphically described, and give interest and vitality to the book.
When, however, the romancer leaves the chronicles
behind and relies upon his own imagination, he fails
dismally; because, as Poe had said of him before,
he cannot distinguish between what is merely repulsive and what is genuinely pathetic and tragic.
His heroine is calculated to move our pity and our
regard, save for the horrible relation she sustains to
her brutal uncle, through no fault of her own, but
rather through the morbid imagination of her delineator. The hero, Philip de Vasconselos, would
excite our admiration for his virtues, and our indig-
nation for the wrongs he undergoes at the hands of
De Soto, — the defects of whose character are un-
pleasantly exaggerated, — were it not that Simms
will not let him bear those wrongs as a true knight
should, but makes him become a traitor to his
countrymen, content to sink into a savage chief,
who finds a solace for the disappointments of love
and ambition in the embrace of a loving and noble,
yet still barbarian princess. Bird, though far inferior to Simms in general power, did not make
this last fatal mistake when he might easily have

done so. Juan Lerma, in "The Infidel," suffers as much from the jealousy of Cortez as Vasconselos does from that of De Soto; nevertheless, with stronger temptations to become a traitor, he remains true to his race, and so preserves our regard. Vasconselos forfeits it, and so Simms's romance fails to fulfill the chief condition of the existence of any romance, namely, that it should purify and elevate the minds and hearts of its readers.

But "Vasconselos" had merits to which Simms's next book can lay no claim. "Southward Ho! a Spell of Sunshine," which was published towards the close of 1854, has been described as a kind of Southern "Decameron," but there is no real reason for so handicapping a book already weighted down. It is true that its effects upon the morals of undisciplined readers are less questionable than those of Boccaccio's masterpiece; but then no one ever accused the "Decameron" of being dull, and "Southward Ho!" certainly is. It was simply a device to enable its author to publish once more some of his long-forgotten short stories. They are told by a party of passengers who are traveling by sea from New York to Charleston, and their only merit lies in the fact that they are welcome interruptions to the would-be facetious conversations which these passengers carry on. It must be admitted, however, that as noted points upon the coast are passed, the book lights up with an occasionally felicitous description; and it is interesting to find Simms prophesying that in fifteen years the mountains of

North Carolina, a region with which he was thoroughly familiar, would be a fashionable resort for Northern invalids and pleasure seekers. Could he wake up now at Asheville he would probably rub his hands, and think himself a better prophet about the future of health resorts than about the future of his proposed Southern confederacy, a subject on which he permitted himself to say a few words in this very *olla-podrida* we are considering.

But although the only portion of "Southward Ho!" which would be likely to interest a modern reader has been pointed out, it would not be fair to dismiss it without the statement that some of Simms's friends, like Duyckinck, Hayne, and Cooke, found it charming, because, as they said, it was written just as Simms tálked. I for one am willing to believe that the hearty, genial author was a much better raconteur over a glass of punch than I have found him to be in the pages of his pseudo-Decameron.

In the meantime, Redfield had been bringing out a revised edition of the best of the romances. Darley was engaged to illustrate them, and Simms occupied his spare hours at Woodlands in correcting obvious blunders and youthful extravagances, and in writing new and affectionate dedications to old friends like Yeadon, who had stood sponsor to "The Partisan" nearly twenty years before. "Martin Faber," "The Damsel of Darien," "Pelayo," and a few other immature efforts and failures, were allowed to sink into oblivion, but most of the border and revolutionary romances were given a fresh circulation and were favorably received by the press. Perhaps it was this revival of interest in his work that made Simms produce four romances in the next few years, three of them worthy to rank with any he had previously written.

In the spring of 1854 he was evidently at work on a new revolutionary romance, for he was getting the minute information he always required from correspondents like Jamison. The following spring this romance, " The Forayers, " was finished, and he was working on its sequel, " Eutaw, " — slowly, indeed, as he wrote to his friend John J. Bockie, of Brooklyn, for he had a multitude of smaller matters on his hands ; still he hoped to finish it by July. He did not do this, probably because he went to work on "Charlemont," the sequel to "Beauchampe," — a romance which should never have been begun and which has been noticed sufficiently. But "Eutaw" was finally finished in February, 1856; for its author had had a respite from some of his duties and could at last concentrate his attention upon it. His round of lectures at the various villages of South Carolina was over, and he had cleared some money and increased his reputation. His editorial career also was over, for ten years; for the last publisher of the "Quarterly," Mortimer, had insisted on quarreling with his editor, and had presumed to think that he himself could edit as well as publish. That he did not

carry out his threat was due in part to the fact that
the creditors he had made as publisher determined
to sue him. How much Simms got of his hard
earned salary, which may have been increased after
the first year to fifteen hundred dollars, is not to
be ascertained, but is easy to guess at.[1]

Probably no other man in the South could have
done as much as Simms did between the inception
of "The Forayers" and the completion of "Eutaw." As we have seen, he was editing his review
during most of the time, was writing "Charlemont," was delivering lectures and addressing female seminaries, and was revising his old romances.
In addition to this he was taking his usual trips,
talking politics, having a play represented at
Charleston, contributing to Duyckinck's "Cyclopædia of American Literature," and superintending
all the planting at Woodlands, owing to the protracted ill health of his father-in-law, Mr. Roach.
In the face of all this, could he be expected to
write anything that should be worthy of the attention of posterity? It would hardly seem so; and
yet "The Forayers" and "Eutaw" show no sign
of flagging powers, and are among the most interesting of all the Revolutionary romances.

They take up the history of that exciting period
just where it was left at the close of "Katharine
Walton," — at the point "when, for the first time,
the British were made to understand that the con-

[1] The *Southern Quarterly* was published for one year longer
(1856) at Columbia, (S. C.), under the editorship of Dr. Thornwell.

flict was doubtful." The enemy have now contracted their operations to what is called the "low
country," and Lord Rawdon has yielded his command to Colonel Stewart, whom Greene expects to
engage in the last great battle at Eutaw Springs.
The partisans Marion, Sumter, Pickens, Horry,
Lee, and the two Hamptons are dashing about the
country, harassing the enemy almost as much as
does the intense heat of the season. It is with
these rapid and daring movements that "The Forayers" is chiefly concerned, and we perceive the
appropriateness of its sub-title, "The Raid of the
Dog-Days." "Eutaw" of course concerns itself
with the battle and its consequences.

Many of our old friends, such as Marion and
Porgy, reappear, and we once more glide through
dark lagoons and tangled undergrowth until we
find ourselves at rest in a partisan camp. We are
present for the twentieth time, perhaps, at the midnight sally, and witnesses of Tory and British atro-
cities. But new characters are introduced who
soon win our regard, even though they are by no
means to be considered creations. Again we have
the story of the true love that does not run smooth
because a villainous Tory will presume to fall in
love with our hero's sweetheart. As usual our hero
insists on falling in love with the daughter of an
enemy, and in running all sorts of risks to obtain
a meeting with her. Another old manor house is
besieged by ruffians, and once more the commonplaces of romances in general are brought in to eke

out the materials which have already stood Simms in good stead for a dozen or more volumes. But we read on, and grow excited when the heroine is carried off, and when her little brother is subjected to a captivity the rigors of which he contrives to abate by interesting his jailer, Hell-Fire Dick, in the adventures of a gentleman of a somewhat different persuasion, Bunyan's immortal Pilgrim. We find ourselves marveling at the scouts who pursue impossible trails over impossible places; we grow boys again, and long to shoot with such unerring precision and to ride such races and fight such battles as these hearty partisans do every day without thinking that there is anything unusual in it. Of course if our blood is cool, we are apt to pause over tangled sentences, and to wonder why Simms would fancy he was writing romance when he was really writing history. But many a boy has read "Eutaw" without stopping for these things, and there are probably older readers who do the same.

As romantic in its incidents as either of these stories, but much fuller of faults, was the play "Michael Bonham," which was produced at the Charleston Theatre on the nights of March 26 and 27, 1855. But for the curious fact that the hero of the play was then living in Carolina, and that it was the only one of Simms's numerous dramas that was ever performed, all mention of it could be safely omitted. Simms had written it some three years before, and had published it both in the

"Southern Literary Messenger" and in pamphlet form. This latter fact does not seem to have been remembered in Charleston, for the "Courier" of the morning of the 26th stated the contrary, and proceeded to give its readers some idea of what they might expect. General Milledge L. Bonham, the hero, was a well-known man. He had been one of the most daring associates of Bowie and Crockett and Travis, or, as the "Courier" somewhat magniloquently put it, of "the small, but hardy band of crusaders who first planted near the 'Great River' of the American Spaniards the lone-star flag, which has been lovingly and blandly absorbed by the standard sheet of Stars and Stripes." More recently he had served with distinction in the Mexican war, and it was probably this fact which suggested to Simms the propriety of writing his drama. No thought of having it performed seems to have entered Simms's mind until Dickinson put "Norman Maurice" in rehearsal and the manager of the Charleston Theatre applied for permission to have "The Golden Christmas" dramatized.

The faults of "Norman Maurice" are all conspicuous in "Michael Bonham," and how the original of the romantic hero could have been flattered at finding himself carried through a series of duels and intrigues and cut-throat adventures is hard to conceive. It is true that in some respects it was an acting play; that is, it might have suited a non-critical audience who wanted plenty of movement and striking situations, and who did not care a straw whether the dramatist observed the laws of dramatic construction, or whether he borrowed wholesale from other dramatists. This is the most that can be said for it. The only character that is at all interesting is David Crockett, who is absurdly represented as following Bonham into San Antonio as a subordinate when the latter could not have been much over twenty years old. In short, when read in the closet the play seems to be the work of a precocious youth of eighteen rather than of a practiced writer and constant student and spectator of the drama.

Still, as one performance was to be given in aid of the Ladies' Calhoun Monument Association, and as the newspapers had pronounced it to be admirable, a large audience greeted it with "frequent demonstrations of applause," which "testified their gratification at this offering from the pen of one who " had "ministered to Southern readers in all the modes of authorship." "The cast was a good one," continued the "Courier," "and the general effect was more than creditable."

Simms was so nervously interested in the success of his offspring that he could not be induced to attend; but he wrote his friend Major Hammond an account of the two performances, and intimated that a third might be given which would put some much-needed money into his pocket. Whether his expectations were realized does not appear, but it is certain that he was slightly chagrined at the fact that the audience did not call for the author. To this Hammond replied rather humorously: "What author was ever called out in your goodly city? I never heard of one. The folks did not know the compliment, — they paid the very highest known to them, and quite unusual, too, that of encoring *scenes!* A song might do. But scenes! it is surely a *rara avis.* Saw Bonham (M. L.) yesterday. His vanity is flattered. He was gratified at your success, of which I told him."

But the good people of Charleston who applauded Simms's scenes were fast preparing to become actors in a much more serious drama. It must not be imagined that, because little has been said of politics lately, the atmosphere about our fiery Southerner was clearing. Not a whit of it. It is true that he no longer had Beverley Tucker's letters to stir him up; but he had the two Hammonds and Jamison to talk to, and the "Charleston Mercury" and his review to write for, and numerous squabbles among the politicians at Washington to keep up with, so that he was by no means free from nightmares even while he was indulging in his most delightful romantic dreams. When Tucker died, it occurred to Simms that a biography of such a distinguished exponent of the states-rights school would be an excellent handbook of politics for the rising generation. He accordingly set to work to secure information, but for some unknown reason soon forebore the task. He was by no means idle, however, in sowing the seeds which Tucker had scattered broadcast. Besides his

published articles and editorials, and the stray
allusions made to politics in his books, he used
his lecturing tours and his vast correspondence as
means to the desired end. Young politicians outside of South Carolina wrote to him for advice.
One, a Mr. Henry Hughes, of Port Gibson, Mississippi, author of a "Treatise on Sociology" which
Simms had praised in the "Mercury," addressed
him as the acknowledged head of the new school of
Southern thinkers, and remarked, "When we Mis-
sissippians want to reason about home matters, we
turn towards South Carolina as naturally almost as
pagans to an oracle."

His correspondents upon this subject were not
all Southerners. When good, facing-both-ways
gentlemen from the North wrote school histories
of the United States, they were always particularly
anxious to get a statement from Simms that their
books contained nothing that would shock a Southern mind. When a fiery editor of Columbia,
South Carolina, attacked the "Lady's Book" for
an article containing alleged abolition sentiments,
Mr. Godey, after wringing his hands and exclaim-
ing that he had published his magazine for twenty
years and not one line against the South had it
contained, wrote to Simms beseeching that he
would testify to the standing of the "Lady's
Book" on all such questions and pacify De Leòn,
the editor of the "Telegraph." Simms did pacify
De Leon, but Godey wrote presently to say that
he wished some one would help him out of the

scrape he was in at the North for having declared
that he had never published a line against the
South. The poor man was deeply aggrieved that he
could not be allowed to face both ways forever.
Yet he was no worse than thousands of his countrymen, who by their submission to the adherents
of the false god of the country did almost as much
to rivet his chains upon that country as his more
vociferous priests and worshipers, and who have
received their due reward for all time at the hands
of the author of "Uncle Tom's Cabin." Certainly
nothing that he wrote to Simms was worse than the
following sentence which is taken from a letter
written by an author not unknown to fame : "I am
half a Southerner myself; and although I happened to be the son of honest Northerners, I am
not averse to a single item peculiar to your part of
our common country." It really seems as if some
of his Northern friends were a little afraid of
Simms's vehement way of expressing opinions
which were natural enough in him, but which were
rather unnatural in persons born in colder lati-
tudes. It may be suspected that he liked better
those friends who, like Bryant, could hold to their
own opinions and still be sincere in their affection.
That he was vehement enough in expressing his
opinions, no matter where he was, is evidenced by
the fact that General James Grant Wilson once
heard him say, suiting his gestures to his words:
"If it comes to blows between the North and the
South, we will crush you [the North] as I would
crush an egg."

He was soon to be taught that a man can go
too far in the expression of opinions very honestly
held. Although some stray lectures delivered in
Northern cities had not been very favorably received, he conceived the project of undertaking an
extended lecturing tour in the winter of 1855.
He does not seem to have matured his plans, although he gave several lectures in small Southern
towns; but in the fall of the following year he did
succeed in arranging quite an elaborate programme.
He was to begin his lectures in New York in response to an invitation signed by George Bancroft,
with whom his relations were always friendly, William Cullen Bryant, Evert A. Duyckinck, Dr.
John W. Francis, and others. Then he was to go
as far east as Boston and as far west as Detroit,
taking in many of the intermediate towns.

Accordingly, on the night of Tuesday, November 18, 1856, he addressed a fair audience in Dr.
Chapin's Church of the Divine Unity, on a subject identical with that of a volume heretofore
criticised: "South Carolina in the Revolution."
The "Herald" of the following morning described
him as being prepossessing in appearance, with a
very rapid and forcible delivery. The "Tribune"
said that the lecture lasted for an hour and a half,
and was heard in silence save for a round of applause at the end. It closed its notice with a brief
comment on the bad taste of the lecturer in introducing his subject with some remarks derogatory
to Mr. Sumner.

The second lecture was fixed for Friday, November 21. The "Herald" of Saturday, under the head of "City Intelligence," contained the following reference to it: "Simms's Lecture. W. Gilmore Simms, according to advertisement and previous announcement, was to deliver the second lecture of his course in the Rev. Dr. Chapin's church last evening; subject, 'The Appalachians: a Southern Idyll, descriptive of Southern Life, Manners, Scenery, etc.' Five minutes before eight o'clock, the time appointed for the lecture, there was an audience of three persons present. The church was well lighted and warmed, but none of the committee having appeared, the sexton only admitted the people to the vestibule of the church. At eight o'clock, there was an audience of six persons, not including the reporters. From eight to eight and a half a few others dropped in, making an audience, all counted, of thirteen gentlemen and four ladies. The lecturer still not appearing, the gas was turned off, the doors locked, and the assembly adjourned *sine die*, looking at their tickets."

Two days later the "Herald" commented editorially upon Simms's failure, declaring that he had received fair treatment and that his undertaking had been a quixotic one. It remarked that a South Carolina audience would not have let off so easily any Northern lecturer that might have gone thither to defend Charles Sumner. The "Tribune" of the same day, November 24, gave nearly two of its editorial columns to a defense of the position

previously taken by Sabine as to the services of
South Carolina in the Revolution. It also advised
Simms to omit his allusions to Sumner, adding:
"It will be quite time enough to vituperate Mr.
Sumner after having first refuted him." The
"Evening Post," in consideration, no doubt, of Bry-
ant's friendship for the lecturer, alluded to the
dismal affair as briefly and favorably as was pos-
sible under the circumstances.

Simms naturally felt deeply hurt at what had occurred. He acted quietly, however, and canceled
all his other engagements, refusing to accept invitations from certain quarters where it was believed
that the New Yorkers had dealt too harshly with
him. The Southern press took up his cause and
several strictly Southern lecturing tours were
mapped out for him. But he was in no humor for
public speaking at present, even to friendly audi-
ences, and he returned to the quiet of Woodlands
with a sigh of relief. After two months' rest he
took the platform again, and lectured at Baltimore,
Washington, Richmond, Petersburg, Norfolk, and
other Southern towns, with decidedly more success.
At some of these places he eschewed political subjects, preferring such unobjectionable themes as
"The Choice of a Profession" and "Early Southern
Discoverers."

It is impossible not to sympathize with our impulsive lecturer in his troubles, even though they
were of his own making. It was so natural to him
to think that any cause he espoused must be right,

that he never stopped to think whether it would be expedient to endeavor to convince other people of the truth of that cause. In his eyes Sumner had been guilty of the grossest of crimes in slandering the South and its institutions, and although he would probably have hesitated to use the historical bludgeon himself, he had no hesitation in saying that Sumner had got only what he deserved. In the South it was common enough for a man's body to be responsible for the indiscreet use of his tongue, and not many Southerners could understand how a few blows had made Sumner a hero throughout the North. We can see now, of course, that it was in the worst possible taste to make any allusion, save one of regret, to the horrible occurrence which had deprived Massachusetts of her able and fearless senator. And yet if slavery could make a man who was dearly beloved and esteemed by those who knew him best descend to such un-called-for violence, it could make an eager partisan defend that violence even in the house of its victim's friends. We do not know exactly what Simms said,[1] for his remarks were extempore, and he probably went further than he had intended; but it is almost certain that if he were living now, he would be one of the first to condemn his own utterances. For the man, if an impetuous partisan and a good hater, was nevertheless as honest as the day, and full of that true courage which is never

---

[1] The *Times*, which gave the longest account of the lecture, did not give the language used in reference to Sumner.

ashamed to make confession of wrong-doing. He really thought that he was doing the New Yorkers a great favor in opening their eyes to the baseness of Sumner and the abolitionists, and when he found that he would not be listened to, he was more hurt and sorry than angry. He could not show his face even to his friends, and he apologized to one of them for not visiting him in the following pathetic words: "I had been so defeated, so disappointed of my expectation, that I was in no mood for society, even that of friends; and I hastened home to my forest cover, with the feeling of the wounded hart flying to the thicket."

From the time of this retreat from the hostile North to the day of his death, Simms was in many respects an altered man. Hitherto he had borne up against unfavorable criticism on the part of strangers and of his own people, and against constant pecuniary embarrassments, with a strength and cheerfulness that were sometimes marvelous. His constitution had seemed to be herculean; no amount of labor could daunt or fatigue him. In his amusements as well as in his routine work he had always shown a vim and zest that had been the envy and despair of milder and soberer spirits like Timrod and Hayne. But now a change comes over him, which is probably more visible to the biographer who has studied his correspondence than it was to the friends who saw him from day to day. It is a gradual change, premonitions of which are not wanting even before this memorable autumn of

1856. He begins to refer to the state of his health, declares that he is overworked, and that what he has already accomplished has been to little or no purpose. He is becoming a great sufferer from catarrh and from some of those painful although not dangerous complaints which are natural to sedentary men, — dyspepsia and its attendant ills. He becomes more querulous, although he can never conceal his natural kindness of heart. He complains of imaginary slights from old friends like Thompson of the "Messenger; " he exaggerates a brief depreciatory notice of his poetry in the New York "Tribune" into a persistent endeavor on the part of the North to destroy his literary reputation. He takes a gloomier view of the political situation, for which he had abundant cause apart from any predisposition to paint things in dark colors, and finally he allows over two years to go by without publishing anything of note. This last fact will be perhaps accepted as sufficient proof that something was wrong with him.

Nor was he suffering entirely from a morbid fancy, as some of his friends tried to assure him. His health was being gradually undermined by the great strain to which he had been subjecting his constitution for years; his wife and children, too, were not infrequently ailing, and his father-in-law was a chronic sufferer from the gout. Unless he could keep his eye on everything that went on at Woodlands, he was certain to lose money. The negroes were lazy and pampered, the overseers were thoroughly unreliable. He had come to the plantation with a debt on his shoulders, and in twenty years he was still in arrears, although probably not to the same parties. His romances were no longer in such demand as when "The Yemassee" went through its three large editions in a year, nor were the magazines so glad to take his pieces or to pay as good prices for them. And yet his family was a large one, and his children were year by year becoming a greater expense to him. It is no wonder, then, that a tone of despondency becomes noticeable in his letters, which deepens as fire sweeps away his possessions, as his children die of dread diseases, as, to crown all, the storm bursts upon his beloved South and changes the whole face of things.

Yet although despondency masters him at times, he still has many things to make him happy, and is far from succumbing to his fancies and drifting into an idle, purposeless life. He still plans new romances even if he does throw all save one aside; he still dreams of dramatic success, and writes several acts of a Spanish tragedy, "Don Carlos;" he still collects Revolutionary letters and documents, and slowly revises his history of South Carolina; and finally he still dabbles in poetry and amuses himself by collecting his fugitive "Areytos" from forgotten magazines and from no less forgotten volumes of his own. But while this work was pleasant if not profitable, he had another and a greater source of pleasure. He had always been a sociable man, and had longed for intellectual companion-

ship, which up to this time he could get only at
the North. As a young man he had never been
freely admitted to the cultured society of his native city, and although this exclusiveness had re-
laxed as he had grown older and had made his
mark, it had nevertheless continued to wound him,
and to render him uncomfortable even in the company of such of his contemporaries as had long since
acknowledged his worth. · Now, however, he had
gradually gathered around him a band of younger
men, all ambitious and some devoted to that severe
mistress, Poetry, whom he had himself served with
such devotion and with so little success. These
men looked up to him, and were zealous in fighting
his battles. They formed a club and placed him
at the head, and many were the rubbers of whist that
were played amid the clinking of glasses and the
clatter of tongues eager to improve the few rare
moments when "Father Abbot" was not addressing his disciples. At such meetings Simms was in
his element. There was no one to contradict him,
hardly any one to criticise him, and he discoursed on
every imaginable subject with equal ease and vol-
ubility. What cared he if neighbors two blocks
away astonished his host the next morning by smiling, and saying, "So you had Simms with you
last night. We could hear him declaiming as far
away as my house." He went on, and thundered
out one of Daniel Webster's speeches, or a backwoods joke, or a poem of his own, as the case might
be. And the club applauded, even if Timrod did

occasionally give vent to an undertone expression of weariness.

Among the leading members of this little coterie were Paul Hayne, Henry Timrod, John Dickson Bruns, Samuel Lord, Junior, F. Peyre Porcher, Richard Michel, Hayne's brother - in-law, Samuel Y. Tupper, and Benjamin J. Whaley. Of these, Bruns, Porcher, and Michel became physicians, and Lord and Whaley followed the law. Mr. Tupper was the business man of the party, and Hayne and Timrod were the literary Bohemians. It is strange that of these nine men the only three that have died are those who were specially inclined to lead a literary life, — for Dr. Bruns wrote some pleasant verses and was a man of great taste and cultivation.[1] Of the survivors, all save Dr. Michel are representative citizens of Charleston, that gentleman having made Montgomery, Alabama, his home. The club they formed was a purely informal affair, which met in turn at the houses of the members; but when he was in Charleston Simms would generally have the meetings in his own house, which he facetiously called his "wigwam."

In the mornings, when he was not at his printer's, he would while away the hours in the office of one of his protégés, generally in that of Lord, who doubtless was not as overrun with clients in the

---

[1] Since the above was written, Mr. Tupper has died, full of years and honors. I have to regret the fact that on my visit to Charleston to gather materials for this book, I was unable to have a conversation with Mr. Tupper. Extracts from letters written by that gentleman will be given hereafter.

latter part of the fifties as he is to-day. In the afternoons Russell's book-shop was the rendezvous.
It was situated on busy King Street, and looking
out from it one could get a glimpse of Charleston's
best people passing and repassing. Seats were
arranged in the rear of the shop for special guests
such as Simms, Petigru, Mitchell King, who used
to buttonhole Russell and repeat long passages from
the Latin poets, to the worthy bookseller's great
bewilderment, Alfred Huger, Dr. Samuel Henry
Dickson, and Father Lynch. There, too, might
be found Simms's spare and ascetic friend, the
Rev. James W. Miles, and the Hon. William J.
Grayson, Petigru's biographer and the apologist
for slavery. Of the younger men, besides Hayne
and Lord, one has been spared to win a world-wide
reputation for the classical knowledge of which he
had just laid the foundations in Germany, Dr.
Basil L. Gildersleeve. Another recent graduate
of a German university was David Ramsay, a
grandson of the historian, destined soon to lose his
life at Fort Wagner; and as brilliant as any of
those that have been mentioned was William R.
Taber, the young editor of the "Mercury," who
was killed in a duel in September, 1856.

One outcome of these gatherings at Russell's was
the appearance in April, 1857, of the first number
of "Russell's Magazine," the best publication of
the kind ever undertaken in Charleston. Hayne
and a Mr. W. B. Carlisle were the editors, but
Hayne did all the work. He was gallantly assisted

by Simms, Timrod, Bruns, Grayson, and others, and the magazine ran for three years. It died in March, 1860, and it excites our admiration for having lived so long in such days of confusion. It stood up stanchly for everything Southern, particularly for Simms; whenever Hayne got a chance to praise his friend, he did so, and did it well and honestly. Sometimes he overdid the matter, as when he wrote or allowed to be published a severe critique on Dana's "Household Book of Poetry," because Simms had not been represented therein. And when the "Courier" refused to publish Dana's calm and fair letter of remonstrance, which was afterwards sent to Simms and is still preserved, a further proof was furnished of the harmful effects of the spirit of sectional hatred and suspicion that was abroad in the land.

But Hayne, though at times a partisan where his friends were concerned, was essentially a noble spirit; the noblest and most charming character, with the exception of Simms, to be found among Southern writers, one is almost tempted to say, among Southern gentlemen. He wrote the most delightful letters of all of Simms's correspondents. He was always loyal, always frank, always the gentle lover of what seemed to him to be true and beautiful. When he traveled from home his genial nature won the love of men like Fields and Longfellow. No more simple and refined gentleman was ever nurtured in the old South. If he lacked Simms's vigor and powers of varied accomplishment, or Timrod's artistic self-control, his genius was, nevertheless, more receptive, more keenly alive to the beauties of nature and of art. Without lacking virility, he charms chiefly by his possession of traits of character distinctively feminine. His gentleness, his receptivity, his delicacy of feeling, his facility in surrendering himself to the domination of master minds, are all feminine traits, some of which have impaired the value of his poetry, but which have combined to give a unique charm to his personality.

"Russell's" was not Hayne's first editorial undertaking. He had helped W. C. Richards on the "Southern Literary Gazette," a weekly published in Charleston during the early fifties, and had been associate editor of a Washington weekly, the "Spectator," which was published by a certain Augustus Harvey. This position had been got for him by Simms, who never tired of helping his friends; but it may be inferred from Hayne's letters that he reaped neither honors nor pecuniary rewards from his connection with the short-lived "Spectator." It is pathetic to learn that after all his exertions he could secure only five subscribers for Harvey's journal in the whole city of Charleston. But Hayne was primarily a poet, and whatever may be thought of the quality and permanence of his work, the brave struggle he made to live for the sake of his art will always endear him, not only to his own people, but to all who can appreciate heroic self-devotion to noble ends.

Now a man who could deliberately set himself
apart in the old South to lead a literary life needed
constant encouragement, and there was no one
more willing and able to give this encouragement
than Simms. His acquaintance with Hayne began
early in the fifties, and to the day of his death
he never ceased to urge the latter on to new
achievements, or to prophesy great things of him.
Hayne has left on record his youthful veneration
for Carolina's greatest writer, and he never failed
to acknowledge how much Simms had done to
stimulate him to creative efforts. It was not the
mere puffery of a clique when Hayne wrote rever-
ently and lovingly of Simms in "Russell's," and
when Simms reviewed Hayne's poems in two long
articles in the "Mercury." Both men felt what
they said; both knew that they were striving for a
common end, — for the advancement of their art,
and especially the art of their section. And if
their efforts were immature, if they are destined to
be far surpassed by the creations of writers nurtured under more favorable conditions, it is idle to
think that they worked in vain, — no honest work
is ever in vain, — for their examples must stimulate future workers along the same lines, and their
productions must be credited with having at least
kept in exercise the literary faculty, whatever it
may be, of the Southern people at a time when it
looked as if that faculty must perish from disuse.

A man of greater genius than Hayne, but
equally indebted to Simms for both sympathy and

substantial help, was Henry Timrod, son of the poet-mechanic, William H. Timrod. Simms had known Timrod's father, and he was among the first to acknowledge the genius of the son. His relations with Timrod do not seem, however, to have been as constantly cordial as his relations with Hayne; and it is safe to say that the fault was not entirely on Simms's side. Hayne, in a letter written from Charleston on February 9, 1860, alludes to one unpleasantness between them as follows: "When leisure and inclination coincide, will you not oblige *me* by a brief review of Timrod's Poems? I know, after what has occurred, *he* can urge *no possible* claim upon your notice, but, nevertheless, I wish you *would* notice him."

This unpleasant little matter would deserve oblivion were it not for the fact that it is typical of the kind of treatment Simms was constantly receiving from men who ought to have been his friends. It is gratifying, however, to know that the estrangement did not last long; and we shall see hereafter that Simms was able to render great assistance to Timrod in the terrible years that immediately followed the war. Although Hayne does not assign a cause for the breach between the two writers, it is easy to infer what the true cause was. Timrod was critical by nature and Simms was vulnerable in many places. Timrod knew that he could write real poetry, while Simms could not, and it probably vexed him to hear the elder man airing his often crude views upon poetical subjects in his positive

Johnsonian manner. Then again the contrast between Simms's magnificent physique and his own puny frame was not likely to make the rough and ready favors and approbation of the veteran author very acceptable.

Be this as it may, Timrod's was probably the most finely endowed mind to be found in Carolina, or indeed in the whole South, at this period. His German blood and his inherited qualities had given him a greater artistic endowment than any other Southern writer, save Poe, had been blessed with. He was able, except in the case of his sonnets, in which he evidently came under Simms's influence, to control himself; was able to devote time and patience to the polishing and perfection of his verse; and, more than all, was able to distinguish between subjects that were proper and subjects that were alien to his art. In these respects he was slightly, but only slightly, superior to Hayne. But where Hayne and the generality of Southern poets possessed a delicate fancy, for the most part exercised on subjects not far removed from the commonplace, Timrod possessed an imagination which, if not lofty and wide embracing, was within its narrow range characterized by a singular intensity. He has not left much work behind him, and that work is marred by the effects which constant sickness and poverty and the stress of war necessarily had upon his genius; but he has left a few singularly beautiful poems, and one at least, the ode written for the occasion of the decoration of the Confederate graves in Magnolia Cemetery, that approximates perfection, — the perfection of Collins, not that of Lovelace. That he was dominated by Tennyson, just as Hayne was dominated by Tennyson and William Morris, and Simms by Wordsworth, is perfectly true; but his poetic powers were not only greater than those of his brothers, but also more akin to the powers of the great model he set himself. Hence I cannot but believe that a day will come when his work will be more generally known than it is at present.

But although Timrod sometimes resisted Simms's influence, neither he nor any other member of this interesting group could wholly escape that influence or fail to look up to Simms as the chief representative of Southern literature, as the standard bearer of a high cause which had experienced failure oftener than success. The more intimately they knew the man, the more they loved him, and the more they could overlook his pomposity when he folded his cloak around him, and began to discuss the topic uppermost in his mind.

Some members of "the club" preferred his idle talk, which, in the words of one of them, Mr. Tupper, "was ever entertaining and frequently instructive." "His estimate of prominent politicians and little great men about us was singularly correct," continues the same authority. "He had a great contempt for cant and affectation; nothing irritated him more than the solemn, ponderous talk of a blockhead affecting the dignity and wisdom of a bishop or judge."

Mr. Tupper also describes how he used to sit and watch Simms prepare an article for immediate publication. "He would write page after page without stopping a moment for reflection or revision, and, without altering a word or reading what he had written," would let it go to the printer, occasionally writing at the end of his sheets the following direction to that functionary: "Carefully revise; I have no time to correct your errors." On one occasion Mr. Tupper and Simms were preparing to go to a festival or ball of the volunteer fire department, when the latter suddenly inquired who were to be the invited guests. Mr. Tupper gave him the names of the most prominent, whereupon Simms called for pen and paper, and in half an hour wrote about twenty stanzas of facetious poetry, each stanza giving some well-known characteristic of a separate guest. These he read at the proper time with such effect that he was obliged to reread them before the night was over. He then walked to a fireplace and burned them, resisting Mr. Tupper's importunity to save them, by declaring that he would not preserve anything that reflected on the infirmities of friends.

Naturally the stories told about Simms are not always so pleasant as this one. Yet, while some of them are calculated to raise a smile at his expense, not one of them will make a discriminating hearer forget the real excellence of the man. Sometimes even his young admirers were tempted to make his peculiarities the subject of a practical joke. For example, Simms prided himself on his gastronomic attainments, and in the person of Lieutenant Porgy once allowed himself to grow eloquent over the delicacy of a stew made of alligator terrapins. But there were some heretics in "the club" who did not believe that Simms had ever eaten an alligator terrapin, and they determined to try him on the dish for which he had given so elaborate a receipt. They procured one of the monsters after some delay and trouble, and, having arranged for the proper making of the stew, invited Simms to supper. The veteran came, and was bountifully helped to his favorite dish. At the very first mouthful he made a wry face, and exclaimed: "For heaven's sake, boys, where did you get this rancid stuff?" "That is alligator terrapin, stewed à la Porgy, Mr. Simms," was the reply. "Ah," said the discomfited romancer, "you must have made some mistake with the receipt."

The literary inactivity which characterized Simms after his return from the North in the autumn of 1856 has been already described. He wrote for "Russell's" and the "Mercury," and supplied Appleton's "New American Cyclopædia" with biographical sketches, but he began new romances only to throw them aside. One of his reviews in "Russell's" deserves notice because it shows that he could at times point out defects in Southern literary work. The person who received this unfavorable but just criticism was a small poet named Howard H. Caldwell, who, according to

Hayne, instigated in revenge a nasty attack upon Simms in the columns of the New Orleans "Delta." Hayne in his loyalty turned the cold shoulder to Caldwell, and wrote to Simms as follows: —

"It [Simms's career as a writer] has been a fight against bitter prejudice, miserable provincialism of tone and sentiment, mean jealousies, and, worse than all, that species of ignorance which is so invincibly blind and presumptuous. . . . And just *such* a contest, modified in detail, but the same essentially, awaits every true literary athlete, whose intellectual battlefield happens to be in any part of this material, debased, provincial, narrowminded South! God help all such combatants. 'T is *almost* enough to make one forswear his country. I cannot refrain from picturing to myself your fate, had you removed at any early age to Massachusetts or Europe. Prosperity, praise, 'troops of friends,' and admirers, but *not* what you now possess, and which must be a proud consolation, — the consciousness of having been true to the Penates, of having illustrated, as none other has, the *genius loci*, under disadvantages which would have sunk a weaker mind and corrupted a less manly and heroic heart." (January 14, 1859.)

Some months previously (October 30, 1858), Simms, while jotting down the personal memoranda which were cited in the first chapter of this book, commented as follows on his father's advice that he should remain in Mississippi: —

"Thirty odd years have passed, and I can now

mournfully say the old man was right. All that I
have [done] has been poured to waste in Charleston,
which has never smiled on any of my labors, which
has steadily ignored my claims, which has dispar-
aged me to the last, has been the last place to give
me its adhesion, to which I owe no favor, having
never received an office, or a compliment, or a dollar at her hands; and, with the exception of some
dozen of her citizens, who have been kind to me,
and some scores of her young men, who have honored me with a loving sympathy and something
like reverence, which has always treated me rather
as a public enemy, to be sneered at, than as a du-
tiful son doing her honor. *And I, too, know it
as a place of tombs.* I have buried six dear children within its soil! Great God! what is the sort
of slavery which brings me hither!"

It was not a morbid temper alone that inspired
these gloomy words. Simms had just been through
trials that would have unnerved any man. The
year 1858 had been ushered in by the death of his
father-in-law, Mr. Nash Roach (February 28), and
more untimely deaths had followed. Mr. Roach
had reached the age of sixty-six, and on his death
Woodlands had passed to Simms and his wife for
their lives, and on their deaths to their eldest son,
William Gilmore. But Woodlands, which had
been especially bright to Simms ever since the
birth of his second son, Sydney Roach, in August, 1852, and of his third son, Beverley Hammond,
in August, 1854, was to be bright no longer. The

family had removed as usual to Charleston, and Simms had gone North for a short trip, when the yellow fever made its appearance in the city. "A terrible prescience," as he afterwards styled it, hurried the father home. He arrived only in time to find his two favorite sons stricken with the disease. All efforts of father, mother, and devoted friends like William Porcher Miles, who gave himself up to nursing them, failed to save them, and they died on the same day, September 22, 1858.

The loss of these boys was probably the greatest blow that Simms had ever had. Children of his maturer years, they had entered like sunshine into his clouded and chequered life. One of them had combined the names of two dear friends (Tucker and Major Hammond), and both had seemed up to this time the embodiment of health and spirits. He had loved all his children, and, besides those mentioned in the previous chapter, he had had two born to him within the past two years; his eldest daughter, too, had just married, or was about to marry, her cousin, Mr. Edward Roach, and he might look forward to having grandchildren at his knees; but he could not be comforted, and in poems and letters he poured forth the bitterness of his grief.

In such a state of mind it was natural for him to turn for relief to his proper and congenial occupation of writing romances. He took up the unfinished "Cassique of Kiawah," and by the spring of 1859 had it ready for the printers. Except for the touching prefatory sonnet to Miles, no traces are to be found in it of the effects of his great sorrow upon his mind and heart. There is hardly a sign of flagging powers, although he has been writing romances for twenty-seven years. Sometimes, it is true, he proses more than is usual with him; but when he wakes up from his doze and pushes off on the trail of his plot, he runs like an old hound who is anxious to show that he is still worthy to be called the leader of the pack. In short, although the Revolutionary romances have at times a greater charm for the reader who loves the wild, free life of swamp and forest, "The Cassique of Kiawah" maintains an average standard of excellence which makes one hesitate before determining that it is inferior to any of Simms's romances.

Like "The Yemassee" it is a colonial story, but of a still earlier period — 1684. Unlike "The Yemassee" it does not confine itself to the woods, or make its Indian characters prominent; but gives an admirable description of the infant Charlestown and of life on a gallant privateer, the Happy-go-Lucky, terrible to Spanish galleons and dear to colonial dames who purchase its contraband silks and laces. Its author is nowhere out of his element, and does not, as in so many of his other works, allow his historical knowledge to impede his progress. If his descriptions of events at sea display no special familiarity with seamanship, they are nevertheless spirited and full of action, not mere colorless imitations of Cooper. And if

the fact that a romance of six hundred pages does
not seem tedious to a reader who has already gone
through twenty odd romances by the same author,
be a sign of success, then Simms certainly succeeded in "The Cassique of Kiawah."

This last of Simms's worthy romances had fallen
upon bad times; for the country was too much
stirred up over the great questions of slavery and
secession to pay much attention to literature.
Nevertheless many who read it expressed their admiration in the warmest terms. Cooke and Hayne
were especially pleased, and Professor W. J. Rivers, perhaps the best informed man in Carolina on
matters of local history, wrote to bear his testimony
to the accuracy with which Simms had delineated
the historical period in which he had set his romance. Stately Charleston bought a few more
copies than usual; and even the "North American
Review" made some amends for its former unpleasantness by giving a favorable notice of the book.
Thus encouraged, the veteran shook off his troubles
and his ill health sufficiently to revise and enlarge
his "History of South Carolina." Scarcely had
he finished this task, before his nerves were again
shattered by the severe illness of his baby daughter,
Harriet Middleton, whose beauty had been the
pride of the family. She was Miles's god-daughter, and after the crisis was over Simms wrote the
former, then member of Congress from Charleston,
a pitiful account of the anguish that had racked
him for weeks past. After her recovery he was

cheered by a visit from his old friend Lawson, and perhaps by an invitation, got for him by Miles and others of his friends in Congress, to deliver the oration at the unveiling of Clark Mills's equestrian statue of Washington. It was undoubtedly a pleasure to be requested to undertake such a task; but Simms wrote back dolefully that he was sick, despondent, poor, and out at the edges generally. So he felt obliged to decline, and the Hon. Mr. Bocock, of Virginia, was finally chosen to fill his place. His despondency was further increased by the accidental burning of his house in Charleston early in May, 1860. Here many of the pleasantest months of his life had been spent with Hayne and other friends, and here he had lost his two boys. "You will feel a little yourself," he wrote Miles, "for a wigwam, in which you have seen us so bitterly tried." Other letters followed, telling his friend of plantation losses, of the illness of another child, of the rascalities of politicians, and of the evil of things in general; but he was not enough of a pessimist to avoid an expression of paternal pride when his namesake Gilmore stood "Number One" at the Arsenal Academy of Columbia.

Meanwhile his revised "History of South Carolina" had been published, and he went to New York in August, 1860, to superintend the printing of his last ante-bellum book, his enlarged "Areytos, or Songs of the South." There was, of course, no need for the volume, — youthful love songs are hardly the kind of poetry with which to usher in a revolution, — but Simms took an almost feverish delight in publishing, and if he ever needed pleasure, he needed it in this trying year of 1860. To do him justice it must be said that he expected no praise for his poems, but he did expect great things of his history, and he was much disappointed when he found that scarcely a newspaper in South Carolina took any notice of it. The "North American Review" gave him another compliment; but the South Carolinians were too busy applauding violent secessionist speeches to pay any attention to their own history, even though Simms had written his book with the avowed purpose of furnishing the young men of the State with an ample stock of arguments with which to defend the cause of states-rights. He laid great stress upon this last point in his letters to Congressman Miles; but, although he is certainly more outspoken about nullification than he was in his first edition, it is hard to discover why he should have thought that he had prepared a manual for a statesman, when he had only written a good school history or an interesting sketch for a general reader. It is true that, as President C. K. Adams of Cornell has said, "it shows an intense local patriotism," but South Carolina politicians hardly needed lessons in that regard in the year 1860. Still, as the above quoted authority says, the book "has several distinctive merits above all other histories of South Carolina. It covers the whole period down to our civil war. It has all the beauties of the author's character-

istic style. . . . From beginning to end the narration is spirited and graphic, but the sketch is
too brief for details even on the most important
points." This is high praise, and it is in the
main well deserved. One can only wish that
Simms could have seen it just after he had written
one of his lugubrious letters to Miles on the subject of his people's neglect of his patriotic book.
For, however sectional it may seem nowadays,
Simms certainly made it patriotic in his sense of
the term. Yet it was not the first time his efforts
for South Carolina had been slighted by the people
for whom they were made, and after a short stay in
New York, during which he advised his friends,
like Lawson, to unload their Southern securities as
speedily as possible, he returned to Woodlands
to await, with what patience he could muster, the
breaking out of the war he had long foretold.

But as we began with nightmares we may as well
end with them, even though this chapter has already stretched out to an unconscionable length;
and as it began with extracts from Simms's correspondence with Beverley Tucker, it may close with
similar extracts from his correspondence with his
young friend Miles. Before these interesting letters are examined, however, it will be well to refer
briefly to a ridiculous action on the part of one of
those useless and demoralizing Southern conventions which were stirring up strife in the decade
preceding the war.

The convention held in December, 1856, at Sa-

vannah appointed a committee to prepare a "series
of books in every department of study, from the
earliest primer to the highest grade of literature
and science." The books were to be free, of course,
from abolitionist teachings, and were to show the
world the beauties of slavery and the indefeasibil-
ity of states-rights. The committee appointed to
prepare this literature — and there are some good
people in the South to-day who dream of manufac-
turing a similar product — contained some excellent
men like Bishop Elliott, of Georgia, and Professor
Bledsoe, but, strangely enough, the only representative man of letters the South could boast of was
omitted. This remarkable action was noticed in a
sarcastic article in "Putnam's Magazine" for February, 1857, the writer inquiring why the name of
William Gilmore Simms, LL. D., had been so un-
ceremoniously passed over. He went on to say:
"In respect, however, of constructive talent and
affluence of product, Mr. Simms takes precedence
of any other of our distinctive Southern authors.
Mr. Wirt and Mr. Legaré, who are usually quoted
as the Pillars of Hercules of our Southern literature [*ex pede* NON *Herculem*], were both polished,
and graceful, and accomplished essayists; but they
displayed none of the verve or continuity of
Simms."

It is a little amusing to recall at this point the
notion Simms had latterly taken up that the Northern press was endeavoring to undermine his reputation. His sturdiest supporters and the major-

ity of his readers had always been at the North,[1]
and it was not until he began to meddle in politics
that he ever got any severer criticism there than a
man of his careless literary habits might have expected. If it had not been for the encouragement
which the North gave to "Atalantis," "Martin
Faber," "Guy Rivers," and "The Yemassee," he
might have gone on publishing "Early Lays," and
other such volumes, to the end of time without anybody's being the wiser except a few Southern bibliophiles. If he had not visited the North summer
after summer, mingling with her literary men, his
work would have been far more provincial, if indeed he had found sufficient incitement to keep
working at all. The neglect he had had to complain of had come chiefly from the South, for reasons which have already been given at length.
This recent ignoring of his claims by the Southern
convention, while really an unintended compliment,
was but of a piece with the constant slights he had
received from his own people for thirty odd years.
It was but feeble amends for this treatment that
he was afterwards made a member of the Southern
Board of Education appointed by the Knoxville
Convention, or that he was named by the governor
as a delegate from South Carolina to the Southern
Commercial Convention which met at Montgomery,
Alabama, in May, 1858.[2]

[1] Redfield stated this to General J. G. Wilson, with regard to
the revised edition.

[2] This action of the Savannah Convention has been twisted into

In his correspondence with Tucker, Simms had deferred to the former's age, and had allowed him to lead the discussions they kept up on politics, but in the case of his young friend Miles he was disposed to be leader himself, and to play the part of adviser. It is somewhat amusing in view of his former prophecies to find him writing from Woodlands, February 3, 1859: —

"Don't touch Cuba. She is the bait which the Democratic party holds out to the South. Beware how you enter this field. The Democratic party has but one chance left for life, that of involving us in foreign war. It is a mere delusion to suppose that our chances of getting Cuba are less, if separate, than as a whole. *If separate, we control the whole commerce, — all the shipping of the North! It is better to be separate before we take Cuba.* Take it now, and we have a burning brand we shall never extinguish. It is the only process for bolstering up the Democratic party, and while that party lives the South can never be secure. But I forget, my dear Miles, I am too spasmodic now for a politician. I have hurts and cares, which keep me from thought. Make the most you can of this scribble, for there is truth in it. I see a thousand miles ahead in this matter. God bless you. Yours ever, SIMMS."

a joke which has come more than once to my ears. "*Resolved,*" so the Convention is reported as voting, " That there be a Southern literature. *Resolved,* That William Gilmore Simms, LL. D., be requested to write this literature." This humorous perversion of an action silly enough to need no perversion is due to the article in *Putnam's* quoted above.

Writing from Woodlands, May 21, he says: "My own opinion is that the people of all the South are monstrously ahead of all their politicians, as the latter will be made to see and feel. It is only the trading politicians that care about a president at all. The people of the South want their rights, not office. Those who want office scarcely can understand them [the people]. Mark me, the politician now, who would maintain himself long, must endeavor to get ahead of the people, not to arrest their momentum, but to direct it in the very path they are pursuing. . . . We in the South at this juncture can condense all our political creed into one brief formula: 'We know but the South, and the South in danger!' And no more tampering with the enemy; no more campaigns bolstering up a driveling [?] party to the ruin of the South. Write me. I need it."

At the end of the same year, December 28, writing of ex-governor, then senator, Hammond, he says: "He is friendly to Buchanan and will support him, but only so long as Buchanan shall prove superior to the stupid ambition of trying to win over the Northern democracy at the sacrifice of everything. In brief, Hammond will support the Democratic party only while it is tributary to the interests of the South." In the same letter he gives Miles this laconic advice: "Let all your game lie in the constant recognition and assertion of a *Southern nationality.*" On February 8, 1860, he gives him better advice when he tells him

not to let the Southern members "mouth and splut-
ter," — a bit of counsel which should have been
given to them years before, as the pages of the
"Congressional Globe" abundantly prove. Writing March 21, of a speech recently delivered by
Senator Hunter, he remarks that it is "a true,
timid, compromising one, though well written. It
will not do for the time. We want thunderbolts,
not gossamer, for the combat. This of course is
all *inter nos.*"

During the summer of 1860 he is mainly occupied in speculating about the presidential election
of the coming autumn.[1] He thinks Breckinridge's
chances good, declaring that Douglas will not get
the vote of a single Southern State. But after all
he does not attach as much importance to the election as he does to the fact that the cotton States
have been brought "to act together, independently,
irrespectively of the North," — that the conflict has
been brought to the only issue that could possibly
come, "a purely sectional issue," from which only
one result can arise, a struggle for independence on
the part of the South. Apropos of this consummation he writes, July 15: "I had a long and earnest talk with Jamison, begging him to see Rhett
and urge strenuously upon him what I should say.
I told him that, while I was anxious, like himself,
for the formation of a Southern confederacy, I saw
clearly that such a declaration would drive our

---

[1] He approved of the breaking up of the Charleston Convention, but did not think that the Southern leaders went *far enough.*

people from us, — at this time the fruit is not ripe,
— but that we should really retard the final day
of deliverance." He then goes on to point out how
hard it is to make politicians and common people
conduct a campaign on abstract principles, and
concludes that even if the "Black Republicans"
win this time it will be better for the South. For
the successful party will go ahead in its madness
until at the South both politicians and people will
feel that there is no bearing their insolence any
longer, and all will move toward the formation of
a "Southern confederacy." Therefore "it is to be
wished that Mr. Rhett could take no active part in
the canvass," and the "Mercury" will do well "to
forbear as much as possible and to expend its thunder rather upon Lincoln than Douglas." In this
way Lincoln may be defeated, and if not, the Republican party will become still more odious, and
then will come the separation.

There is a good deal of shrewd political sense
mixed up with these nightmares, as the reader has
doubtless perceived. Simms evidently did not see
clearly how far the people of the South had been
led to dread the success of the Republicans, but
he was quick enough to perceive that in the success
of that party he and his friends must base their
hopes for the speedy separation of the sections.
Nor was he at all inclined to mince matters, as some
honest persons were then and have been since, by
proclaiming that the South was merely engaging
in a struggle for her constitutional rights. He saw

plainly enough that people do not fight for abstract
principles, and that if constitutional questions came
into play at all, it would only be in a secondary
sense. He boldly based his desire for separation
on the hatred existing between the sections and on
the menace which the preponderance of power on
the part of the North gave to the South's peculiar
institution. In other words, he saw that the coming war would be one for the preservation of slavery, however much men might consciously or unconsciously disguise the fact. He had echoed
Tucker's words: "If we will not have slaves, we
must be slaves," and in doing so he showed himself to be a clearer thinker than the conscientious
but befogged theorists around him, who were forever speaking and writing as if the constitutional
theories which were held on account of slavery
were more potent over men's minds than the destroying institution itself. We may regret that
such a clear-headed man should have been so de-
luded in respect to the true nature of the cause for
which he was struggling, but it is as well to remember that he did not claim to be fighting for one
thing when he was really fighting for another.

And so when Lincoln was elected and the call
came for a convention of his State, Simms was not
found napping. He wrote to Miles that he hoped
they would carry the South "through what the
Germans call the *Landsturm*." "It will be a popular rush," he added, "as I have always predicted,
as soon as the national party should have perished;

the momentum given to the people being such as no popular leader or politician would venture to head, or, heading,[1] which would be sure to run over him." Then he goes on to point out that the descendants of Revolutionary heroes should be put forward to engage the popular sympathy, and that a proper man should be found for the governorship, which "will be for a time at least the presidency of a new republic." He proposes a bill of rights for the convention to draw up, and wishes Miles to consider whether in the new confederacy the States should not have equal representation in the lower house as well as in the upper, the great principle of safety being the protection of minorities or feeble States. Not content with these suggestions, he sends some patriotic poems for insertion in the "Mercury."

Nor does he forget to keep his Northern friends like Mr. Bockie, of Brooklyn, informed on the state of affairs at the South. On November 20, he writes to him from Woodlands: "Never was a people so thoroughly aroused and resolute before. . . . South Carolina will secede first, Alabama and Mississippi, Georgia and Florida, in order next, and before the 1st of February, all these States will be out of the Confederacy.[2] South Carolina will be out before Christmas. Her legislature was unanimous, and every member of the convention

---

[1] Two commas have been inserted to make the meaning plainer, but the construction of the sentence is hopelessly bad.

[2] That is, the Union, which was a Confederacy according to Simms.

nominated is for secession unreservedly. South Carolina alone can bring 60,000 men into the field, sixty Palmetto regiments; and we have already 50,000 volunteers from other States, should any attempt be made at coercion. Such an attempt will help us and force all the other Southern States to take their places by our side. . . . The Union had survived its uses, had got to be a mere shop [?] of faction, fraud, and peculation, was no longer a guardian of the feeble, was a bold, impudent aggressor upon the rights of others, an usurper, waxing fat and kicking in its lustihood, and needed to be taken down and driven to short commons." [1]

In a word, he was thoroughly aroused. Ill health and lassitude seemed to have left him. He waited impatiently for the passage of the "Ordinance of Secession," and soon after singing his "Nunc Dimittis" wrote Miles a brief undated epistle which concluded as follows: "I have been making stump speeches. Everybody right in this region. Minute men in arms. Go to the convention [at Montgomery] if you can. Of course, Congress is nothing to you now. Identify yourself with the movement. But do not fatigue yourself." [2]

[1] Simms, of course, had his constitutional arguments, but slavery was the chief question with him. Most Southerners then believed, as Dr. Gildersleeve has since expressed it (*Atlantic Monthly*, January, 1892, p. 87), that they were fighting for "the cause of civil liberty, and not the cause of human slavery," — forgetting that it was human slavery which largely determined the nature of a Southerner's ideas of civil liberty.

[2] Alluding to Miles's recent illness.

CHAPTER VII.

THE WAR.

"I AM here, like a bear with a sore head, and chained to the stake," wrote Simms to Miles on the last day of 1860. "I chafe, and roar, and rage, but can do nothing. Do not be rash, but do not let the old city forget her prestige. Charleston is worth all New England."

But if he could not be up in arms, he could do more than roar and curse New England. He could write letters by the dozen to Jamison and Miles, pointing out mistakes that had been made by those in authority, making military suggestions of all sorts, and showing himself dowered with a large supply of common sense and of genius for affairs, as well as with the poet's "hate of hate, the scorn of scorn, the love of love." Only one of these letters can be given here, but all should some day be published.

Sunday [1] Night, 12 P. M.

I am sleepless, my dear Miles, and must write. If you should be sleepless also, it is not improbable but that my letters will help you to a soporific con-

[1] Probably the Sunday that followed the firing on the Star of the West, *i. e.* January 13, 1861.

dition. It seems to me that you will have a little respite. The opening fire upon the Star of the West changes materially the aspect of things to the Federal government, and they will hardly think to send supplies to Sumter except under cover of armed vessels, which is the inauguration of open war upon the State, which the President and cabinet will hardly attempt unless under authority of Congress. Congress alone, I believe, has the power to declare war. There is no telling, however, what may be done when the power is under the hands of a weak administration, counseled and governed, in fact, by a person whose whole training has endowed [him] with military ideas as paramount to all.[1] We must, of course, prepare for two dangers, treachery and assault. But it strikes me that the *unexpected* fire of Fort Morris will compel a pause in the Federal councils, for the better maturing of plans, and some respite for preparation will be allowed you. Not an hour should be lost in preparation. To have numerous guns, to bear equally upon an assailing squadron and Fort Sumter, seems to be the necessity. Looking at the map, I note that Mount Pleasant is distant from Fort Sumter some two miles, while I estimate Moultrie to be some one and a quarter. A battery at Mount Pleasant, cutting the western angle of Sullivan's Island, seems to be in direct range with Sum-

---

[1] It seems plain that Simms here alludes to General Winfield Scott. Cass had had a military training, but he had resigned from the Cabinet when the above was written.

ter, and if within reach of heavy cannon, then a
battery of earth at this point, with half a dozen
thirty-two pounders, might operate successfully
against it, at all events compel a very useful diver-
sion of its fires. So I find that on the sandhills
below Fort Johnson, and on the sandhills at the
extreme western verge of Fort Morris, batteries of
say three heavy cannon each might face Fort Sumter, framed of logs faced with iron and filled in
with sand, which could contribute largely to its
distraction, if not its injury. On these sandhills,
also, you possess an advantage in their elevation,
which will tend to reduce the superiority of Sumter
in height. Two or three batteries along these hills
and at these points, mere bastions, having two or
three guns each of heavy calibre, could be thrown
up very suddenly, assuming, as I do, that you can
command, from the popular patriotism, any amount
of slave labor. I would have them so planted as
not to face the portholes of Sumter, yet be able to
take them at an angle. Shot entering a porthole
obliquely would be more mischievous, perhaps,
than if direct, since the zigzag course they would
pursue would be likely to kill every man on one side
or other of the guns, besides abrading the embra-
sure very seriously. In reference to Wappoo Cut,
let me mention that, as the obvious entrance to that
cut is by the Stono, there is an old fort, once
thought a pretty strong one, at the mouth of the
Stono, on Cole's Island. This might be manned
by volunteers from the precinct, officered by some

good military man. It covers Bird Key [?] and
is very well placed, though still, I think, it would
be good policy to stop up Wappoo Cut, or keep an
armed schooner in Ashley River, at the mouth of
it. I am writing, you perceive, without the slightest knowledge of what *has* been done; and it is
quite probable that all my suggestions have been
anticipated. If, however, you fancy there is anything in them, communicate with Jamison and any
military friends on whose judgment you rely.
Ranging timbers properly mortised might be prepared by the mechanics of the city, and the iron
bars laid on, if desired, before shipment to the desired points. It is my impression that old Fort
Johnson ranges Moultrie in the same line with
Sumter. If so, it is a question how far it would
be proper to use the former place with heavy cannon which might range across the strait. You
should employ all the heavy cannon you can.
Jamison told me that you had an abundance.
Unless Fort Morris has numerous pieces, she could
hardly play any efficient game with many assailing
vessels. I do not know where Fort Morris is
placed, but suppose it to be fronting equally the
Ship and the Twelve-feet channel. In that event,
unless the sandhills interpose, it is under the range
of Fort Sumter, provided the distance be within
three miles, as I suppose it to be. I should have
said four, but for the threat of Anderson to fire
on Fort Morris. A battery between Fort Morris
and the Lighthouse, on the edge of the sandhills,

might rake the Ship Channel with a *plunging* fire, yet I should think be out of range and even sight of Fort Sumter. I think I said, in a previous letter, that in sighting the guns for long distances telescopes should be used; of course, I meant only the ordinary ship spyglasses, of which a sufficient number for each battery could be obtained in the city. With another battery to second Fort Morris, each of twelve guns at least, and heavy ones, you could give a telling account of all entering vessels. They might all be sunk with good gunnery. But two shot only taking effect out of eighteen fired, would seem to show that the gunnery was not sufficiently practiced. I write only from report. To-night, I learn that (*on dit*) there has been a mutiny in Fort Sumter, and that Anderson has had to shoot one of his men, and put ten more in irons; and that *this* was the reason why he did *not* fire on Forts Morris and Moultrie. By the "Mercury" it is said that some negotiations are on foot which will prevent bloodshed. The inference is that Fort Sumter will be given up. This is hardly probable. I suspect treachery. We should suspect nothing else. Anderson wishes communication with the city. If opportunity is allowed him to see what we are doing, or to hear of it, or if he is allowed to corrupt mercenaries, we shall have worse mischief. We must not be too confiding, too easy of faith, too courteous, even to an enemy, who, if he had the right feeling, would at once resign his command and throw up his position on the distinct ground of his Southern birth and associations. He should be kept corked up closely, until we are quite ready to draw him off. If he still keep his position, and we are to have an attempt by the war steamers, Fort Sumter must and will take part in it; the vital point is how to neutralize his action in the engagement. I see but the one suggested, to keep as many batteries at work on him, breaching and otherwise, and a cloud of vessels and men ready for scaling, as will effectively divert his regards from those forts which are designed for the defense of the harbor. And unless Fort Morris be made strong in guns, I see that vessels of heavy draft in deep water may shell it *ad libitum*, while the smaller craft passes in. I am very doubtful whether a fort on the east end of Sullivan's can do more than cover the Maffit and Rattlesnake channels, if these. It can hardly do much mischief to vessels entering the Ship Channel. Something will depend upon the calibre of its guns. Do, if you can spare a half hour, write me, in charity, how we stand, and with what degree of preparation, and believe me

W. GILMORE SIMMS.

To this long letter Simms added a by no means short postscript, in which he detailed a scheme for approaching Fort Sumter by rafts in case an escalade should be attempted, a proceeding which he deprecated upon the whole. The two head rafts were to be covered with thick plank and tin, and to be painted dark. They would thus be protected from hand grenades, and at low water the whole chain of rafts would form an almost solid bridge. But the main point was to wear the garrison out. "So long as we can effect this," he concludes, "and keep them in a state of siege, there is no discredit to the State. We should do nothing rashly now, to the peril of our brave young men, which we can possibly avoid. But you will think me interminable. Once more, good-night." [1]

[1] Any elaborate comments upon this letter, or upon the similar ones that succeeded it, would be out of place on the part of a writer who can make no claim to special knowledge of military matters. Yet it would be unfair to Simms not to point out how far he seems to have anticipated in his correspondence the plan of operations subsequently pursued by the State and Confederate authorities in reference to the defenses of Charleston harbor. The floating battery which operated against Sumter, and which Beauregard commended to the Confederate Secretary of War (*The War of the Rebellion*, etc., Series I. vol. i. p. 316), was one of Simms's earliest suggestions. The battery proposed at Fort Johnson was erected, and a second added ; a ten-inch mortar was also used at Mount Pleasant. The iron-clad battery at Cummings Point, on the extremity of Morris Island, looking toward Sumter, which was the chief subject of many of his letters, was erected almost entirely in accordance with his plans, as is evident from a comparison of his letters with those which Major Anderson was sending at the time to the authorities at Washington. This battery worked well, but the credit of its conception has been wrongly assigned. *The Charleston Year Book* for 1883 (p. 549) states that "the first thought of the modern iron armor now in use originated in Charleston, with the late Col. C. H. Stevens, Twenty-fourth South Carolina Volunteers, who, as a private citizen, in January, 1861, began the erection of an iron-armored battery of two guns, on Morris Island, built with heavy yellow pine timber of great solidity, at an angle of 40°, *and faced with bars of*

On February 20, besides his remarks on a copy-right law, — a subject which had been discussed by him in the "Southern Literary Messenger" several years before, — he referred as follows to the question of restricting the slave-trade: "We ought to frame no organic law touching the slave-trade. We may express a sentiment, if you please; but no law. Either negro slavery is a beneficent, merciful, God-chartered institution, or it is not. If beneficent, why limit it? Is it better for the negro to be a barbarian and savage in his own country, than to work out his deliverance [sic] in this? If better, why be at the pains to cast censure on the morale of the institution? Regulate the trade, but do not abolish."

In the same letter he asks why the three-fifths rule in regard to the representation of slaves should be adopted, — "a rule forced upon us by a people about to abandon slavery, and, in surrendering to

railroad iron." The attempt to find in this experiment the germ of the modern iron-clad is, of course, idle, as armor-plated vessels were constructed by the French in the Crimean War. It would seem to be equally erroneous to assign the conception of the idea of the iron-clad battery to Colonel Stevens. The battery was not begun until the last days of January, and it was on February 5 that Major Anderson discovered that it was being covered with railway bars. But at least a month before, Simms had detailed the whole plan of such a battery to Jamison, then acting as Secretary of War to the State of South Carolina. Jamison spoke of the plan to military men, and perhaps Colonel Stevens deserves the credit of having first determined to act upon it. The subject cannot be pursued, but it is at least apparent that Simms's long letters were not without influence, and that he was no mere dabbler in matters outside his sphere.

which, we gave them the power to conquer us," —
except to conciliate border States like Maryland
and Missouri, which will soon hold the relation
toward the cotton States, if the latter induce them
to enter the new confederacy, which the North
formerly held towards the South. He thinks the
border States will only weaken the new government, that they had better form a middle confederacy, which they must do if they do not join the
cotton States. "Count the votes for yourself,"
he concludes, "and see where, in a few years,
the cotton States would be with such an arrangement. On one hand, Virginia, Maryland, Kentucky, Tennessee, North Carolina, and Missouri,
versus South Carolina, Georgia, Florida, Alabama
[Mississippi], Arkansas, Louisiana, and Texas.
Verb. sap. I am sleepy. It is two o'clock in the
morning."

He must have been very sleepy if he could have
gone to bed without reflecting what a commentary
his own predictions were upon his beloved doctrine
of secession. Why three groups of States, rather
than four, five, or any number? Why not single
cotton States after a while, rather than a group of
them? And why, if Cotton was king and slavery
a divinely appointed institution, should eight States
fail to manage six? But he evidently did not think
the matter out, for two days later he wrote to em-
phasize his views, declaring: "If we move steadily
forward, they [the border States] cannot help themselves, and must come into our fold and on our

own terms. *We should make no organic law, and pass no provision under it, having their case in contemplation at all.* I would rather have a compact empire than a very extensive one, and our future secret of safety and success must depend wholly upon the homogeneity of our society and institutions. Were the territory occupied by the border States an inland sea, a waste of waters, it would please me better." Had this last wish been realized, he would not have had his present biographer pointing out that in the above sentences there is no mention of a union of States holding certain views of the Constitution, but that there is a pretty plain mention of States forming a union to perpetuate slavery. But to continue our extracts. Why, he asks, should we "conciliate States into our alliance whom we shall have to support just as we have supported [sic] New England?" Still they may be of use after all in making "an imposing front which *might* discourage the hostility of the North." And yet he fears that the cotton States will in the future be much more troubled with the question, "Who shall we keep out?" rather than with the question, "How many will come in?" For "in process of time all Mexico is destined to be civilized [sic] through the medium of negro slavery." He further fears that it will be difficult to keep New Jersey and the other Middle States out of his new confederacy, and he prophesies that in three years California will "set up for herself." Let us, then, "not bother our heads to please England and

the North on the score of negro slavery and the
slave-trade. They have already voted us barbarians. But we have them in our power." It seems
a little like the irony of fate that this letter should
have been written on Washington's birthday.

In his next letters he urges for low taxes on im-
ports, describes how he is adapting the sword bay-
onet to the old musket, and refers as follows to
his battery: "I find that Jamison has adopted my
suggestion of using ranging timbers with facings of
railroad iron for batteries; but I am not satisfied
with the shape of the battery, nor with the manner in which the iron is laid on. . . . It presents
too long a plane surface to a plunging fire. Besides, the rails are not spiked down. I counseled
that they should be spiked, but loosely, so as to allow some working of the rail under the shock of
shot or shell." And so he went on, giving minute
details, illustrating his points by diagrams, and
showing at every word how all his faculties were
aroused for the defense of the cause he had labored
for so long. On April 17, he wrote again about his
batteries, concluding with these pathetic words:
"To-day, my dear Miles, I am fifty-five! But my
gray beard is sixty-five. I have grown very old in
two years."

He had been through enough to make him grow
gray, and just two weeks before the letter last
mentioned was written he had had fresh proof of
how hard it was for him to gain any credit for his
labors. Certainly one would think that at such a

time patriotic services would have been recognized, and that men would have been glad to give credit to one another for any exertion, however small, in behalf of the common cause. And yet we find Simms adding a postscript to his letter to Miles of April 2, which runs as follows: —

"I suppose you have seen how quietly all my agency in the suggestion of the battery of rail iron and ranging timber has been ignored. In my letters to you and to Jamison, — and the letters to you were all transferred to him, — I planned batteries for land and water, went into details, showed all the advantages, showed how the structure should be made casemate, bomb-proof, how the plane should be inclined to the rear, how the '*rat trap*' in the rear might be made to improve upon everything hitherto used. In your letters to me you professed to know nothing of these things, and to have no such intimacy with military men as to justify you in approaching them on the subject. In Jamison's letters, he spoke of the great difficulty which he had in persuading military men to consider the subject; all seemed to doubt and to distrust everything which was novel, and from the hands of a civilian. But gradually, as public opinion *abroad* began to speak of the conception as working a revolution in such structures, I find the battery a subject of great attention, and all my poor agency in it ignored wholly. And yet my plans and suggestions covered this and the floating battery, and covered other schemes for temporary structures, by

which I proposed a covered approach to the walls
of Sumter, which should be as secure against hand
grenades as against cannon — Well! it is not
much — More:[1] If there was any strategic device
for the relief of Fort Sumter, I argued and anticipated it in my letters to Jamison written almost
nightly· for months! Enough! Yet one feels a
little sore that there should be no record of a
patriotism and a devotion to his country, which has
left him little time or thought for anything else.
Ever since the moment of secession, and for years
before, in my labors of political literature, I had
the same fate."

Poor old man! — but his friend Miles at least
stuck by him and declared that to Simms more than
to any one else were due the preparations made in
Charleston for the reduction of Sumter. And
while displaying this intense, but to us misguided
patriotism, the zealous partisan was striving to inform himself of all that was being written against
his favorite doctrine of the right of secession. In
the letter to which the above postscript was added
he had written: "I could wish to get every publication which in any degree related to the secession
movement. I wish to fortify myself in regard to
the controversy, as well from the opposite standpoint as from our own." The results of his studies were seen in editorial after editorial in the

---

[1] The effects of his excitement are to be seen in the style of
Simms's letters at this time. His ellipses are often confusing, as
in the above sentence.

"Mercury." For no ignoring of his labors could prevent him from giving up his heart and soul to the cause of his State, and, as we have seen, he did not even stop writing about his batteries.

The war was now fairly begun, and, if his correspondence did not naturally decrease, it is at least certain that few of his letters for the next four years have been preserved. From such as have come to light we see that he was in a constant state of anxiety both for his country and for his family. There was no chance now for summer trips, and although in August, 1861, he wrote to his friend Dr. Porcher that the country about Woodlands was perfectly healthy, there being only one case of fever to seventy negroes, we are inclined to doubt his statement when we find him in the same year losing two of his children from fever of a malignant type. One of these victims was his fifth son, Sydney Hammond, aged two years, the other was Miles's god-daughter Harriet, aged nearly four.

But though mistaken as to the healthfulness of Woodlands, he knew the place well in other respects. Dr. Porcher had just published an essay on the plants of South Carolina and their use in time of war. Here he touched a hobby of Simms's, and the latter wrote him long letters full of suggestions. Sojourns among the Indians and backwoodsmen had enabled our versatile author to pick up much botanical knowledge and many curious recipes for the compounding of medicines and of other useful articles. Soap, cartridge boxes, ink,

bonnets, and peanut chocolate, are among the
things that can be made easily, the last-named
concoction being a very good substitute for coffee,
as Porcher can learn for himself if he will run up
to Woodlands, where there is no scarcity as yet of
"hog and hominy" (April 14, 1863).

If Porcher had made the visit, he would not
have found the Woodlands at which Simms had
passed so many years of pleasure and of pain. The
old house, with its broad piazza, and the study where
so many romances had been written, was no more.
For about the first of April, 1862, the main house
took fire from some unknown cause and burned to
the ground; and if its owner had not some months
previously built a wing to accommodate his over-
flowing library, the family would have had no shelter save an outhouse or two.

Simms had driven with General Jamison to Midway, to learn what was happening at the seat of
war. They got back about one o'clock at night,
and Jamison drove away home, while Simms went
quietly to bed, little dreaming that in three hours
he would have to flee for his life. Beginning in
the attic, the fire made such headway that when it
was discovered at four in the morning, there was
no chance to save the house. The slaves, however,
worked with a will, and in response to Mrs.
Simms's urgent cries, "Boys, save my husband's
library," the fire was prevented from spreading to
the wing. The resulting desolation can be best
comprehended from the following letter to Miles: —

WOODLANDS in Ruins, *April* 10.

Thanks, dear friend, for your kind letter. It is the most perfect solace I have, to find gathering to me at this juncture troops of friends. Your words are most precious among them. You have been beside me in previous and, I think, worse trials. Gladly now would I give my dwelling and all that I have saved, for the restoration of my two boys. And since then, a third boy, and a girl, your own protégé, and, I think, one of the most promising and lovely of my children. Truly, I am pursued by a hungry fate! But I will not succumb. It may crush, but shall not subject me, no [sic] more than Yankeedom shall subject our country. I am happy to tell you that I have saved all my manuscripts, and nearly all my library. I fortunately built, only the last year, a wing to the dwelling, connected by a corridor, twenty feet in length. The wing was saved. But for this removal of my books, they must have been all lost. And only a few days before the fire, I gathered up all my manuscripts — matter enough for fifty volumes, — and packed it into trunks, not knowing how soon I should have to fly, — thinking more of the Yankees than of midnight fires, and wishing to be ready. Had I lost my library and manuscripts the blow would have been insupportable. As it is, I mean to die with harness on my back.

My family is occupying my library and two outhouses. I write you this letter from a corner of my carriage house. I am building two rooms in a

board house, which will afford me tolerable shelter
from the summer, and if the insurance company
will pay, as I am promised, seventy-five in the
hundred, I shall get enough, with my own bricklay-
ers and workmen, to rebuild the walls and roof of
my old mansion. But to restore is impossible.
My loss in money is about $10,000. I have lost
the best part of my furniture, — every bedstead
but one, — half of my bedding, bed and other
clothes, drawers, wardrobes, crockery, medicine
case, and pictures, statuettes, candelabra, ornaments, and a thousand toys, ornaments, mementos,
such as can never be replaced, — the accumulations
of two or three families, for five generations. All
the stores in my pantry were destroyed. Luckily
my meat house and other outhouses were saved.
My negroes worked zealously and with a loving
devotedness, which was quite grateful to me. I had
them on the roofs of corridor, library, and kitchen;
narrowly escaped myself by a ladder from an upper
window, while the floors overhead were falling in.
I do not despair, do not despond, but verily it
tasks all my courage and strength to endure such
repeated strokes of fortune. . . .

So far he writes of himself; the rest of the letter
is occupied with complaints of the neglect of his
counsels by the authorities and with new counsels
as sure to be disregarded. He asks "why artillerists should not be armed with pikes, instead of
with short swords which are of no use;" since

"pikes in the hands of artillerists could protect a battery against any dash of cavalry." "The art of war," he continues, "is no more perfect than any other art, and is susceptible of a thousand improvements, which are not to be expected from the mere soldiers of drill and routine."

But if his counsels were disregarded by "drill and routine" officials, his losses were not forgotten by his friends, some of whom raised a subscription of three thousand dollars to help him to rebuild. He also tried to make a little money by his pen, which had of late been idle, for he sent the proprietors of the "Southern Illustrated News" — Richmond gentlemen who were rash enough to promise their subscribers original contributions by Dickens and Thackeray — certain poetical "Sketches in Greece," which he had had by him for six years, as well as a serial entitled "Paddy McGann, or The Demon of the Stump," — a tale of a humorous Irishman who fancies himself haunted by a demon, but who is really worried out of his life by a shrewish spouse. Simms was writing this story at the time of the battle of Fredericksburg, December 13, 1862, and the following sentences, taken from the first chapter, give a vivid picture of the hopes which the victory raised: —

"Even as I write the thunder rolls westward from the east. There is storm along the heights of Virginia. The cry is havoc; the war-dogs are again unleashed! The tempest rages, and the bloody banner of the foe goes down in its own blood. We are victors, and this time the route[1] is complete. Thirty thousand [sic] of the insolent invaders bite the dust. Our triumph is secure, our independence! and Peace, with her beautiful rainbow, plucked from the bosom of the storm, and spread from east to west, from north to south, over all the sunny plains and snowy heights of our beloved Apalachia, sends our gallant sons back once more to the calm blessings of each hospitable home." And the fierceness of his exultation is explained when we read on: "It is not all over, our happy life, my friend! We shall enjoy the old sports of our sweet little river once more, in communion with our noble-hearted companions. It cannot be that God will deliver us into the hands of these atrocious heathens. As between us and the Deity, there is no doubt a sad reckoning to make; but as between us and these accursed Yankees, no reproach lies at our doors, unless that single one of having too long slept within the coil of the serpent. I have faith in God, my friend. He may punish us, and we must suffer, for this is the meed of our desert; but he will not let us sink. I have faith in his promise, in his mercy, and I know that after this tribulation, our peace shall return once more, our prosperity, our friends ; and the 'song of the turtle shall be heard in the land.'"

It is pathetic to read these heartfelt utterances,

---

[1] One of the numerous typographical errors of which Southern authors were constantly complaining. It is hardly probable that Simms intended to use the obsolete spelling.

committed with such conviction of righteous intention to the worn type and wretched paper familiar
to all who have interested themselves in Confederate literature. Those men of the old South felt
that their existence as a primitive people was at
stake; they felt that the easy, picturesque life they
led depended for its perpetuation upon their good
swords, and they fought as the soldiers of Charles
fought the Saracens at Tours, or as Goth and Roman fought Attila and his Huns at Chalons. In
their patriotic songs they spoke of the Northern
troops as Huns and Vandals; for they knew too
well that a Northern conquest meant the destruction of their peculiar civilization. But they did
not and they could not realize that the parallel between themselves and the soldiers of Aetius was
apparent only. They did not and they could not
realize that they were fighting, not for the true religion and the higher civilization, but for the perpetuation of a barbarous institution and of anarchy
disguised.[1] And yet who that sees their mistake
to-day would be so rash as to declare that if he had
lived in their times and in their environment, he
would have acted differently? And who shall deny
that they were brave men, pouring out their blood
for a cause which to them was true and holy and
blessed of God himself? It is idle to deny their
bravery, although that, like most of their qualities,

---

[1] It is meant, of course, that this would have been the result of
their victory — not that they consciously fought for any such result.

was a "survival," and it is equally idle to affirm
that a whole people can astonish a world by their
heroism in defense of a cause in which they do not
believe.

To return, however, to our wrought-up romancer.
"Paddy McGann" lies in the dingy pages of the
pretentious Richmond weekly, and no one will ever
endeavor to resurrect it. There is no need to do
so, unless one wishes to get a pleasant description
of the Edisto, — the "sweet little river" of the
above extracts, — and of the easy-going life which
Simms and Jamison and their neighbors lived on
its banks. But all these good men are gathered to
their fathers, and few will care to know how Jamison excelled any man in the State in making a
cocktail, and Simms in making a punch. The old
life is gone, and as Simms felt it going his outcries
against the devastating "Northern hordes" became
shriller and shriller. As one reads some of the
poems he was in the habit of dashing off, as the
newspapers brought an account of a new battle, one
can fancy that one is listening to the wail of a Ro-
manized Briton telling of the cruel deeds he has
seen perpetrated by the yellow-haired barbarians
from over sea.

However exaggerated these poems might be, they
came from his heart, and were all that he could
write. His drama on "Benedict Arnold," which
he published in the "Magnolia," another Richmond weekly, bored him greatly, as he confessed
to Hayne. "My heart," he continued, "is too

full of anxiety to suffer me to write, and though I
have a contract for some two hundred dollars'
worth of prose, I find myself unable to divert my
thoughts from the crisis in which the country trem-
bles in suspense. What I write is in a spasm, a
single burst of passion, — hope, or scorn, or rage,
or exultation " (July 29, 1863).

Six weeks later a nearer grief assailed him. On
September 10, 1863, his wife died, in her forty-sev-
enth year. Not quite a year before, she had given
birth to her sixth son and thirteenth child, Charles
Carroll, the namesake, probably, of the gentleman
in whose office Simms had studied law. For some
time previously Simms had mentioned in his letters
that his wife was not well; but he had no idea that
her condition was critical. He wrote later to Doctor Porcher, that the calamity fell upon him like a
bolt out of a clear sky. He was "seized with mental paroxysms of great violence, which threatened
the integrity of " his brain. For four days and
nights he neither ate nor slept; and but for opiates
would have gone mad. This attack was followed
by a fever which prostrated him for a month.

Nevertheless, the thought of his children brought
him at last to his feet, and he determined for their
sakes to battle with the world once more. How
the winter was passed is not known, but it appears
from a letter to Hayne that early in May he went
to Columbia with his eldest son and namesake,
whose furlough had just expired. Gilmore was
now of age, and whatever his fears for his son's

safety, the father was proud to have at least one
of his name and blood battling for the Southern
cause. The young man went to Virginia, and
nearly lost his life at the battle of Trevilian's. A
kind lady of the neighborhood nursed him, and sent
him home to even harder labors than campaigning
had been, — labors of which there will be occasion
to speak before long.

While in Columbia Simms saw Timrod, and
when he got back to Woodlands, he wrote to
Hayne, May 8, 1864, as follows: "I saw Timrod,
and was glad to find him in better health and spirits than he has had for years. . . . If his situation
lessens his opportunities for verse writing, it at all
events gives him the creature comforts, and with a
young wife, he has need of all he can earn in these
perilous times. Besides, he is making himself a
fine prose writer, and the practice in a daily newspaper will improve his energies, without materially
disparaging [?] the proprieties and graces of his
style. His tendency is to the tragical, but a daily
newspaper will modify this. A daily newspaper
in a village like Columbia is far different from
that of a great commercial city, and the very limited space accorded by our papers now, lessens the
strain upon the mind. The labor is not exhaustive,
nor very various. He has only to prepare a couple
of dwarf essays, making a single column, and the
pleasant public is satisfied. These he does so well
that they have reason to be so. Briefly, our friend
is in a fair way to fatten and be happy, though his

muse becomes costive and complains of his *mésal-
liances.* . . . I did not meet with Tim's wife,
though he gave me an invitation to see her. But
the walk was too much for me; I am scarcely good
for a mile heat nowadays."

In the same letter he referred to a poem on Stone-
wall Jackson, which was still unfinished (it remained
so), and which he regarded as fine in conception and
good in execution. He added: "I should not forget to say that recently I finished what I think a
very creditable poem, entitled 'Midnight Chaunt in
Autumn.' It was begun several years ago, and
shortly after I had lost two noble boys, in one day,
by yellow fever. But then after writing a dozen
stanzas, my heart failed me, if not my head, and
the manuscript was thrown aside. Happening recently upon it, and under similar circumstances of
suffering and season, I finished it. It makes some
eighty verses, quatrains. You will like it, I think,
though whether it sees the printers in a hurry is
very questionable. With the plantation upon me,
the cares of the family, anxieties without number,
tithes and taxes to be provided, and a still heavy
burden of correspondence, life seems escaping from
me, frittered away in small things and — [?] details." Then follow brief references to the pri-
vations of the times. They have enough food at
Woodlands, but no variety. Stimulants, too, are
wanting, — though Rhett has recently sent him a
gallon of whiskey,— and consequently he cannot
put a stop to his chills and fever. But the war will

end this year, and if Hayne wants to make money
he had better desert poetry for a while and turn to
prose.

So the days passed. On September 17, 1864,
he wrote to Hayne that he was worn out, having
just returned from Columbia, whither he had been
to attend the funeral of his old friend Jamison, who
had died of the yellow fever. The disease was all
over Charleston, and so were the enemy's shells.
Hood, he hears, has been miserably outgeneraled
by Sherman. Unless Johnston or Lee or Beauregard is sent against the latter, the enemy will
penetrate to Macon, Augusta, Andersonville, etc.
He foresees the end, unless imbecility in office, civil
and military, be checked. On November 21, he
writes to the same friend that he has been harvest-
ing his sorry crop. Another year of war, and the
planters will produce nothing. He has lost two
horses and two mules within the year and cannot
replace them, and all his agricultural implements
are worn out. In literature he does little or nothing. A few short poems are all he has done in
eighteen months. And still he has to work for the
public, for he goes to Columbia next week as a
member of the Board of Visitors of Military Acad-
emies.

Whether he stayed at Columbia from this time
on, or whether he returned to Woodlands and made
arrangements for moving with his younger children to the city, is uncertain; but it seems clear
that by the first of the new year, 1865, he was no

longer residing at his plantation. The place was
not deserted, however, for a Mrs. Pinckney and
her family were left as occupants. Simms, of
course, thought that Sherman would soon leave
Savannah on his northward march; but he probably fancied, as many did, that Charleston would
be the object of assault, and that the middle country,
in which Columbia lay, would either be fairly safe
from the ravages of the main body of the enemy,
as lying out of their line of march, or else that the
Confederate government would send Johnston to
defend South Carolina's capital city. If such were
his expectations, — and it is fair to infer from a
subsequent publication that he did indulge them, —
they were destined to be cruelly disappointed.
Barnwell and Midway lay directly in the path
taken by the conquerors, and suffered accordingly.
Fugitives began to pour into Columbia, bringing
heart-rending tales of the desolation that followed
every step that Sherman took, and it was not many
days after the memorable first of February, when
the northward march began, before Simms learned
that his newly built house, his library that had but
recently escaped so narrowly, and all his outhouses
had been completely destroyed by the same element that had so often proved his foe. But his
private losses were nothing when contrasted with
the horrors that were enacted under his very eyes
on that Black Friday (February 17), which saw
the beautiful old town of Columbia given up to
pillage and the flames.

It is not proposed to give an account here of these horrors or to enter upon any discussion of the much vexed question, " Who burned Columbia? " All who desire to know what Simms saw and what he thought of the conduct of the Northern general and his troops are referred to a pamphlet entitled "Sack and Destruction of the City of Columbia, S. C.," published by our author from the ruined city itself shortly after Sherman left it. Simms never wrote anything more graphic than this account of what he had seen and heard. Doubtless his vehemence induced him to exaggerate in places, but it is hard to read his stirring pages without coming to the conclusion that the sack of Columbia is one of the greatest crimes ever perpetrated by the troops of a civilized country.

Simms himself did not fare badly, but when he saw the magnificent library and scientific collections of his friend Dr. R. W. Gibbes, the antiquarian, fired in the owner's presence amid the jeers of rude soldiers, he doubtless thought of the fate of his own library at Woodlands, and ground his teeth in impotent rage. He saved his watch by his presence of mind, for when accosted by soldiers and asked the time of day, he would look innocently to where the city-hall clock once stood, and reply, "Our city clock is gone, you see, but it must be near —." Twelve hundred less astute citizens, anxious to please, are said to have pulled out their watches only to have them snatched away. Another and pleasanter incident has been recorded by Mr. Aldrich, Simms's neighbor. A young Northern officer knocked at the door of the house where Simms and his children were staying. The novelist answered the summons in person, and after the usual formalities, the visitor said, "Sir, I have enjoyed too much pleasure from your works not to feel grateful. You belong to the Union, and I have come to see if I can render you any service." Simms thanked him and said that he desired only to have his family saved from intrusion. The officer departed, and in a few moments a guard appeared, who were polite and efficient in performing their duty. It is but fair to add that this is by no means the only instance of courtesy on the part of individual officers and soldiers of the Union army to the oppressed inhabitants of Columbia.

Another incident recorded by Mr. Aldrich may be referred to. Shortly after the destruction of Woodlands he met Simms at Columbia, and naturally began to sympathize with him over his losses; but Simms turned around almost fiercely, and exclaimed, "Talk not to me about my losses, when the State is lost." He was not the man, however, to think anything lost for long, and in little over a month after the burning of the city, he had persuaded a printer, Mr. Julian A. Selby, to undertake a triweekly newspaper under the appropriate title of the "Columbia Phœnix." Paper, press, and type had to be procured from a distance, but after toilsome trips Selby succeeded in getting the necessary supplies, and on March 21, 1865, the

first number made its appearance. Some of the
earlier numbers are now before me. Curious,
badly printed sheets they are, about six by eighteen
inches, intended to fold so as to give six small pages.
No subscriptions are taken, but each number retails
for one dollar. After number nine, the paper becomes a daily as well as a triweekly, and persons
are allowed to subscribe for a month at twenty and
ten dollars respectively, strictly in advance. The
veteran editor of nullification times is, of course,
at the head of the editorial staff, — probably is the
staff, — and is in his element. Through the first
twelve numbers runs the account of the sack of
Columbia, which has been already mentioned in
its pamphlet form. Besides this there are stinging
editorials, and, what is more surprising, hopeful
prognostications of the future of the war. An occasional telegram makes its appearance, and a fair
number of advertisements, among which is one that
offers for sale a set of Simms's romances. But an
editorial entitled "Woodlands," which appeared in
the issue for Wednesday, April 12, 1865, concerns
us more narrowly, and we note that just four years
have elapsed since that firing on Sumter which
Simms so earnestly counseled.[1]

This editorial is nothing more than a long account, evidently from Simms's hand, of the final
burning of Woodlands. From it we learn that
Mrs. Pinckney, the lady in charge of the place,
sent a note to General Blair requesting protection

[1] The *Phœnix* is, I believe, still published in Columbia.

for the dwelling and library. Before an answer could be received, bands of stragglers had entered the house, only six rooms of which had been rebuilt, and begun their work of destruction. In the midst of this turmoil, a guard arrived, which was shortly followed by General Blair himself, in company with other officers. The gentlemen spent some time examining the library, and when they retired they took away with them only some maps of the State and a couple of fowling pieces. While the guard remained, nothing was disturbed, but with the departure of the soldiers, frequent attempts were made to burn the house, and the ladies occupying it fled to Midway for protection. At daybreak the servants discovered that the building was in flames, and that all their labors to preserve it would be fruitless. The library was the first to burn, and not a volume was saved. The larger and better furniture had been previously sent off, and many of the choicer books had been packed in boxes, to be removed whenever transportation could be obtained. Thus the thievish incendiaries, who did not care for books, got little for their pains, and in view of this fact some of the neighbors conceived the idea that the house must have been fired by Simms's own negroes, particularly by his trusted body servant. This man was actually tried by a court of freeholders, but was acquitted. Simms evidently did not believe the charge, but it was repeated by Mr. Aldrich five years later. For the credit of human nature it may be hoped that Simms was right.

Before Simms wrote the description of his losses, which has been abridged above, Lee had surrendered at Appomattox, and the war was practically at an end. Probably it was because he could not bear to think of his people's losses that he occupied himself in writing minutely of his own. He did it with a calmness which it is difficult to imitate. For who shall describe how the old partisan, who had once in his imagination crushed the North like an egg, felt during those last weary months, when the defeat of all his hopes stared him in the face? He had entered the period of struggle with confidence in the justice as well as in the success of his cause; he came out still confident of the justice, but struggling in vain to reconcile the two ideas of a just cause and an unsuccessful one. Many honest people have since his day been trying with equal futility to effect a similar reconciliation. But it will not do. The facts of universal history warn them that any such attempt is futile. No people, however brave and true, can wage an eventually successful war with advancing civilization, and this is what the South was trying to do. It is vain to talk of constitutional rights that date from a century back; it is vain to say that deep and honest conviction in the truth of a cause makes a cause true; it is vain to say that mere money and cowardice and wrong are on the successful side, and all bravery and right on the defeated side. Civil wars do not divide a people on such lines; if they did, it would be idle to speak of a nation's fulfilling

its destiny under the direction of God. But if
nations do not fulfill their destinies under the direction of God, what need is there to speculate about
the past or the future at all; what has history to do
in such a reign of Chaos and old Night?
No! the most loyal Southerner may as well
make up his mind to face the fact that the cause
for which Simms labored, and for which so many
thousands of brave men died, was a losing cause, in
consequence of the fact that the people that upheld
it were fighting to perpetuate an institution opposed to progress, an institution that blocked the
path which a great nation had to take. In view
of this truth, it does not seem necessary to insist
upon the part played by the North in the great
contest. It is idle to deny that many things were
done by her zealous sons, and many things left undone by her lukewarm sons, that tended to hasten
the South upon her downward course, and to add
to her frenzy and blindness. For it is one of the
curses of an institution like slavery that its baleful
effects are not confined to its upholders, but react
upon its opponents. "Sweetness and light" are
virtues that are rarely to be traced in the history
of the American people between 1820 and 1865. It
could not have been otherwise. "Sweetness and
light" had little place in a struggle against slavery; for civilization was never known to go forward
in satin slippers. Doubtless many good people,
reading the record of these pitiful times, have fancied that if a little "sweetness and light" had ap-

peared, a few more concessions been made, the result would have been different. Such fancies are
idle. An old order of things had been planted in
a portion of this country by perfectly natural pro-
cesses; and the time had come for it to give way
to a new order of things. But in history there is
no beneficent Despot who says, "Let the old order
vanish and the new be born." All life is a struggle ; and the higher planes of existence, individual
as well as national, are reached by toil, by slow
degrees, by pain. The war of secession, therefore,
having been inevitable, it is not necessary to point
out all the false steps made by the North. These
false steps delayed the day of change, and made
the ordeal through which the South had to pass
more bitter and terrible, while reacting, as such
steps are sure to do, upon the people that made
them. The South, also, took false steps of her
own accord, and, as in the case of the North, those
false steps were fearfully atoned for. But it was
the forces of destiny in the main that placed the
South in her direful position; and it was the forces
of destiny that made the North the instrument by
which the whole country, North and South, was
finally saved for what we all believe will be a glorious future.

This view of the matter cannot of course be a
popular one, and it has its historical limitations.
Most readers prefer the historical method of Carlyle to that of Buckle, because it is pleasanter to
praise and blame men than to stand dumb before

the inscrutable workings of law. Then again few readers, and few historians, see how it is possible to use both methods at one and the same time. Yet this has to be done. It is just as essential to point out the importance of representative men like Garrison and Simms as to point out the fact that both North and South were merely fulfilling their respective destinies. Law and the individual that embodies its workings are the two foci around which the historian must move; and, if the curve he traces is not a perfect circle, it is not his fault. He is saved at any rate from much erratic wandering; from dropping downwards into the regions of the commonplace, the base, and the low. He is saved, in the particular instance we are considering, from the absurdity of representing two sections of practically the same great race as being entirely the children of light and the children of darkness respectively. He is saved from imagining that all virtue concentrated itself to the north of a certain historic line and all vice to the south of it, or *vice versa*, and that if, since the war, there has been some drifting of the virtues southward or northward, they are promptly recalled and installed in their proper places on the eve of a presidential election. He is saved from all this, and at the same time is allowed to grow eloquent over truly great men like Lincoln and Lee, and also to render the negative service of pointing out that not all the popular heroes of either side are worthy of the homage they are receiving. He can also point out the instructive parallel that exists between the struggle of Cavalier and Puritan on either side of the ocean, can show that the qualities of neither are thoroughly great and lovable, but that in their amalgamation a great people must be produced. But he can also grow tedious.

Yet before this chapter closes, attention should be called once more to the trials that befell Simms during these terrible years. He had done much to bring on the war that ruined him, and yet he had only done what seemed to him to be just and right. If he had been conscious of wrong-doing, it would be time to speak of retribution; but the word would be out of place in connection with an honest man. As a mistaken man he suffered from the natural consequences of his mistakes; but who can recount his losses without feeling that his lot was indeed a pathetic one? His calling gone, his stereotype plates confiscated, his dwelling twice burned down, his books destroyed, friends, two children, and wife taken from him, and his State and section in the dust of humiliation and defeat, who shall say that he was not a sorely tried man? And yet he never proved himself a truer or nobler man than in these days of adversity, — days which to him were hardly cheered by the vision of the new order that was to be.

For out of the ashes of the old South, a new and better South has arisen. A disintegrated and primitive people have become united among themselves and with their former foes. and are moving forward upon the path of progress. Instead of the past, they have the future to look upon; instead of a mere State, they have a nation to trust in and to maintain. They have retained all that was good in the old South, and to their inherited virtues and powers they will add, as the years go by, vir- tues and powers that must come to any people that move forward with civilization. If they have not yet shaken themselves loose from the clogs of prim- itive custom which they have inherited from their ancestors; if the slave in the person of the freed- man still stands in the way of their progress, they will nevertheless push on, and in the course of years the clogs will fall from them and the freedman will be a help instead of a hindrance. They have the energy of a new people, and they have a terri- tory almost boundless and inexhaustible. They have awakened from their nightmares and gone out into the fresh air of the morning, and the breeze has driven the fever from their brows. They have ceased to lament the tossing hours, the fitful anguish of the night when they called upon God and thought he did not hear them, and the burden of their song of deliverance rolls ever up to his throne: —

"Yet I doubt not thro' the ages one increasing purpose runs,
 And the thoughts of men are widened with the process of the
    suns."

CHAPTER VIII.

LAST YEARS.

No precise statement can be made about Simms's movements between March and November, 1865. Only one scrap of writing in any way connected with him has been discovered; and that is the order signed by Colonel James C. Beecher, giving the negroes on Simms's plantation permission to gather the growing crops. Early in November he went to New York in order to renew his relations with his publishers, a purpose which was only partially accomplished. From the St. Nicholas hotel he addressed notes on November 5 and 7 to his two Brooklyn friends, Mr. William H. Ferris and Mr. John J. Bockie, asking if they were afraid that they would be compromised by coming to see him. They went immediately, and showed him by many acts of kindness that nothing that had happened could affect their friendship for him. Nor were his other friends, like Duyckinck and Lawson, less anxious to show him that they saw in the gray-bearded, sad old man only the strong and vivacious good comrade of twenty years before. His visit was probably a short one, and in a pecuniary sense unprofitable; but it must have done him a

world of good to see that his misfortunes could not
alienate his friends. In December he was back in
South Carolina and in editorial harness, this time
in Charleston, as associate editor with Timrod of
the "Daily South Carolinian," a paper of which
Mr. Felix G. De Fontaine was chief editor and
proprietor. It was a sad editorial that he wrote
for his readers on the first Christmas morning after
the return of peace. Peace! the word was a mock-
ery to men and women living under the terrors of
military and, what was worse, negro rule.

With the new year our materials again become voluminous. Simms writes to Bockie and
Duyckinck to negotiate in any way they can with
his publishers, for newspaper drudgery is terrible.
De Fontaine is absent most of the time, and Timrod does not contribute a line for weeks together.
Five columns of editorials are not prepared in a moment, and it is not pleasant to think that there is a
rumor on the streets that the authorities are going
to suppress the "Carolinian" for being a little too
free in its criticisms of passing events. Still more
unpleasant is it to work till the wee small hours,
and to hear nothing said about pay day. But as
he manages to give a whist party to eight old
friends, with plenty of oysters and whiskey punch
to solace such as do not care for the rigor of the
game, one perceives that his condition is not alto-
gether cheerless. Then, too, one finds that no
amount of civil or political troubles can put a stop
to weddings, and one feels that Simms must have

been glad to give away, in his old age, his daughter Chevillette to a man whom he respected and admired, Major Daniel Rowe. He also found time to write several chapters of a new romance, "The Brothers of the Coast," a pirate story; and if he soon laid this work aside, it must have been some comfort to feel that he could work at his old trade at all.

But in February, De Fontaine and Timrod removed with their newspaper to Columbia, and Simms, after taking a brief trip to Florida, formed a connection with the "Courier." He was all the while, however, meditating a permanent removal to the North, where he would have a better market for his wares. Woodlands was practically useless now, and his eldest son, Gilmore, who was also studying law, had great difficulty in getting any negro hands to work for him. They moved to their labor, Simms wrote, like elephants with the gout. They stole all the growing crops, and shot down the hogs and cattle that happened to stray into the woods. They all carried guns, and insulted every white man and woman they met, provided they thought they could do it with impunity. In brief, the Devil was let loose again, to quote the emphatic language of our author.

Yet Charleston was no better. Nobody knew what to expect from the conquerors or from the insolent freedmen. Provisions were at famine prices. The richer a man had been before the war, the poorer he was now likely to be; and his previous training rendered him unfit for any active work whereby he might better his fortunes. Those who had saved plate and other heirlooms were gradually parting with them for bread. Those who fancied that they could write spent almost their last penny for paper and scribbled away quires of pathetic trash. Then they bought a stamp and mailed a letter to Simms, begging that he would get their books published. He did try to oblige them in some cases, but without success; and yet he had no money, to say nothing of his time, to waste on such correspondents. He wrote to Bockie: "There is not a young author or authoress in the whole South that does not call upon me for counsel and assistance. I shall have to go North, if only to escape these calls upon my time, my thought, patience, and physique." Moreover, his friends were leaving Charleston. Dr. Bruns was to go to New Orleans; Timrod had gone to Columbia, and Paul Hayne to his little cottage in the pine woods near Augusta. It is true, his daughter, Mrs. Roach, with whom he was now living, would have to be left behind, along with some of his other children; but as he was obliged to contribute to their support, as well as to support himself, it seemed as if it were folly to stay at the South any longer.

So he went North in June, and stayed three months, negotiating with publishers and visiting old friends. But for some reason or other, partly because, no doubt, he did not wish to abandon his people, he gave up, or rather postponed, his plan

of making a permanent settlement in New York or
New Jersey, and came home to Charleston once
more. Before he left New York he wrote the
preface to a collection of Southern war poetry
which he had long been making, and also entered
into a contract with the publishers of the "Old
Guard," a violent magazine, edited in the interests
of the South, for a serial to run through the twelve
numbers of 1867. He also occupied his spare
hours by writing long letters to the "Courier" on
the state of literature at the North, and republished
his story "Marie de Berniere" as "The Ghost of
my Husband."

From Charleston he wrote, on October 22, to
Hayne at Copse Hill. He had just run up to
Woodlands and found the ruins the same. If he
ever despaired, he should do so now. But such is
not his wont, and he adds: "I am now cudgeling
my brains at a new romance, the first scene of
which opens at the sandhills of Augusta. I have
done some one hundred and twenty pages, and hope
by the close of the week to have done one hundred
and fifty more! *Nous verrons*, as old Ritchie [1] was
wont to say; as Burns says, 'Perhaps it may turn
out a song, perhaps turn out a sermon.' [2] I am
more in the mood to sermonize than sing."

Then he adds some details about their common
friend Timrod. "Poor Timrod is the very Prince

[1] Probably Ritchie of the Richmond *Enquirer*, but some local
celebrity may be meant.

[2] *Epistle to a Young Friend*, stanza 1.

of Dolefuls, and swallowed up in distresses. He now contemplates separation from his wife, that she may go forth as a governess and he as a tutor, in private families. He can earn nothing where he is [Columbia]; has not a dollar, goes to bed hungry every night, and suffers from bad health. It is the mortifying thing to all of us, that *none of us can* help him. Bruns and myself are both living from hand to mouth, and not unfrequently the hand carries nothing to the cavernous receptacle." Still Simms hopes to be able to seize a week at Christmas in order to visit Hayne and the Hammonds at Augusta.

On November 27 he again writes to Hayne and assures his friend of his intention to visit Copse Hill. "Timrod," he adds, "has been on the verge of starvation. He is now acting as private secretary to [Governor] Orr." His own story for the "Old Guard" is progressing, but he will have to work prodigiously to finish it by Christmas. He then mentions his volume of war poetry, — a production which, in view of all that has been previously said about Southern poetry, needs little comment.

The poems that composed it had been collected mainly from newspapers, and Simms had had great difficulty in communicating with the various authors, owing to the wretched condition of the Southern mails. In consequence, a number of mistakes crept into the volume; but it was the editor's own fault when one poem was printed twice. Simms's

preface, however, deserves high praise for its calm
tone. He has accepted the inevitable. The Union
is now the nation, and the war poetry of the South
belongs to this nation as truly as the captured cannon. The poems themselves are naturally not so
calm. Most of them are mediocre, and they con-
tain a large amount of bathos. Good models such
as Campbell and Drayton are seldom followed except by the editor himself, but of course his contributions do not rise to the standard set by Timrod
and Randall. On the whole the metrical facility
shown by some of the writers is striking, and in
spite of the thin quality of the poems themselves
they frequently give evidence of culture and true
feeling on the part of the Southern cavalier.

Hayne was not the only struggling Southern
man of letters with whom Simms was in correspondence. Timrod wrote him doleful letters, generally
in pencil on scraps of paper. In one of these
he acknowledged a power Simms always possessed
over despondent and yielding natures. "Somehow
or other, you always magnetize me on to a little
strength." Cooke also wrote, complaining of the
criticism that "Surrey of Eagle's Nest" had received at the North, and giving an account of his
other literary labors. Judge Gayarré, too, wrote
from New Orleans, giving a disheartening description of the condition of that city. And so Simms
could work away at his romance, feeling that after
all he was no worse off than the rest of his craft,
and that Charleston, with all its misery and suffer-

ing, was the proper place for his cheerful and indomitable spirit to move and work in.

At Christmas he broke away from the city, and
paid his promised visit to Hayne at Copse Hill.
There he found his noble friend living at peace in
a little cabin, cultivating his garden and his muse.
Hayne had made a wise choice. Years of war time
had familiarized him with poverty and hardship;
he had a contented nature, — why, then, should
he plunge into active life and endeavor to grow
rich by outwitting or trampling down his neighbors? Why, if he could sell his verses and raise
vegetables, should he undertake some respectable
but dull trade or profession? So he had come to
the pine woods of Georgia and made himself a
home. It was only a cabin, but within its narrow
precincts he was destined to do his best work, and
to show to the world that it was possible for a
Southern writer to be a conscientious and serious
artist, as well as a man of tenacious will and un-
flagging energy.

It was with a sad sort of pleasure that the two
friends met to exchange their views of the present,
and recount mournfully their recent experiences.
Simms was changed in many respects, but he was
still as eager as ever to pass the night in profitless
though pleasant discussions when he should have
been trying to regain his strength through sleep.
Nor did host or guest forget to fill their glasses
while the talk flowed on. But pleasant visits do
not usually last long, and in two weeks Simms was

back in Charleston, working as hard as ever. He
had sent on five hundred pages of his story "Joscelyn" to the publishers before leaving Charleston
for his holiday, and the first few chapters had already appeared; but now he had so much to do, in
helping the poor people around him, that he felt
that the romance was dragging on his hands. His
judgment was right. One feels as one reads this
last of the revolutionary romances that even Simms
himself has broken down. Only here and there
can any touches of his former power be discovered, and but for the fact that he got a few dollars
by it, one could wish that he had never written
it. And yet how could the worn-out old man have
done anything better under the circumstances? It
seems a shame to criticise his work at all.

Nevertheless, he could still write strong and pathetic letters. Here are a few sentences from one
written to his friend Bockie, on March 20, 1867:
"But no language can describe the suffering which
prevails, especially among that class, accustomed
to better days, whose pride compels them to *starve
in silence.* There are hundreds, in this city, as I
learn from good authority, who are daily making
sale of such remnants of plate, crockery, furniture,
etc., as have been left them, to provide the daily
bread. And there are very few of us who do not
require the exertion and labor of every hour, far
into the night, to keep above the water. You
know already that I am finding bread for my children only out of my brains, and you can readily

guess how pitiable is the result. One of my literary friends [Timrod], of fine capacity, is literally dying by inches, of poverty and disease together; having wife, and widowed sister, and several nephews and nieces in the same condition of distress from poverty. But the subject is too terrible, and I gladly turn from it."

He then goes on to thank Bockie for his kindness in sending presents to himself and his daughters, — all of his intimate Northern friends were delicately generous to him during these trying years, — and he is especially grateful for the gift of a sewing machine. He writes: "Fortunately my daughters have all been taught to do their own work, fit their own dresses, and they go to work cheerfully, and sing merrily while they toil; and their elasticity helps to encourage and strengthen me in my labor. The picture of Irving, etc., will help to cover the bomb-shell holes still in our walls. The room in which I sleep is still excoriated with those missiles. Please advise me, whatever is sent me, of the names and addresses of the parties to whom I should be grateful." Then he goes on to recount how his publishers are straitened for money; how his son Gilmore is sick; how he himself will have to go up to Woodlands soon, to pay the taxes and look after things; finally, how he suffers with now chronic complaints, and divides his time between taking medicine and writing twenty pages of foolscap per day. "For the last three nights," he adds, "I have written till two in the morning. Does not this look like suicide?"

A few weeks later, April 3, he wrote to Hayne,
giving a doleful account of poor Timrod, who, by
the way, was just about to make a visit to Copse
Hill. The letter contained a brief reference to
one of Simms's characteristic acts of generosity,
which deserves recording. " I was fortunate
enough to procure for him [Timrod] one hundred
and fifteen dollars, which is eked out to him weekly
at twenty dollars per week. When that goes, God
knows what the poor fellow will do, as, in truth,
people here are almost as destitute as himself.
We have here [at his daughter's house] three families rolled into one, numbering about sixteen, —
say ten grown and the rest children, — and about
thirty dollars per week is what we have to live
upon. I need not tell you what prices are."
Simms does not tell Hayne how much trouble it
cost him to raise the money for Timrod; but I have
been informed, in a letter from Mr. Samuel Lord,
that he spent days in getting it. And this while
he himself needed to husband all his time and
strength.

In a subsequent letter he gave his friend Bockie
a brief description of Charleston's chief trouble.
"Things grow worse and worse with us daily, and
your Yankee preachers are stirring up the vani-
ties of the negro to such a degree as to keep him
from work, and prompt him to aspire to supreme
possession of the country. His insolence increases
day by day, and your military governors are stimulating it by a studious effort to degrade the whites

in all possible ways." Then he adds a few words
as to his personal discomforts: "I am compelled
to share my room, in which I sleep, work, write,
study, with my two sons, Gilmore and Govan. I
am accordingly cabined, cribbed, confined, — I,
who had such ample range before, with a dozen
rooms, and a house range for walking in bad
weather of a hundred and thirty-four feet. I am
drudging, as a matter of course."

But he had his consolation in the work of distributing the three hundred and fifteen dollars that
had been sent by his friend Mr. Ferris for the relief of the Charleston poor, and he was very proud
to write back that he had supplied for several
weeks the necessities of twelve families, containing
some forty-five persons. He was also busy corresponding with brother Masons, and distributing
the money sent in response to his appeals. Then,
too, he had his own work to look after, especially
the contemplated sale of such of his revolutionary
documents as had escaped his two fires. For years
he had been collecting every letter and paper he
could find that bore upon the Revolution or upon
South Carolina history, and he still had enough
left to make it worth his while to sell them, now
that he needed money. It doubtless hurt him to
part with them, but there was no reason why he
should be more fortunate than his old friend Tefft,
of Savannah, whose magnificent collection of autographs was also for sale. So he secured the services of Duyckinck and Bockie, and eventually sold

his papers to the Long Island Historical Society, in whose custody they still remain. Before he parted with them, however, he prepared a monograph, entitled "Memoir and Correspondence of Colonel John Laurens," which was published as the seventh number of the "Bradford Club Series."

Another piece of work on which he was engaged at this time was a revised "Mother Goose," which was offered to a New York firm, but was respectfully declined. It still exists in manuscript, and one who glances over it can only feel that the publishers were not particularly hard-hearted in rejecting it. One knows not whether to smile or sigh at the thought of the old man cudgeling his brains in order to improve on "Hey diddle diddle, the cat and the fiddle." But it was one of Simms's failings to think that he could do everything, and one is not surprised to find him, a few months later, writing a play, in four days, for a third-rate actor named Bailey, who was going to astonish the Southern public by a series of plays written by native authors and presented by eminent and presumably native actors. Nor is one surprised to find Bailey declaring Simms's drama a fine one, but regretting his inability to put it on the boards just now. It is rather amusing to learn that Simms was induced to write this play by one of his female admirers, — a certain fair authoress of North Carolina, who was so alarmed for the morals of New York city that she submitted to the managers of the "Black Crook" a perfectly proper spectacular

drama to be acted in its stead. Of such may be
the kingdom of heaven, but hardly the great American drama, for which some people are looking as
anxiously as others are for the great American
novel.

In the latter part of June, Simms again went
North, partly on his own business, partly to secure
Masonic aid for his struggling friends. On July
2, he got a characteristic note from Lawson, asking why an impecunious Southerner should insist
on paying five dollars a day at the New York hotel
when good, cheap board could be had at Yonkers,
where he, Lawson, was spending the summer.
Simms took the hint and paid his friend a short
visit. He had his daughter, Mary Lawson, along
with him, and the two were rather oppressed by the
invitations they received from friends old and new.
They paid flying visits to Great Barrington, where
Simms revived old memories, and to Boston, where
he met a new friend who had been previously
known only through an extensive correspondence.
This was Mr. Arthur W. Austin, a stanch opponent
of abolitionism, who shortly after the war began
to write long letters to Simms on political subjects,
and — what was better — to send him many delica-
cies like good old port, that could not be easily obtained in Charleston during the days of reconstruction. While visiting Mr. Austin, Simms fell into
the hands of some Masonic friends, who trudged
him around the streets under an August sun, and
so exposed him to an attack of ague. He had the

consolation, however, of knowing that he had been an object of public curiosity, and that not a few people had taken him for "Semmes the Pirate."

But in spite of sickness and constant traveling he was compelled to keep busy with his pen. His correspondents were pressing for replies, and their letters were not as a rule so humorous as the one in which Hayne described how he had been recently warned by an anonymous note from Richmond never to venture to put his foot in that city again, and all because he had published a poem in which he had spoken more mildly of the Union cause than the anonymous writer thought proper. There is a grim humor, however, to be found in the numerous letters written him by Southern publishers. They are full of compliments to the "Nestor of Southern literature" and of requests that he will become a regular contributor to the columns of a new journal which is certain to be successful. Simms was frequently seduced into making engagements, and he kept his part of the bargain; but the publishers did not keep theirs, — a peculiarity on the part of Southern publishers which Simms, Hayne, and Cooke were in the habit of alluding to in their letters of this period. Had the poor fellows got all the money due them from the publishers of the mushroom papers that sprang up in the South after the war, their circumstances would have been fairly comfortable. As it was, they congratulated themselves when they got a dollar from such sources. Perhaps they thought it the part of patriotism to continue writing for these pretentious and short-lived journals; perhaps, like most good old Southerners, they were slow to learn that a man's word is not always as good as his bond; perhaps they thought that the sanguine publishers would really pay if they could — so they wrote on with a patience and faith that excite our admiration.

Toward the last of September Simms went South again; at least he is found at that time among his favorite North Carolina mountains, shooting deer, listening to hunters' yarns, making notes on the proper construction of bear-traps, — in a word, gathering materials for other stories with his customary care. On his arrival in Charleston he heard the sad news of Timrod's death, and immediately set to work to write a sketch of him for a Baltimore weekly, "Southern Society," and to raise money for the family left in such destitution. The letters he had received from Timrod during the months preceding the latter's decease are too harrowing to bear quotation. The evils inflicted by poverty were bad enough, but the consciousness that he was dying by inches, and the suffering occasioned by a severe and, perhaps, carelessly performed, operation, had rendered the last year of the young poet's life simply unendurable. And yet in the midst of his sufferings he had contrived to write the exquisite poem that will ever preserve his name, — the memorial ode to which attention has already been called.

But scarcely had Simms's correspondence with
Timrod terminated, before he began to write frequent letters to another poet, this time a Northern
one, George H. Boker. Simms had written a review for the "Courier" of S. Adams Lee's "Book
of the Sonnet," and had taken occasion to claim
a high position for Boker as a poet. The latter
wrote expressing his astonishment that he should
at last get some justice done him and that, too,
at the hands of a Southerner. He declared that
Simms's words had filled him with fresh hope, and
added that he would be glad to send his kind critic
other volumes of his poetry, including his "Poems
of the War," unless, indeed, the views expressed in
the latter work would shock Simms too much.
Like the sensible man he was, Simms told him to
send his verses by all means, no matter what sentiments they contained. Then followed a brisk correspondence in which the two men expressed their
views of poetry as an art, and, it would seem, — for
only Boker's letters have been read, — related some
of the difficulties under which they had labored.

Boker confessed that, like Simms, he had published simply to put himself on record. The indifference of Charleston to Simms was paralleled
by that of Philadelphia towards himself. When,
on November 3, he wished to send Simms copies of
"Plays and Poems" and "Poems of the War,"
Lippincott's messenger went over the whole city
and failed to find a copy of either. But Boker
did more than complain and say uncomplimentary

things of New England, — for he does not seem to
have had much more love for that section than
Simms had, or than another Pennsylvanian, Senator William Maclay, had had nearly a hundred
years before, — he got Simms to write for the new
magazine which Lippincott was about to start as a
rival to the "Atlantic Monthly." Certainly one
much needed draft from this source found its way
to our author's pocketbook. It is refreshing to
find him getting good money occasionally for the
work which was surely but slowly undermining his
constitution.

The year closed much as it had begun. Poverty
was still grinding the South down and Simms was
still working more for other people than for himself. He got his friend Austin to send him the
few copies of the 1860 edition of Timrod's poems,
still remaining in the hands of Ticknor and Fields,
and sold them for the benefit of the poet's family.
He did what he could to comfort his daughter
Chevillette, Mrs. Rowe, for the death of her first
son. He lent encouragement to his son Gilmore,
who had just been admitted to the bar. He wrote
lovingly to Bruns, who was despondent over the horrors of negro rule in New Orleans, and the difficulty a gentleman had in making both ends meet.
But he still kept before him the possible necessity
of a removal to some place in Maryland or New
Jersey, where he could work in peace. A letter
from Bruns, however, recalling the merry time the
writer and Simms and Hayne and Jamison had

had at Woodlands, on New Year's night, 1859,
must have made the thought of ever leaving Carolina almost intolerable.

The new year, 1868, opened with an endeavor
to render Woodlands habitable once more, if not
profitable. It was not possible to rebuild on the
ample scale of the old house, but Simms thought
he saw his way clear to erecting a comfortable
frame dwelling which would shelter his declining
years. But carpenters were hard to get and lum-
ber was for a long time unobtainable. It had to
be brought to the place on rafts; and just when the
rafts were expected, the Edisto would be carried
out of its banks by a freshet. Still the work was
persevered in, and by July, Simms could give his
friend Ferris an account of the hunting and fishing
he was having, as well as of the difficulty of getting
the carpenters out of the house. He could complain, too, that his building had cost him twice as
much as he had expected, and that he was almost
penniless. In addition to the robberies committed
by the negroes, he had had to submit to conduct on
the part of publishers which, if given a less harsh
name, was even more trying. One contract which
was to pay him six hundred dollars, and for which
he had written seven hundred pages of manuscript,
failed him just at the time his house building had
to be paid for. So he left for New York to make
fresh contracts in no very cheerful frame of mind.
Death, too, had not spared him this year, for in

February a favorite grandchild, a daughter of Mrs. Roach, had died while he was still living in Charleston. But through it all he had worked away on a new story, entitled "Voltmeier," the scene of which was laid in North Carolina, where, it will be remembered, he had hunted in the preceding autumn. He had even dreamed of becoming a professional lecturer once more, and had delivered one lecture in Charlotte, North Carolina, which had been warmly applauded.

At midsummer he made his Northern trip somewhat more profitable than had been usual with him of late years. He entered into contracts for three stories to appear serially during the next year, and, as he had only one on hand and that not completed, he hastened back to Woodlands and set to work with a desperate energy that was destined to wreck his health and shorten his life. He wrote to Ferris, on November 21, that he had written six hundred pages of manuscript since his return, and that he was keeping two stories going at once. Besides this he was annotating some of Shakespeare's plays, whether for publication or for Ferris's private delectation does not appear. He was also collecting and sending to Ferris, who was fond of autographs, all of the important letters he had saved from his correspondence. It is needless to say that from his biographer's point of view he could hardly have busied himself more usefully than with this last-mentioned labor.

With the exception of an occasional visit to

Charleston, the next nine months were spent by
Simms at Woodlands, with the respite of scarcely
a single day from hard and grinding labor. A letter to Hayne, written probably in February, 1869,
gives a pathetic account of the way he was spending his time and strength. After saying that he
has recently had a spell of illness, and after con-
gratulating Hayne on the fact that the latter is able
to support himself on the money his verses bring
him, Simms writes: "I am living quite obscurely,
whether at home or abroad, and you will seldom see
my name hackneyed in the papers. I do not now
write for fame or notoriety or the love of it, but
simply to procure the wherewithal of life for my
children; and this is a toil require [requiring] constant labor. My recent illness is simply the consequence of a continued strain upon the brain for
four months, without the interval of a single day.
In that time I wrote near two thousand pages note
paper of manuscript on two works, to say nothing of
an immense correspondence and numerous asides at
the calls of friends, etc. I am still suffering very
much from debility and the usual concomitants
of student life. . . . I write you now only by an
assertion of dogged will."

Then he goes on to give particulars about his
work: "Year before last I wrote a Revolutionary
romance for the 'Old Guard' magazine, called
'Joscelyn.' . . . This year I have been writing for
the same work a story called 'The Cub of the Panther,' which will be completed in seven or eight num-

bers. Half a dozen are already written. I have also
written, between last spring and last Christmas, a
romance of the mountains, called 'Voltmeier, or the
Mountain Robber,' which is now in course of publication in the 'Western World.' This is a long
story, making some thirteen hundred pages note
paper closely written. I am brooding now over a
third work of length, for which I have a contract,
and should have had a good deal of it ready by this
time, but for my illness. *Voilà tout!* I write
[or wrote], by the way, for two Baltimore journals,
from neither of which have I got any pay. I have
balances due by both, which I fear I shall never get
a cent of." The condition of Woodlands is then
briefly alluded to: "I am again, as you see, at
Woodlands. I have rebuilt one wing of my house,
a little cottage of only four rooms on the old foundation. I tried to do six rooms, but my money
failed me. Gilmore and my son-in-law, Major
Rowe, are farming here on a small scale. . . . I
arrived in Charleston, from New York, the 20th
of October last, spent one day in the city, and then
came on to the plantation, which I have not left one
day since. To-day I am expecting guests from the
North. But for these and other visitors preceding
them, I would have gone for a week to Charleston,
in the hope of benefit from change."

In July he did go to Charleston, and then to New
York and Boston. It was the last time he was to
visit his old friend Lawson and his new friend Austin. But he was sick and depressed, had little

money, and found the publishers reluctant to advance more. He returned to Woodlands early in the fall, and after some desultory work resolved with the new year to take up his permanent abode with Mrs. Roach, in Charleston, where he could be sure of the nursing he needed. Before his removal, he wrote a long letter to Hayne, December 22, giving an account of his condition: "For my part, and for the last six months, I have been literally *hors de combat* from overwork of the brain, — brain sweat, as Ben Jonson called it, — and no body sweat, no physical exercise. In the extremity of my need, I took contracts . . . for no less than three romances, all to be worked at the same time. I got advances of money on each of these books, and the sense of obligation pressing upon me, I went rigidly to work, concentrating myself at the desk from 20th October, 1868, to the 1st of July, 1869, nearly nine months without walking a mile in a week, riding but twice, and absent from work but half a day on each of these occasions. The consequence was that I finished two of the books and broke down on the third, having written during this period some three thousand pages of the measure of those which I now write to you " [large note]. He then goes on to say that he has written a few pieces for a new magazine that has been started in Charleston, the "Nineteenth Century." It does not pay, but still he wants the South to have an organ. Poor fellow! as if the Reverend Mr. Hicks could give it an "organ" when he himself had tried

repeatedly and failed; as if "organs" were needed
in those dreadful days when what was wanted was
not sentimental gush or vain vindictive howlings,
but the energy and faith he had always shown, and
which, sooth to say, were to become virtues of that
new South which he was not to be permitted to see
and rejoice over.

So he went to Charleston, declaring that he had
few objects now in life save to see his children
happy. Only six had been left him of fifteen, and
of his six grandchildren, three had died. He had
fought a good fight, and was weary, but still he
prayed that he might die with harness on his back.
No lean and slippered pantaloon for him, so he
wrote Hayne; he would rather die now than drift
into helpless imbecility. And he feels that he
ought still to support himself, and yet he can make
little or no money. It was a boon when on December 1, 1869, he was invited to write a prologue
for the opening of the new Academy of Music in
Charleston. A flash of his old strength shot
through him and he wrote some vigorous couplets,
for which he received thirty dollars from the managers and five and twenty as a compliment, from
some unknown source.

Before an account is given of the last months
of this active and heroic life, a few words must be
said about the three romances which had been published as serials in 1869. "The Cub of the Panther: a Mountain Legend," or, as Simms subsequently put it, "A Hunter Legend of the Old North

State," ran through the year in the "Old Guard," and deserves only one comment. It shows plainly that Simms was beginning to realize that the day of the romancer was over, and that that of the realist was dawning. He did his best in the early chapters, and indeed throughout the story, to give a plain description of the life of a peculiar mountain people. He did not succeed, as a matter of course, in cutting himself loose from his earlier methods of composition, nor did he succeed, as some later writers have done, in making a minute and at the same time charming study of the primitive people among whom the scene of his story was laid. But he did his best, and while doing it, showed that his mind had by no means crystallized.

The second romance, "Voltmeier, or the Mountain Men: a Tale of the Old North State," ran for several months in a New York sensational weekly. In this, too, especially in the early chapters, Simms endeavored to lay aside the stately robes of the romancer, but he soon fell into his old ways and wrote an exciting story after the style of "Border Beagles." There is the usual plotting and counterplotting, the mystery, intrigue, and adventure, familiar to readers of sensational stories, and the wonder is how a man in Simms's condition could have written it all. The name of the third story, on which he broke down, is not known, but he seems to have partially kept his contract by letting George Munro republish in his "Fireside Companion," under the title of "The Island Bride," the novelette issued twenty-five years before as "Helen Halsey."

Such were the last romances of the man who had once been considered Cooper's not unsuccessful rival. Through no fault of his own he had been driven to become a mere penny-a-liner to fourth-rate publications. When "Guy Rivers" was published, he was able to declare that it should pass through no reader's hands. There is now among his papers a bundle of manuscript, — a story evidently written during or after the war, — on which the rather curt comments of a reader, advising against publication, are still to be read. But the change of fortune that had come to him is too pitiful to dwell upon.

On the second day of the new year Simms wrote to Hayne to inform him that he had reached Charleston and that he was still holding out against his bodily infirmities. As of old he felt that he must be Hayne's mentor and give him advice about his poetry. "For myself," he added, "nothing need be said. I am rapidly passing from a stage where you young men are to succeed me, doing what you can. God grant that you may be more successful than I have been. . . . I have little money left, and my last days would be cheerless in the last degree but for numerous good friends, who will hardly allow me to suffer. . . . But I am weary, Paul, and having much to say, I must say no more; but with love to all, God be with you in mercy." On March 26, he wrote Hayne that he had made a short trip to Woodlands, and had seemed at first to improve, but that at the end of his stay another acute attack (probably some kidney trouble) had come on. He was now slowly improving, but since his return to the city had been out of the house but once, and then only for an hour. He was almost too feeble to quit his sofa. He added that he had been told that the "Cosmopolitan," which was publishing a story of his, had been abandoned by its editor. The story was unfinished, and he had written to try to get his manuscript back, but had failed. Would Hayne please try his hand upon the neglectful editor?[1]

But though so feeble, Simms kept valiantly to his determination to die in harness. He wrote editorials for the "Courier," among them one commemorating the death of his old friend Richard Yeadon. He could hardly have helped feeling that his own time was drawing near, and that soon one of his friends would be performing a similar service for him. Almost his last appearance in public was on May 3, when he delivered the opening address at the Floral Fair held by the Charleston County Agricultural and Horticultural Association. It was fitting in more ways than one that he should have been asked to deliver this address, for he had always been a lover of flowers, and it was a feeble sign that the people of Charleston were at last be-

---

[1] What the name of the story was, or where the *Cosmopolitan* was published are matters about which I am in the dark.

ginning to appreciate his worth. The address, which was entitled "The Sense of the Beautiful," was printed in the "Courier" and warmly praised, too warmly for its intrinsic merits, but not too warmly for its author's services to his State and city. It showed that Simms's mind was in his latter days turning often toward the ideal, and endeavoring to find in the consciousness that he had always loved the true and the beautiful a solace for his present disappointments, for the "brute and baboon and barbarous days," in which he avowed that he and his hearers were living.

On June 2, he wrote his last letter to Hayne, describing himself as having suffered from "a long and exhausting malady," and as "worn to such diminutive proportions" that his friends would no longer recognize him. On June 6, his illness, which seems to have been a complete physical breakdown combined with kidney and stomachic troubles, took an alarming turn. By Thursday night, June 9, all hope was given up, but he lingered on until Saturday, the 11th, when he died at five o'clock in the afternoon. He was conscious to the last, and he seemed to die peacefully, as if glad to be at rest. His children and friends were around him, and every comfort had been supplied him during his illness. One of the last persons to talk with him was his old friend the Reverend James W. Miles, who, almost as feeble as himself, had left a sick bed in order to come to his side.

When the news of his death reached the public,

the bell of St. Michael's was tolled and expressions
of sincere grief were heard on all hands. Charleston in her adversity was slowly becoming conscious
of how cruelly she had treated her ablest son. The
"Courier" of Monday was in mourning, and contained an appreciative editorial upon him from the
pen of Dr. Porcher. The funeral took place on
Monday, at five o'clock in the afternoon, from St.
Paul's Church. The church was thronged, in spite
of the threatening weather. A heavy rain came up
just as the coffin reached the building, where it was
met by the two officiating clergymen, the Reverend
J. W. Miles and the Reverend C. C. Pinckney.
Nor did the rain prevent a large number of those
present at the church from following the body to
that Magnolia Cemetery, at the consecration of
which Simms had read a poem twenty-one years
before. There the worn-out body was committed
to a grave in a corner of a plat that had been set
aside for the erection of a monument to John C.
Calhoun.

The country at large was so much occupied in
retrieving the losses caused by the war and in welcoming the birth of a new school of fiction, that
the death of a romancer whose day was passed did
not attract any widespread attention. Still some
notice of the event was taken by the press, and the
animus of the opinions expressed was generally
favorable. But as the years have rolled by, the
man and his work have been more and more for-

gotten. It is true that his romances have been kept before the public in a cheap form, and have been popular with boys, at least with Southern boys. But a great many well-informed Southern men and women have never heard of Simms, and others are apt to make the mistake made by the curious Boston populace and confound him with "Semmes the Pirate." It may be doubted whether many Northern readers of culture open his romances, although they may be familiar with his name from references made to it in histories of American literature. It is true that two years ago an appreciative article treating of his revolutionary romances appeared in the "Atlantic Monthly," but it was doubtless something of a revelation to many of the readers of that magazine. As a rule the meagre references that have been made to him in text books and elsewhere have been somewhat depreciatory, without any very clear reason being given for the depreciation.

If his name has been thus eclipsed in America, it is no matter of surprise to learn that it is hardly known in England. It is a little strange, however, to be assured, as I have been,[1] that two such widely differing personages as Lord Beaconsfield and Mr. Martin Farquhar Tupper should have expressed a warm admiration for Simms's romances. It is also pleasant to find an anonymous writer, in the "London Quarterly Review" for January, 1885, in the

---

[1] By General James Grant Wilson and by the late Mr. Tupper of Charleston, a cousin of the English author.

course of an article on American novels, doing
Simms the justice to declare that he was an author
whose works were far less known in England than
they should be, "but who produced numerous powerful sketches of genuine American incident," —
sketches which "are much better worth reading than
many of the novels which have made fame and
fortune for inferior writers." The same critic concluded his notice by saying: "The United States
have thus far produced few imaginative, writers of
greater desert than Simms in his particular line."

But we have left South Carolina and the year
1870 somewhat far afield, and must return to them
for a moment. Perhaps the sincerest mourner
among all the old novelist's friends was Paul
Hayne. On July 9, he wrote as follows to Dr.
Porcher: —

"Behold, also, how our old circle of ancient
friends and comrades is thinning! One by one
they have quitted our sides, until at length old
Simms himself, whom I had got into the habit of
regarding as *immortal*, has finished his course, and
said his final farewells! . . . Gallant old man!
whatever his faults, I, for one, loved him with all
my heart! And there is no doubt that his time
had *fully* come. He had fought a good fight and
kept the faith, at least the faith he had plighted to
his own genius and will.

"Yet, as Pierpont says of his deceased child,
'I cannot *make* him *dead!*' So much *vitality* was
there in the man, so vivid is his image before the

'mind's eye,' that all attempts at a *realization* of his death utterly fail! . . . Simms's genius *never had fair play!* Circumstances hampered him! Thus, the *man* was greater than his *works.*"

In a letter to the same gentleman, of August 4, he expressed himself freely as to the merits and demerits of Simms's work, his criticism being saner than his excessive underscoring would lead one to expect: —

"A really *great author* (whether in *prose* or verse) *Simms emphatically was not*, and there is no use in maintaining so fulsome a proposition. But his *talents* were splendid, and his whole life seems to me *noble*, because of the 'grit,' the perseverance, the indomitable energy which it displayed.

"I 've not the remotest idea that his *works* will endure. They were too carelessly written. They lack the *'labor limæ'* to an extent which is distressing. Nevertheless Simms is worthy of *all honor*. 'God rest his *soul*.' "

While Hayne, whose own sense of the necessity of artistic training had grown wonderfully during his residence among the Georgia pines, was writing thus of his comrade's memory, steps were being taken in Charleston to perpetuate that memory in an enduring fashion. About two weeks after his death, a meeting of Simms's friends discussed the propriety of raising a monument to him as soon as possible. Committees were appointed and speeches were made, but the times were still too hard for an undertaking of the kind to succeed. After some

years and various meetings, however, enough money
was raised to warrant the committee's engaging
J. Q. A. Ward to prepare a bronze bust of the romancer, which it was proposed to erect on the Battery. Simms had once been heard to express a wish
that he should have no other memorial than a simple shaft of South Carolina granite broken at the
top. But the committee preferred the bust, and,
after it had been inspected and approved by some
of Simms's Northern friends, Bryant, Lawson,
Bockie, and others, it was mounted on a pedestal
of native granite, and was duly unveiled, with appropriate ceremonies, on the eighth anniversary of
his death, June 11, 1879. At the time of its erection it was the only memorial of the kind in Charleston, the Powers statue of Calhoun, in the city hall,
having been destroyed during the war, and the twig
planted in the centre of the city-hall park, to mark
the site of a proposed monument to Robert Y.
Hayne, having grown to a tree. There is still nothing to mark the spot where the remains of the
noble old man lie, save the name "Simms" carved
on the granite curbing that marks off the family
section. This should not be. Charleston owes
it to herself to do what she can to atone for the
long years of neglect which were all the reward she
gave to her devoted son during his lifetime. His
wish should be carried out, and on the broken shaft
should be carved the epitaph which he composed
for himself: "Here lies one who, after a reason-
ably long life, distinguished chiefly by unceasing

labors, has left all his better works undone." And to these sad words should be added some expression of regret by his people for their long neglect, and of belief that the work he did and the example he set can never wholly die.

Our task is well-nigh ended. It only remains to endeavor to summarize briefly the chief personal characteristics of the man whose career has been the subject of these pages, and to estimate the value of the work he accomplished. It is to be hoped that on both of these points enough has been given to enable the reader to form his own conclusions; but it is always to be expected that the biographer who has made a special study of a man and his writings should record his own conclusions in a compact and intelligible way. And first of Simms as a man.

From both his parents Simms inherited a sanguine, impulsive, and impressible temperament. It would seem that the father's traits were more strongly impressed upon the son than the mother's; for there was little in Simms's nature that was feminine. The most obvious effects of the father's roving nature and passion for adventure have been noted already; but it should be remarked that to this source is possibly due much of the intellectual restlessness which drove Simms from one style of composition to another, and which never let him rest long enough to polish and perfect his work. It is true that he always gave as an excuse for his hurried manner of writing the necessity he was under of earning his daily subsistence; but it would seem that the cause of his unartistic methods of work lay deeper in his own inherited temperament. Nor should we forget in this connection the effects upon him of the turmoil and struggle of his early years, of the humiliating treatment he underwent at the hands of a cold and unsympathetic aristocracy, and finally of the general tone of good-natured vulgarity and conceited ignorance so characteristic of America during the earlier years of this century. All these influences affected his character as much as they did his literary work. They made him dogmatic, opinionated, eccentric, capable at one time of doing great things and at another of doing something unexpectedly foolish. To adopt Mr. Matthew Arnold's terminology, they made him oftentimes appear to be a mere Philistine, when in reality the whole of his life was given up to the endeavor to make himself a man of culture, permeated with "sweetness and light." A barbarian he could not be, since he was not an aristocrat by birth. Perhaps there has never been a man whose development was so sadly hampered by his environment; and that he succeeded as far as he did in escaping from the effects of his environment should move our admiration and respect.

It is needless to dwell upon the native kindness of heart, the buoyant spirits, the superb physical and moral energy of the man, for these have been fully set forth already. Though at times seem-

ingly eaten up with self-conceit, he was never either
really conceited or selfish.   He was never ashamed
to acknowledge his own deficiencies; never so busy
with his own affairs as to turn a deaf ear to a call
for help or sympathy.   The amount of good he did
in his last feeble years cannot be calculated.
Those who saw his eccentricities only, laughed at
him; those who knew him well, loved him more
and more until their love almost grew to reverence.
If he often did a foolish action, he never did a
mean one; and though not symmetrically great, he
was essentially noble.   He had virtues, too, not
specially common in his time and section.   While
fond of stimulants and excitement, he refrained
always from intoxication; while fond of the story
that is told to men only, he was irreproachable in
his private morals.   In religious matters he was
often charged with infidelity, but the charge cannot
be sustained.   Although he never joined a church,
and although he held opinions which most people
would pronounce unorthodox, there is every reason
to conclude that he believed in the essential inspiration of Christianity.   If this be not so, then he
was far less radical in his unbelief than might have
been expected from a knowledge of his character.
On the whole, one forms the impression that Simms
was a vigorous, hearty man, with a versatile and
talented mind, a very large heart, an indomitable
will, and keen if not always delicate, sensibilities.
His weaknesses and eccentricities were partly due
to inherited tendencies, partly to environment, but,

though they marred the symmetry of his character, they nevertheless could not efface the strength and loveableness of his personality.

There is little reason to differ from Hayne with regard to the quality of Simms's literary work. "A really great author," he "emphatically was not;" a talented author he undoubtedly was. His failure in poetry was marked because the unfavorable influences of his environment, combined with the unfavorable characteristics of his inherited temperament, naturally showed to their fullest effect in that region of art where individual peculiarities are least tolerable. It has been shown already how impossible it was that the ante-bellum South should produce a great artist in verse; and Simms's failure is rendered all the more conspicuous from the fact that he endeavored to excel in forms of poetry that require the highest artistic skill. But even if he had written poetry, it would still have been *English* poetry, which would not have suited his patriotic American heart. So after all there is no great reason to be sorry for the fate of his verses. Yet it should not be forgotten that his poetry was a great solace to him, and that it lifted him above this earth and its cares, and that as no one need read it who does not wish to, no one is any the worse for it.

With regard to his prose, attention must be confined to his revolutionary and colonial romances. If the quality of permanence is to be found in his work, it is to be found here. His miscellaneous critical, political, and biographical work has served its transitory purpose and is already forgotten. His historical work will be consulted occasionally by special students, but is of little general value. It is of far more value, to the Southerner at least, to know that Simms never ceased to bewail the indifference of his people to their own history, and that he never failed to encourage local students like Pickett and Meek of Alabama to prosecute and publish their researches. When the Southern people get a true history of themselves, they will find that they have many things to learn and to unlearn; and one of the things they will vainly wish to forget will be their utter indifference to the unseconded and uncheered efforts of men like Simms, to rescue the history of their State and section from the dust of oblivion.

To return however to the main question: Will the revolutionary and colonial romances be read, say fifty years hence? The border romances are omitted from consideration for the already expressed reason that they should never have been written, since they have nothing ennobling in them. If the friends of romance are to make any firm stand against the attacks of the realists, they must make it right here, on the essentially ennobling qualities of great romances. That the romance, in its old form at least, will play again a serious part in the history of literature is open to grave doubt. Literary forms, like nations, seem to play their parts and then retire from the stage. But because no Englishman will ever again write a great epic is

no reason why "Paradise Lost" should cease to delight us. And so, because we shall see no more
Scotts or Coopers is no reason why we should
prophesy a day of oblivion for their works. If
their works fill any one of the world's various
needs, they will be preserved in the world's memory and regard. Yet it would seem that their
works ennoble all who read them in the right spirit,
and that therefore their works will live; for it is
no little thing to ennoble a man's mind and heart,
and it is perhaps as useful a thing to ennoble a
boy's mind and heart. Hence, if Scott and Cooper
become more and more the authors of boyhood,
their place will be no less honorable and secure.

But was Poe right when he ranked Simms above
the herd of American romancers, just after Cooper
and Brockden Brown, and are Simms's best romances ennobling? It would seem that Poe was
right. Cooper at his best is superior to Simms at
his best, and there is no need to compare them at
their worst. Brockden Brown, though a follower of
Godwin, had a narrow vein of real genius, which
can hardly be asserted of Simms. In versatility
and talents Brown was Simms's inferior, and in
estimating the work of the two writers one is almost
inclined, in balancing quantity with quality of work
(a process which most critics neglect), to place the
two men upon the same level. Any comparison
with Hawthorne is of course out of the question.
With regard to romancers like Dr. Bird, Kennedy,
and Paulding, to say nothing of writers like Miss

Sedgwick or Dr. Mayo or Melville, Poe would appear to have stated Simms's position correctly. Both with regard to quantity as well as quality of work he is their superior. His style at its best is not inferior to theirs, and with none of them is it safe to make much question of style. He was more frequently slipshod than they, but that is all that can be said in their favor. In imaginative vigor, in power of description, in the faculty of giving movement to his stories, he leaves them behind. He strikes one as being a born writer, a professional; their works read like those of amateurs.

To consider now the second question: Are his best romances ennobling? In some respects it would seem that they are. They deal with an eventful period, when a young people was struggling for its rights. They show how high and low, rich and poor, were animated by a common patriotism, how they suffered for the cause they espoused, how they triumphed through their bravery and faith. They make the reader familiar with great characters like Marion, and with historic events of no little importance to a nation destined to greatness. Moreover they are full of the freshness of swamp and forest, of the languorous charm of Southern climate and scenery. Then, too, they are full of the heroic deeds of common, unlettered men, and are thus more stimulating than many of those high-flying romances in which lords and ladies undergo their remarkable adventures. It is true, on the other hand, that they are full of an unregulated patriot-

ism which regards every Tory and Englishman, with
a few exceptions, as a brute and a villain; that
they deal with bloodshed and crime *ad nauseam;*
that they are in many places commonplace and
dull. Still, after all is said, it would seem that
the balance stands in Simms's favor. He has described with vigor, and sometimes with charm, the
events of an interesting epoch; he has reproduced
the characteristic features of a life that is gone;
he has painted a landscape, which, if it still exists,
has nevertheless been subject to many changes.
No one will ever do the same work as well, and it
was worth doing. Hence I cannot conclude with
Hayne that his works will die. They will never
be very popular, at least with older readers, but
boys will continue to delight in the daring deeds of
scout and partisan, and cultivated and curious persons will turn to them as faithful pictures of interesting epochs in their country's history.

But here, too, it must again be noted that Simms
was more English than he thought himself. There
was of course more room for originality in his essays in prose fiction than in his poetry, — his excursions into the realms of what Mr. Theodore Watts
is fond of denominating "essential art." His methods were, however, those of his English predecessors,
and whenever he took his eye off his local subject he
wrote like an Englishman. He made constant use
of the stock materials of former and contemporary
romancers, and the comparison which more than
one writer has instituted between him and the Eng-

lish G. P. R. James is in many respects admissible.
But Simms had what James had not: a small particular field which he made his own, and that field
was essentially American.   For this reason he will
live longer than James, and for this reason he deserves a place among American men of letters.
His place is not a high one; but it should never
be forgotten that he was not only a pioneer, but
the pioneer, of American literature, whose destiny
forced him to labor in the least favorable section of
all America for successful literary work.   When his
environment is considered, the work he did will be
deemed worthy of admiration rather than of fault-
finding.

Yes, Hayne was right.   The man Simms "is
worthy of all honor."   Whether as a literary toiler,
working successfully under most harassing conditions; whether as a misguided patriot, striving for
what he believed to be his section's good; whether
as a defeated, worn-out spirit, laboring to relieve
the distresses of his children and his friends, the
man Simms ceases to be a mere man and assumes
proportions that are truly heroic.   His State may
still point to her Calhouns and McDuffies, and
his section may point to politicians and soldiers,
contemporary lights that have cast and still cast
him in the shade; but it is doubtful whether
South Carolina, or indeed the whole South, has
produced in this century a man who will better
stand a close scrutiny into his motives and his life-
work than William Gilmore Simms.

APPENDIX.

A PARTIAL BIBLIOGRAPHY OF SIMMS'S WRITINGS.

LACK of space rather than of materials has necessitated the omission of many bibliographical details. Every entry has been reduced " to its lowest terms; " and only such notes as appear to be indispensable have been admitted. Simms was such a voluminous writer that had full title pages been given, and had all his known contributions to periodical literature, encyclopædias, etc., been chronicled, this appendix would have exceeded all reasonable bounds. It is believed, however, that it will be found to be freer from errors than any previous attempt at a Simms bibliography, as well as more complete. Of such previous attempts that of Allibone is the best. Other bibliographies are to be found in James Wood Davidson's "Living Writers of the South " (1869) ; in John C. Stockbridge's "Catalogue of the Harris Collection of American Poetry " (1886) ; in the " International Magazine " (v. 432 f.) ; in the " Literary World " (Boston, xiii. 351) ; and finally in Duyckinck's and other cyclopædias. These bibliographical lists have been freely consulted, but the bulk of this appendix is the result of individual investigation. Every book (or article) mentioned, except translations and such books as are marked with an asterisk, has been personally examined in the first edition ; and of those so marked only two (Numbers 1 and 78) have been inaccessible in any form.

I. POETRY.[1]

1. * Monody on General Charles Cotesworth Pinckney. (Charleston, 1825. 16mo. [?]) Anonymous.
2. Lyrical and Other Poems. (Charleston, 1827. 18mo.)
3. Early Lays. (Charleston, 1827.)
4. The Vision of Cortes, Cain, and Other Poems. (Charleston, 1829. 16mo.)
5. * The Tri-Color, or The Three Days of Blood in Paris. With Some Other Pieces. (Charleston, 1830. 8vo.)
6. Atalantis: a Story of the Sea. In Three Parts. (New York, 1832. 8vo.) Anonymous.
7. Southern Passages and Pictures. (New York, 1839.)
8. Donna Florida. A Tale. (Charleston, 1843. 16mo.)
9. Grouped Thoughts and Scattered Fancies. A Collection of Sonnets. (Richmond, 1845.)
10. Areytos, or Songs of the South. (Charleston, 1846.)
11. Charleston, and Her Satirists. A Scribblement. By a City Bachelor. (Charleston, 1848.) A hasty satire in reply to a pamphlet entitled " Charleston, a Satire," by a female abolitionist of unknown name.
12. Lays of the Palmetto. (Charleston, 1848.)
13. Atalantis: a Story of the Sea. With the Eye and the Wing; Poems chiefly imaginative. (Philadelphia, 1848.)
14. The Cassique of Accabee; a Tale of Ashley River. With Other Pieces. (New York, 1849. Sq. 18mo.)
15. Sabbath Lyrics, or Songs from Scripture. A Christmas Gift of Love. (Charleston, 1849. 8vo.)
16. The City of the Silent. (Charleston, 1850. 8vo.) Poem delivered at the Consecration of Magnolia Cemetery in Charleston, November 19th, 1850.
17. Poems Descriptive, Dramatic, Legendary, and Contemplative. (2 vols. New York and Charleston, 1853.)
18. Areytos, or Songs and Ballads of the South. With Other Poems. (New York and Charleston, 1860.) Much fuller than No. 10 of this list and contains most of No. 12, as well as a few revised pieces from earlier volumes.

[1] All titles represent 1 vol. 12mo., unless the contrary is indicated.

Dramas.

19. * Norman Maurice: The Man of the People. An American Drama. (Richmond, 1851. 8vo.)
20. Michael Bonham, or The Fall of Bexar. A Tale of Texas. In Five Parts. By a Southron. (Richmond, 1852. 8vo.)
21. Benedict Arnold. A Dramatic Essay. (Richmond, the "Magnolia Weekly," 1863.)

Edited by Simms.

22. A Supplement to the Plays of William Shakespeare. Comprising the Seven Dramas, etc. (New York, 1848. 8vo.)
23. War Poetry of the South. (New York, 1867.)

II. ROMANCES, NOVELETTES, AND COLLECTED STORIES.

24. * Martin Faber. (New York, 1833.) Anonymous. Martin Faber, the Story of a Criminal; and Other Tales. (2 vols. New York, 1837.)
25. The Book of My Lady: a Melange. By a Bachelor Knight. (Philadelphia, 1833.)
26. Guy Rivers: a Tale of Georgia. (2 vols. New York, 1834)
27. The Yemassee: a Romance of South Carolina. (2 vols. New York, 1835.)
28. The Partisan: a Tale of the Revolution. (2 vols. New York, 1835.)
29. Mellichampe: a Legend of the Santee. (2 vols. New York, 1836.)
30. * Richard Hurdis, or The Avenger of Blood. A Tale of Alabama. (2 vols. Philadelphia, 1838.) Anonymous.
31. Carl Werner: an Imaginative Story; with Other Tales of Imagination. (2 vols. New York, 1838.)
32. Pelayo: a Story of the Goth. (2 vols. New York, 1838.)
33. The Damsel of Darien. (2 vols. Philadelphia, 1839.)
34. Border Beagles; a Tale of Mississippi. (2 vols. Philadelphia, 1840.) Sequel to "Richard Hurdis."
35. The Kinsmen, or The Black Riders of the Congaree. A Tale. (2 vols. Philadelphia, 1841.) Afterwards known as "The Scout" (New York, 1854.)
36. Confession, or The Blind Heart. A Domestic Story. (2 vols. Philadelphia, 1841.)

37. Beauchampe, or The Kentucky Tragedy. A Tale of Passion. (2 vols. Philadelphia, 1842.)

38. The Prima Donna: a Passage from City Life. (Philadelphia, 1844. 8vo.) A short story (24 pages) forming the first number of "Godey's Library of Elegant Literature."

39. Castle Dismal, or The Bachelor's Christmas. A Domestic Legend. (New York, 1845.)

40. Helen Halsey, or The Swamp State of Conelachita. A Tale of the Borders. (New York, 1845.) Republished as "The Island Bride," in Munro's "Fireside Companion." (New York, 1869.)

41. Count Julian, or The Last Days of the Goth. (Baltimore and New York, 1845. 8vo.)

42. The Wigwam and Cabin. (2 vols. New York, 1845-46.)

43. Flirtation at the Moultrie House, etc. (Charleston, 1850.) A short skit (46 pages) describing, in the letters of one Miss Georgiana Appleby, a ball at the Moultrie House of which Simms was a manager.

44. Katharine Walton, or The Rebel of Dorchester. An Historical Romance of the Revolution in South Carolina. (Philadelphia, 1851. 8vo.)

45. The Golden Christmas: a Chronicle of St. John's, Berkeley. Compiled from the Notes of a Briefless Barrister. (Charleston, 1852.)

46. As Good as a Comedy, or The Tennessean's Story. By an Editor. (Philadelphia, 1852.)

47. * The Sword and the Distaff, or "Fair, Fat, and Forty." (Charleston, 1852.) Afterwards known as "Woodcraft, or Hawks about the Dovecote." (New York, 1854.)

48. Marie De Berniere: a Tale of the Crescent City, etc. (Philadelphia, 1853.) Contains besides the leading tale two stories, "The Maroon" and "Maize in Milk." In 1855 precisely the same volume was issued as "The Maroon: a Legend of the Caribbees, and Other Tales." "Marie De Berniere" was afterwards issued as "The Ghost of My Husband: a Tale of the Crescent City." (New York, 1866.)

49. * Vasconselos: a Romance of the New World. (New York, 1854.) Published under the *nom de plume* of "Frank Cooper."

50. * Southward Ho! n Spell of Sunshine. (New York, 1854.)
51. The Forayers, or The Raid of the Dog-Days. (New York, 1855.)
52. Charlemont, or The Pride of the Village. A Tale of Kentucky. (New York, 1856.) Sequel to "Beauchampe."
53. Eutaw: a Sequel to the Forayers, or The Raid of the Dog-Days. A Tale of the Revolution. (New York, 1856.)
54. The Cassique of Kiawah: a Colonial Romance. (New York, 1859.)
55. Paddy McGann, or The Demon of the Stump. (Richmond, the "Southern Illustrated News." 1863.)
56. Joscelyn: a Tale of the Revolution. (New York, the "Old Guard," 1867.)
57. The Cub of the Panther: a Mountain Legend. (New York, the "Old Guard," 1869.)
58. Voltmeier, or The Mountain Men. A Tale of the Old North State. (New York, the "Illuminated Western World," 1869.) Numbers 55, 56, 57, 58, are serials which do not seem to have been published in book form.

III. History and Biography.

59. * Memoir of Maynard Davis Richardson in "The Remains of Maynard Davis Richardson, with a Memoir of his Life." By his Friend. (Charleston, 1833.) Simms probably edited this volume.
60. * The History of South Carolina, etc. (Charleston, 1840.) Second edition, enlarged. (Charleston, 1842.) Third edition, much enlarged. (New York and Charleston, 1860.)
61. The Geography of South Carolina, etc. (Charleston, 1843.) Companion volume to the foregoing.
62. The Life of Francis Marion. (New York, 1845.)
63. * The Life of Captain John Smith, the Founder of Virginia. (New York, 1846.)
64. The Life of the Chevalier Bayard. (New York, 1847.)
65. The Life of Nathanael Greene. (New York, 1849.)
66. The Lily and the Totem, or The Huguenots in Florida. A series of Sketches, Picturesque and Historical, of the Colonies of Coligni. 1562–1570. (New York, 1850.)
67. South Carolina in the Revolutionary War. By a Southron. (Charleston, 1853.)

68. Memoir of Colonel John Laurens in "Memoir and Correspondence of Colonel John Laurens." (Bradford Club Series, No. 1. New York, 1867. 4to and 8vo.)

IV. MISCELLANEOUS.

69. Slavery in America, being a Brief Review of Miss Martineau
on that Subject. By a South Carolinian. (Richmond, 1838.
8vo.) Appears also as "The Morals of Slavery." Simms's
contribution to "The Pro-Slavery Argument." (Charleston, 1852.)

70. The Social Principle: the True Source of National Permanence. (Tuscaloosa, 1843. 8vo.) Oration delivered at
the University of Alabama, December 13, 1842.

71. The Sources of American Independence. (Aikin, 1844.
8vo.) Oration at Aikin, S. C., July 4, 1844.

72. The Charleston Book: a Miscellany in Prose and Verse.
(Charleston, 1845.) Simms contributed a short preface and
edited the volume, which appeared, however, without his
name.

73. Views and Reviews in American Literature, History, and Fiction. (2 vols. New York, 1845, — really copyrighted and
published in 1846.)

74. Self-Development. (Milledgeville, 1847. 8vo.) Oration delivered November 10, 1847, at Oglethorpe University, Georgia.

75. Father Abbot, or The Home Tourist. A Medley. (Charleston, 1849. 18mo.)

76. Egeria, or Voices of Thought and Comfort for the Woods
and Wayside. (Philadelphia, 1853.)

77. Address at the Inauguration of the Spartanburg Female College. (Spartanburg, 1855.) Address delivered August 22,
1855.

78. * The Power of Cotton.[1] (New York, 1856. 8vo.)

79. Sack and Destruction of the City of Columbia, S. C., to which
is added a List of the Property destroyed. Originally
published in the "Columbia Daily Phœnix." (Columbia,
1865.) Anonymous.

---

[1] Doubtful. Simms's name is written on the copy in the Boston Public
Library, but the handwriting is not that of Theodore Parker, to whom the
pamphlet originally belonged.

80. The Sense of the Beautiful. (Charleston, 1870. 8vo.) An address delivered before the Charleston County Agricultural and Horticultural Association, May 3, 1870.

V. CHIEF CONTRIBUTIONS TO MAGAZINES.

A by no means exhaustive search has resulted in the collection of over two hundred and fifty titles of poems, stories, and miscellaneous articles contributed by Simms to various magazines and annuals. His contributions to newspapers are even more numerous, ranging as they do from a short letter as country correspondent to editorials and reviews three and four columns long. Obviously the most part of these ephemeral productions should be left to oblivion, and the following list will be found to relate mainly to such of his more elaborate articles as were never collected in permanent form. Up to 1851 Simms was in the habit of binding for his own use his longer articles ; after this date his contributions, at least to his own review, are to be determined by internal evidence only, — a hazardous procedure which has not been much indulged in here.

1. American Criticism and Critics. (So. Lit. Jour., July, 1836.)
2. Logoochie, or the Branch of Sweet Water. (Magnolia, annual, 1839.)
3. Early Lays. (Continued in So. Lit. Mess. for 1839–41.)
4. Queen Mary. (Dem. Rev., Feb., 1842.)
5. Bulwer's Genius and Writings. (Magnolia. Dec., 1842.)
6. The Writings of Washington Allston. (S. Q. R., Oct., 1843.)
7. The Moral Character of Hamlet. (Orion, 1844.)
8. Letters on International Copyright. (So. Lit. Mess., 1844.)
9. The New Spirit of the Age. (S. Q. R., April, 1845.)
10. A Year of Consolation. (Review of Mrs. Butler's book, S. Q. R., July, 1847.)
11. John Rutledge. (Amer. Whig Rev., Aug. and Sept., 1847.)
12. Prescott's Conquest of Peru. (S. Q. R., Jan. and April, 1848.)

13. Stevens's History of Georgia. (S. Q. R., April, 1848.)
14. Headley's Life of Cromwell. (S. Q. R., Oct., 1848.)
15. Modern Prose Fiction. (S. Q. R., April, 1849.)
16. Guizot's Democracy in France. (S. Q. R., April, 1849.)
17. Later Poems of Henry Taylor. (S. Q. R., July, 1849.)
18. Recent American Poets. (S. Q. R., Oct., 1849.)
19. Kennedy's Life of Wirt. (S. Q. R., April, 1850.)
20. Ellet's Women of the Revolution. (S. Q. R., July, 1850.)
21. Sentimental Prose Fiction. (S. Q. R., July, 1850.)
22. Tuckerman's Essays and Essayists. (S. Q. R., July, 1850.)
23. Summer Travel in the South. (S. Q. R., Sept., 1850.)
24. Topics in the History of South Carolina. (S. Q. R., Sept., 1850.)
25. The Southern Convention. (S. Q. R., Sept., 1850.)
26. Home Sketches, or Life along the Highways and Byways of the South. (Continued in Literary World for 1852)
27. Charleston, the Palmetto City. (Harper's Mag., June, 1857.)
28. The Story of Chastelard. (Lippincott's Mag., March, 1868.)
29. How Sharp Snaffles got his Capital and Wife. (Harper's Mag., Oct., 1870.) [1]

The following articles, of some interest to students of Southern history, may be unhesitatingly assigned to Simms : —

1. Pickett's History of Alabama. (S Q. R , Jan., 1852.)
2. Domestic Histories of the South. (S. Q. R., April, 1852.)
3. The Baron De Kalb. (S. Q. R., July, 1852.)
4. Literary Prospects of the South. (Russell's, June, 1858.)
5. Marion, the Carolina Partisan. (Russell's, Oct. and Nov., 1858.)

In this connection a chronological list of the various publications with which Simms was editorially connected will not be out of place. They are all Charleston enterprises save Number 7.

1. The Southern Literary Gazette. (1828–29.)
2. The City Gazette. (1830–32.)
3. The Cosmopolitan, an Occasional. (1833.)
4. The Magnolia, or Southern Apalachian. (1842–43.)

[1] Reissued as "The Big Lie," in "Short Stories," May, 1891.

5. The Southern and Western Magazine and Review.   (1845.)
6. The Southern Quarterly Review.   (1849–55.)
7. The Columbia Phœnix.   (1865.)
8. The Daily South Carolinian.   (1865–66.)
9. The Courier.   (1870.)

Simms was also for many years correspondent and reviewer, perhaps literary editor, of the "Mercury."

VI. ENGLISH REPRINTS AND TRANSLATIONS.

Reprints.

1. The Tri-Color, etc.   (London, 1830, 8vo.)
2. Guy Rivers.   (* London, 1835, 3 vols.   1841, 1 vol. 8vo.)
3. The Yemassee.   (* London, 1835, 3 vols.   1844, 1 vol. 8vo.)
4. The Damsel of Darien.   (London, 1845, 1 vol. 8vo.)
5. The Kinsmen.   (London, 1841, 1 vol. 8vo.)
6. Confession.   (London, 1845, 1 vol. 8vo.)
7. Beauchampe.   (London, 1842, 1 vol. 8vo.)
8. Count Julian.   (London, 1846, 1 vol. 8vo.)
9. The Wigwam and Cabin, issued as "Life in America, or the Wigwam and the Cabin."   (Aberdeen, 1848.)

Simms's review of Mrs. Trollope was reprinted in England along with other American critiques in 1833. (See Allibone, art. Trollope, Frances.)

Translations.

Allibone says that many of Simms's works were translated into French and German. Inquiries have been made in Paris, and Lorenz's "Catalogue de la Librairie Française" has been searched, but no French translation has been discovered. According to Kayser's "Bücher Lexikon," the following German translations have appeared : —

1. The Wigwam and Cabin.   (Wigwam und Hütte. Leipzig, 1846.)
2. The Yemassee.   (Der Yemassee-Indianer. Leipzig, 1847. 2 Bde.)

In the "Bibliothek Amerikanische," Leipzig, 1853-64 :

3. Katharine Walton. (Nos. 26-29.)
4. Marie de Berniere. (Nos. 62-64.)
5. The Sword and the Distaff. (Schwert und Spindel. Nos. 100-104.)
6. Richard Hurdis. (Nos. 280-284.)
7. Guy Rivers. (Nos. 323-326.)
8. Border Beagles. (Die Grenzjagd. Nos. 333-337.)
9. The Cassique of Kiawah. (Der Kassike von Kiawa. Nos. 396-400.)
10. The Partisan. (Der Parteigänger. Nos. 411-415.)

Several books which have been assigned to Simms by his bibliographers have been omitted from the above lists for reasons which cannot be given in detail. They are :

1. The Star Brethren and Other Stories. Simms made up a volume of short stories under this title, but Mr. Davidson seems to be the only authority for its existence in printed form.
2. Slavery in the South. (Richmond, 1851.) Allibone mentions this pamphlet, but there are reasons for believing that he confused it with "Slavery in America." (Richmond, 1838.)
3. The Battle of Fort Moultrie : a Discourse. Allibone seems to be the sole authority for this. It was probably a lecture, and may have remained in manuscript as other lectures, such as " Poetry and the Practical," certainly did.
4. The Swamp Robbers. (1870.) Attributed to Simms by the " Literary World." (Oct. 21, 1882.) This may have been confounded with " The Island Bride " or " Helen Halsey," or the latter story may have really changed its name a third time.

Besides the above Simms has been wrongly credited with " Poems of a Collegian " (1833. By Thomas Semmes) ; "Rombert, a Tale of Carolina" (1835. Anonymous) ; "Osceola, etc." (1838. By Seymour R. Duke) ; "Pelayo, etc." (1836. By Mrs. Mowatt) ; Historical and Social Sketch of Craven County (S. Q. R., April, 1854. By Prof. F. A. Porcher).

INDEX.[1]

[1] No references are made to the Appendix.

350 INDEX.

AUTHOR INDEX

*ADAMS, Charles Francis
The Life of John Adams. 2 Vol. (1871).
Begun by John Quincy Adams. Completed
by Charles Francis Adams. Cited in: BCL;
LC68-24969.   **151** Cloth $29.50

*AITKEN, George Atherton
The Life of Richard Steele. 2 Vol. (1889).
Illustrations, facsimiles, genealogical ta-
bles. Cited in: BCL, CBEL; LC68-24893.
152 Cloth $24.95

ALBRIGHT, E.M.
Spenser's Cosmic Philosophy and Religion.
(1929).   **MS 1** $2.25

*ALCOTT, Amos Bronson
Ralph Waldo Emerson: An estimate of his
character and genius in prose and verse
(1882). Cited in: BCL, BAL; LC68-24930.
908 Cloth $4.95

ALLEN, James T.
The Greek Theatre of the Fifth Century Before Christ (1919). A study of 4th and 5th
century Greek theatre with special emphasis on its architecture and stagecraft. Illus.
LC68-2221.   **647** Cloth $7.50

ALLEN, Morse S.
The Satire of John Marston (1920). A study
of the important 17th Century playwright
and poet. An in-depth analysis of the plays
plus a biographical essay. Cited in: CBEL;
LC65-26460.   **500** Cloth $6.75

AMES, Percy W. (Ed.)
Milton Memorial Lectures (1909). A series
of ten lectures delivered before the Royal
Society of Literature to commemorate the
Terecentenary of the birth of Milton
(1908). Cited in: CBEL; LC65-15895.
501 Cloth $5.95

AMY, Ernest F.
The Text of Chaucer's "Legend of Good
Women" (1918). A careful examination of
the various manuscript texts of Chaucer's
first experiment with the heroic couplet.
Includes a full description of the manuscripts. Cited in: CBEL; LC65-21088.
502 Cloth $5.90

ANDERSON, Ruth Leila
Elizabethan Psychology and Shakespeare's
plays (1927). An analysis of the playwright
through the application of contemporary
psychological thought. LC65-15887.
503 Cloth $5.95

*ANDREWS, Alexander
The History of British Journalism, from
the foundation of the newspaper press in
England to repeal of the Stamp Act. 2 Vol.
(1859). Includes sketches of press celebri-
ties. Cited in: DCL; LC68-24958.
154 Cloth $21.95

APP, August J.
Lancelot in English Literature (1929). A
chronological discussion of the role and
character of Lancelot as he appears in
English literature from mythology through
the 20th century. Cited in: CBEL;
LC65-21392.   **504** Cloth $9.95

*APPERSON, George Latimer
A Jane Austen Dictionary (1932).
LC68-24894   **909** Cloth $7.95

ATKINSON, Dorothy F.
Edmund Spenser: A Bibliographical Supplement (1937). Intended as a supplement
to Carpenter's "Reference Guide to Edmund Spenser." An absolute must for
sources; bibliographical, biographical and
critical. Cited in: CBEL; LC67-30806.
705 Cloth $10.95

*AUSLANDER, J. & HILL, F. E.
Winged Horse: The Story of the Poets and
Their Poetry (1928).
LC68-24959.   **328** Cloth

*BABCOCK, K.W. Charles
The Rise of American Nationality, 1811-1819 (1906). Cited in: BCL, L;
LC68-24970.   910 Cloth $11.95

BAILEY, Margaret L.
Milton and Jakob Boehme (1914). A study of German mysticism in 17th Century England. Cited in: CBEL; LC65-15885.
                               505 Cloth $7.50

BAKER, Arthur E.
A Tennyson Dictionary (1916). The characters and place-names contained in the poetical and dramatic works; alphabetically arranged and described with synopses of the poems and plays. Cited in: BCL, CBEL; LC67-30807.   706 Cloth $13.95

BANCROFT, W. Wallace
Joseph Conrad — His Philosophy of Life (1933). The writer's philosophy as revealed through his works. LC65-15867.
                               506 Cloth $5.25

BASTIAENEN, J.A.
The Moral Tone of Jacobean and Caroline Drama (1930). Elizabethan morality as reflected on the contemporary stage. Particular emphasis on Shakespeare and Jonson. LC68-951.   507 Cloth $7.65

BAUMGARTNER, Milton D.
On Dryden's Relation to Germany in the 18th Century (1914). Cited in: CBEL.
                               MS 84 $3.50

BEKKER, W.G.
An Historical and Critical Review of Samuel Butler's Literary Works (1925). Illus. Cited in: BCL, CBEL; LC67-8773.
                               509 Cloth $6.50

BELLOC, Hilaire
Elizabethan Commentary (1942).
LC67-31526.   707 Cloth $8.95

BENNETT, J.W.
The Theme of Spenser's "Fowre Hymnes" (1931). Cited in: CBEL.
                               MS 3 $1.85

BENNETT, Robert
The Wrath of John Steinbeck (1939).
                               MS 4 $1.50

*BENSON & HEDIN
Swedes in America, 1638-1938 (1938). Originally published by Yale University Press, this work has been long out of print. Essential for all libraries of any size.
                               326 Cloth $25.00

BENTLEY, Phyllis
The English Regional Novel (1941).
                               MS 107 $1.85

BERGER, P.
William Blake: Poet and Mystic (1914). Translation of the French edition of 1907 by D.H. Conner. Cited in: CBEL
LC67-31287.   778 Cloth $13.95

BERWICK, Donald M.
The Reputation of Jonathan Swift (1941). An appraisal of Swift by his later biographers, critics, and editors. (1781-1882). LC65-21096.   508 Cloth $7.95

*BETZ, Louis Paul
La Litterature Comparee. Essai Bibliographique (1904). Introduction par Joseph Texte. 2. ed. augm., pub., avec un index methodique, par Fernand Baldensperger. Cited in: BCL; LC68-25307.
                               911 Cloth $13.95

BILLINGS, Anna H.
A Guide to English Metrical Romances (1901). Dealing with English and Germanic legends and the cycles of Charlemagne and Arthur. Cited in: CBEL.
                               509A Cloth $6.50

*BIRNEY, Catherine H.
The Grimke Sisters—Sarah and Angelina Grimke, the First American Women Advocates of Abolition and Women's Rights (1885). Cited in: BCL; LC68-24971.
                               912 Cloth $8.95

*BJORKMAN, Erik
Scandinavian Loan-Words in Middle English (1900-1902). 2 parts. Cited in: BCL; LC68-24897.   913 Cloth $12.95

*BLEGEN, Theodore C.
Norwegian Migration to America, 1825-1860 (1931). Out of print for some years. Essential for all libraries of any size, and for students of sociology. Originally published by the North American Historical Association in Northfield, Minnesota in 1931. LC68-31271.   325 Cloth $20.00

BOAS, Frederick S.
Ovid and the Elizabethans (1948).
                               MS 8 $1.45

*BOAS, Frederick Samuel
Shakespeare and His Predecessors (1904). Cited in: BCL, L; LC68-24898.
                               914 Cloth $16.95

BOGAERTS, A.M.A.
Chesterton and the Victorian Age (1940). G.K. Chesterton's criticism of Browning, Dickens, Stevenson, etc. LC68-754.
                               510 Cloth $7.95

BOKLUND, Gunnar
The Sources of "The White Devil" by John Webster (1957). LC68-1396.
                               648 Cloth $7.95

BOSANQUET, Theodora
Henry James at Work. Cited in: BCL.
                               MS 9 $2.00

BOTTRALL, Margaret
The Divine Image (1950). A study of Blake's interpretation of Christianity. Cited in: BCL, CBEL.   MS 5 $3.95

*BOULTING, William
Tasso and His Times (1907). 25 plates, portraits, facsimiles. Cited in: BCL. L; LC68-24953   **915** Cloth $13.95

BOURGEOIS, Maurice
John Millington Synge and the Irish Theatre (1913). The life and works of the 20th century playwright. Bibliography of his works, translations and unpublished manuscripts. 20 Illus. Cited in: BCL, CBEL; LC68-906.   **511** Cloth $9.00

BRADBY, G.F.
The Problems of Hamlet (1928). Cited in: CBEL.   **MS 6** $3.25

BRANDL, Alois
Samuel Taylor Coleridge and the English Romantic School (1887). A biography of the poet; translated from the German (1886) by Lady Eastlake. Cited in: CBEL; LC68-757.   **512** Cloth $12.25

BRAYBROOKE, Patrick
Some Thoughts on Hilaire Belloc. LC68-1140.   **649** Cloth $5.95

BRECKNOCK, Albert
Byron: A study of the Poet in the Light of New Discoveries (1926). LC67-30808.   **708** Cloth $11.95

*BREE, Mme. Malwine
The Groundwork of the Leschetizky Method (1902). Illus. Cited in: BCL; LC68-25284.   **290** Cloth $17.95

BRENNECKE, Ernest (Ed.)
Thomas Hardy's Life and Art (1925). A collection of Hardy's essays, letters and notes edited with an introduction. Cited in: BCEL; LC68-751.   **650** Cloth $7.25

BRENNECKE, Ernest
Thomas Hardy's Universe (1924). A study of Hardy's poetry. Bibliography. Cited in: CBEL; LC68-689.   **651** Cloth $5.95

BRIDGE, Sir Frederick
Shakespearean Music In the Plays and Early Operas (1923). Nearly all of Shakespeare's plays provide for music, both instrumental and vocal. This scholarly work attempts to reconstruct that music so as to make us more aware of this facet of Shakespeare's art. 17 Illus. plus a Musical Appendix. LC68-358/MN. **513** Cloth $8.35

*BRIDGE, Horatio
Personal Recollections of Nathaniel Hawthorne (1893). Based on 3 papers first published in Harper's Magazine. Illus. Cited in: BCL, BAL, L; LC68-24931.   **916** Cloth $9.95

BRIDGES, Robert
The Influence of the Audience on Shakespeare's Drama (1927). Cited in: CBEL.   **MS 85** $4.95

*BRINK, Bernhard Aegidius Konrad ten
The Language of Metre of Chaucer (1901). 2nd ed., rev. by Friedrich Kluge, tr. by M. Bentinck Smith. Cited in: BCL; LC68-24899.   **917** Cloth $10.95

*BRINTON, Danel Garrison
The Myths of the New World: A Treatise on the Symbolism and Mythology of the Red Race of America. 2nd Ed. Rev. (1876). Cited in: BCL, L; LC68-24972.   **918** Cloth $11.95

BRISCOE, Walter A. (Ed.)
Byron, the Poet (1924). 24 biographical and critical essays. Illus. with 17 facsimiles and portraits. Cited in: CBEL; LC67-30803.   **694** Cloth $12.50

BROERS, B.C.
Mysticism in the Neo-Romanticists (1923). Mystic influences in the writings of William Morris, Payne, Rossetti, Swinburne and other Victorian poets. LC68-767.   **514** Cloth $8.95

BRONOWSKI, J.
William Blake: A Man Without A Mask (1947). Cited in: BCL, CBEL; LC67-30809.   **709** Cloth $8.25

BROOKE, Tucker
The Marlowe Canon (1922). An Annotated Bibliography. Cited in: CBEL. **MS 10** $2.75

BROOKE, C.F. Tucker
Shakespeare's Plurarch. 2 Vol. (1909). Vol. I discusses the main sources of "Julius Caesar"; Vol. II, of "Antony and Cleopatra" and "Coriolanus." **516** Cloth $15.00

BROWN, Arthur C.L.
Iwain—A Study of the Origin of Arthurian Romance (1903). A scholarly investigation into the sources of Cretien's Romantic poem. Cited in: CBEL. **515** Cloth $6.95

BROWN, Leonard
The Genesis. Growth and Meaning of "Endymion" (1933). Cited in: CBEL.   **MS 7** $1.95

BROWN, Stephen J.
The World of Imagery (1927). A study of the many forms of literary imagery. LC65-26462.   **514A** Cloth $6.95

*BROWN, William Garrot
The Lower South in American History (1902). Cited in: BCL, L; LC68-24973.   **919** Cloth $9.95

*BUCKINGHAM, William and Sir George William Ross
The Honorable Alexander Mackenzie, His Life and Times (1892). Portraits, Facsimiles, Woodcuts. Cited in: BCL, AHA; LC68-25225.   **920** Cloth $19.95

*BUCKLAND, Charles Edward
Dictionary of Indian Biography (1906).
Over 2,500 sketches of individuals since
about 175 A.D. Cited in: BCL, AHA;
LC68-26350.   277 Cloth $17.95

BULAND, Mable
The Presentation of Time in the Elizabethan Drama (1912). Time and its treatment in Elizabethan theatre; its roots and
influences, both classical and contemporary. Cited in: CBEL.   517 Cloth $12.50

*BURGESS, William
The Bible in Shakespeare (1903). A study
of the relation of the works of William
Shakespeare to the Bible; with numerous
parallel passages, quotations, references,
paraphrases, and allusions. LC68-24900.
                           921 Cloth $10.95

*BURROUGHS, John
Notes on Walt Whitman as Poet and Person (1867). Cited in: BCL; LC68-24932.
                           922 Cloth $7.95

*BUTLER, William Francis Thomas
The Lombard Communes: A History of the
Republics of North Italy (1906). Illustrated
with maps, plates, portraits. Cited in: BCL,
L; LC68-25226.   923 Cloth $19.95

BUTT, John
Pope's Taste in Shakespeare (1936). Cited
in: CBEL.   MS 11 $1.75

BUTTER, Peter
Shelley's Idols of the Cave. Cited in: CBEL,
BCL; LC68-24118.   781 Cloth $9.95

BUXTON, Charles R.
Prophets of Heaven and Hell (1945). A
study of Virgil's "Aeneid," Dante's "In-
ferno," Milton's "Paradise Lost" and
Goethe's "Faust." Cited in: CBEL, BCL.
                           MS 86 $4.95

*CALLAHAN, Edward W.
List of officers of the Navy of the United
States and of the Marine Corps, 1775-
1900 (1901). 2 Plates. Originally published
in 1901, this work is one of reference in
all libraries. It is the most complete of its
type. LC68-31274.   327 Cloth $25.00

CAMERON, Kenneth W.
Ralph Waldo Emerson's Reading (1941).
A valuable guide for source-hunters and
scholars to some 1,000 volumes that Emerson withdrew from libraries. Bibliography
of the borrowing with a cross-reference
index. Cited in: BCL.   518 Cloth $5.25

CAMPBELL, O.W.
Shelley and the Unromantics, 2nd Ed.
(1924). An important biography of the
poet and a discussion of his works. Illus.
Cited in: CBEL; LC68-1189.
                           652 Cloth $8.25

*CAMPBELL, Thomas
The Complete Poetical Works of Thomas
Campbell (1907). Edited by J. Logie Rob-
ertson. Notes. Cited in: BCL; LC68-24901.
                           924 Cloth $13.95

CARNAHAN, David H.
The Prologue in the Old French and Provencal Mystery (1905).   519 Cloth $7.35

CARPENTER, Frederick Ives
Emerson and Asia (1930). A significant
study of the Eastern influences on Emerson. Cited in: BAL, BCL; LC67-30810.
                           710 Cloth $10.95

CARTER, Frederick
D.H. Lawrence and the Body Mystical
(1932). LC68-910.   653 Cloth $5.95

CARY, Elizabeth L.
The Novels of Henry James (1905). Includes a bibliography compiled by Frederick A. King. LC65-15897.
                           520 Cloth $7.50

CHAMBERS, E.K.
The English Folk Play (1933). Includes a
bibliography of the texts. Cited in: BCL,
CBEL.   521 Cloth $6.50

CHAMBERS, R.W.
Man's Unconquerable Mind (1939). Stud-
ies of English writers from Bede to A.E.
Housman. Cited in: BCL; LC67-30811.
                           711 Cloth $13.95

CHAMBERS, R.W.
The Place of St. Thomas More in English
Literature and History (1937). Illus. Cited
in: CBEL; LC65-15870.   523 Cloth $4.75

CHAMBERS, R. W.
Ruskin and Others on Byron (1925). Cited
in: CBEL.   MS 12 $1.65

CHARLTON, H.B.
The Dark Comedies of Shakespeare
(1937).   MS 106 $2.95

CHARLTON, H.B.
Shakespeare's Comedies: The Consummation (1937).   MS 13 $1.95

CHARQUES, R.D.
Contemporary Literature and the Social
Revolution. An analysis of post-World-War-
I English literature and its relation to so-
cial change. LC68-2035.   654 Cloth $6.95

CHESTERTON, G.K.
Appreciation & Criticisms of the Works of
Charles Dickens (1911). Cited in: CBEL;
LC68-766.   524 Cloth $6.50

CHESTERTON, G.K.
Do We Agree? (1928). A debate between
the critic and George Bernard Shaw with
Hilaire Belloc in the chair. Cited in: BCL;
LC65-15899.   525 Cloth $2.95

CHISLETT, William
George Meredith — A Study and an Appraisal (1925). Cited in: CBEL; LC68-905.
526 Cloth $7.25

CHRISTIE, O.F.
Johnson the Essayist (1924). An examination of Samuel Johnson's essays, writings and opinions of men, morals and manners. Cited in: CBEL; LC68-688.
527 Cloth $8.25

CLARK, Arthur M.
The Realistic Revolt in Modern Poetry (1922).
MS 87 $4.25

CLARK, John
A History of Epic Poetry (1900). A fascinating study of this poetic form from its earliest development through the 19th century. LC65-15876.
528 Cloth $7.95

CLARK, Paul O.
A Gulliver Dictionary (1953). MS 15 $1.90

CLARKE, John H.
The God of Shelley and Blake (1930).
MS 16 $3.00

CLARKE, Sidney M.
The Miracle Play in England (1897). An intelligent account of the development of Religious Drama from the Conquest to the Reformation. Cited in: CBEL; LC65-15874.
529 Cloth $4.50

*CLYMER, William Branford Shubrick
James Fenimore Cooper (1900). Cited in: BCL, BAL; LC68-24933. 925 Cloth $7.95

COFER, David B.
Saint - Simonism in the Radicalism of Thomas Carlyle (1931).   MS 16B $2.45

*CONGLETON, J.E.
Theories of Pastoral Poetry in England, 1684-1798, traces the pervasive transition which took place between the dates indicated. Beginning on the Continent with Sebillet, Colletet, Rapin, and Fontenelle, it delineates the developments, conventions, and revolts of the tradition as specifically treated by Pope, Purney, Tickell, Johnson, Aikin, Saint-Lambert, Gessner, Blair, and Wordsworth as well as by many less important English and Continental critics. (1952. Cited in: BCL; LC68-29735.
329 Cloth $11.95

*CONWAY, Moncure Daniel
Emerson at Home and Abroad (1883). Cited in: BCL, BAL; LC68-24934.
930 Cloth $11.95

*CONWAY, Moncure Daniel
Life of Nathaniel Hawthorne (1890). Bibliography by John P. Anderson. Cited in: BCL, BAL, L; LC68-24935. 931 Cloth $9.95

CONYBEARE, John J.
Illustrations of Anglo-Saxon Poetry (1826). The first scholarly work on the subject. Cited in: CBEL; LC65-15875.
530 Cloth $12.50

*COOK, Albert S. (comp)
A Concordance to Beowulf (1911). Cited in: BCL; LC68-26349   273 Cloth $14.95

COOK, Albert S.
The Historical Background of Chaucer's "Knight" (1916). LC68-1564.
531 Cloth $6.00

COOK, Albert S.
The Possible Begetter of the Old English BEOWULF and WIDSITH (1922). Cited in: CBEL.
MS 18 $3.25

*COOK, Sir Edward Tyas
The Life of John Ruskin. 2 Vol. (1911). Illus. Cited in: BCL; LC68-24903.
155 Cloth $35.00

*CORBETT, Sir Julian Stafford
Sir Francis Drake (1890). Illus. Cited in: BCL, L, AHA; LC68-25228. 932 Cloth $9.95

CORKE, Helen
D.H. Lawrence and the Apocalypse (1933). A study of Lawrence's poem. LC68-1141.
655 Cloth $5.95

CORY, Herbert E.
The Critics of Edmund Spenser (1911). Cited in: CBEL; LC65-15901.
532 Cloth $6.00

*COWPER, William
The Correspondence of William Cowper. 4 Vol. (1904). Arranged by Thomas Wright. Maps. Cited in: BCL, L; LC68-24904.
156 Cloth $49.00

CREES, J.H.E.
George Meredith (1918). A study of Meredith's works and personality. Cited in: CBEL; LC67-30812.   712 Cloth $9.95

CREES, J.H.E.
Meredith Revisited and Other Essays (1921). Articles on Aristophanes, Cicero, Homer, Ibsen, Meredith and others. LC67-30813.   713 Cloth $6.95

CREIZENACH, Wilhelm
The English Drama in the Age of Shakespeare (1916). A comprehensive work on the 16th century theatre. LC65-15873.
533 Cloth $12.50

CROCE, Benedetto
European Literature in the 19th Century (1924). Cited in: L; LC67-30822.
735 Cloth $12.50

CROISSANT, De Witt C.
Studies in the Work of Colley Cibber (1912). A study of the 18th Century Playwright who was made famous by Pope in his "Dunciad." Bibliography. Cited in: CBEL.   MS 88 $3.50

CROLL, Morris B.
The Works of Fulke Greville (1903). Study of the 17th Century Dramatist and Poet. Cited in: CBEL.   MS 19 $2.95

CUMMINGS, Hubertis M.
The Indebtedness of Chaucer's Works to the Italian Works of Boccaccio (1916). Cited in: CBEL, BCL; LC65-21098.
                        534 Cloth $6.95

＊CUMMINGS, William Hayman
Purcell (1881). Cited in: BCL, L; LC68-25285.   285 Cloth $6.95

CURRY, S.S.
Browning and the Dramatic Monologue (1908). An insight into Robert Browning's introduction and use of this literary form in his poetry. Cited in: CBEL; LC65-26455.
                        535 Cloth $8.25

CURRY, Walter Clyde
The Demonic Metaphysics of MACBETH (1933). Cited in: CBEL.   MS 20 $1.60

DAVIDSON, Charles
Studies in the English Mystery Plays (1892). Cited in: CBEL; LC68-752.
                        536 Cloth $6.95

＊DAVIDSON, Thomas
The Philosophy of Goethe's "Faust" (1906). Cited in: BCL; LC68-24963.
                        933 Cloth $7.95

＊DENNY, Margaret and William H. Gilman (eds.)
The American Writer and the European Tradition (1950). Articles on American naturalism and European views of contemporary American literature by such noted critics as Alfred Kazin, Lionel Trilling, and Louis B. Wright. Cited in: BCL, L, GSUSA; LC68-24936.   934 Cloth $8.95

＊DICKINSON, Edward
Music in the History of the Western Church (1902). With an introduction in religious music among the primitive and ancient peoples. Cited in: BCL, L; LC68-25286.
                        301 Cloth

DIXON, W. Macneile
English Epic and Heroic Poetry (1912). History of the epic form in England through the 19th century. Cited in: CBEL, BCL; LC65-15894.   540 Cloth $9.95

DOORN, Cornelis van
An Investigation Into the Character of Jonathan Swift (1931). Cited in: CBEL; LC68-714.   684 Cloth $7.65

DORAN, John
The History of Court Fools (1858). A world history of the court jester from Greek mythology through the 17th century. Cited in: CBEL.   656 Cloth $12.95

DORSET, Gerald
An Aristocrat of Intellect (1959). An essay on Edgar Allan Poe's life and works.
                        MS 89 $3.25

＊DRUMMOND, William
The Poetical Works of William Drummond of Hawthornden. 2 Vol. Edited by L.E. Kastner. (1913). Cited in: BCL; LC68-24906.   157 Cloth

DUCKWORTH, George E.
Foreshadowing and Suspense (1933). Dramatic Devices in the works of Apollonius, Homer and Vergil.   MS 21 $3.85

DUDOK, G.A.
The Development of English Prose in the 19th Century (1925).   MS 21 $2.95

＊DUFF, E. Gordon
Early Printed Books (1893). Illus. Cited in: L; LC68-25309.   936 Cloth $9.95

DYSON, H.V.D.
The Emergence of Shakespeare's Tragedy (1950). Cited in: CBEL.   MS 23 $1.25

＊EARLE, Alice M.
Stage-coach and Tavern Days (1900). An easy-going and gossipy volume on the taverns of yesteryear and the stagecoaches that ran between them. Drawn largely from experiences in New England, Mrs. Earle relates colorful and vivid tales of tavern landlords, tavern fares, ghost stories, highwaymen, and stage drivers. Illus. Cited in: BCL, GSUSA; LC68-26351.
                        280 Cloth $14.95

＊EELKING, Max VON
The German allied troops in the North American War of Independence, 1776-1783. (1933). Translated by J.G. Rosengarten. Originally published by Munsell in Albany in 1893, this book has been in great demand by genealogists, historians and sociologists. There is nothing like it in the field. LC68-31265.
                        321 Cloth $17.50

EKSTROM, Kjell
George Washington Cable (1950). A study of the early life and works of the 19th century American novelist. Cited in: BAL, LC68-1601.   658 Cloth $8.25

ELIOT, T.S. et al
Criticism in America — Its Function and Status (1924). Essays by Babbit, Boyd, Brooks, Eliot, Mencken and others.
                        541 Cloth $9.35

ELIOT, T.S.
Elizabethan Essays (1932). Eliot's writings on Jonson, Marlowe, Marston, Middleton and others. LC65-15878. 542 Cloth $5.95

ELIOT, T.S.
Homage to John Dryden. Three essays on 17th Century Poetry. Cited in: CBEL.
                        MS 24 $2.00

ELIOT, T.S.
John Dryden (1932). Three essays on Dryden as a poet, dramatist and a critic. Cited in: CBEL; LC68-913. **692** Cloth $5.35

ELIOT, T.S. et al
Tradition and Experiment in Present-Day Literature (1929). Essays by Eliot, Sitwell, Symons and others. LC68-761.
544 Cloth $7.85

ELLEHAUGE, Martin
The Position of Bernard Shaw in European Drama and Philosophy (1931). LC68-853.
659 Cloth $13.95

＊ELLET, Elizabeth F.
The Women of the American Revolution. (1848-50). 3 Vol. Originally published in the 1840's, in 3 volumes, comprising over 1,000 pages, the work has never been superseded. There is no other comparable work on the women of the Revolution. Essential reference work in most libraries. LC68-31269. **197** Cloth $37.50

＊ELLIS, Alexander John
On Early English Pronunciation, With Especial Reference to Shakespeare and Chaucer. 5 Vol. (1869-1889). Cited in: BCL, CBEL; LC68-24964. **158** Cloth

ELLIS-FERMOR, Una
Some Recent Research in Shakespeare's Imagery (1937). **MS 25** $1.80

EVERETT, Dorothy
Some Reflections on Chaucer's ART POETICAL (1950). Cited in: CBEL.
MS 26 $1.50

＊EWEN, Frederic
Bibliography of 18th Century English Literature (1935). LC68-25310.
937 Cloth $3.95

＊FARNHAM, Charles Haight
A Life of Francis Parkman (1901). Illus. Cited in: BCL, L; LC68-24975.
938 Cloth $13.95

FARNHAM, Willard E.
The Sources of Chaucer's "Parlement of Foules" (1917). Cited in: CBEL.
MS 28 $1.55

FAURIEL, C.C.
History of Provencal Poetry (1860). Translated by G.J. Adler. LC68-753.
546 Cloth $13.95

＊FAUST, A.B. and G.M. BRUMBAUGH
Lists of Swiss emigrants in the 18th century to the American colonies. 2 Vol. (1920-25). Spanning over the period 1920-1925, this monumental work is the only one which covers Swiss emigration. It was originally published by the National Genealogical Society, Washington, and has long been out of print. LC68-31263.
200 Cloth $27.50

FAUSSET, Hugh l'Anson
The Lost Leader: A study of William Wordsworth (1933). Cited in: BCL, CBEL; LC68-914. **547** Cloth $8.50

FAUSSET, Hugh l'Anson
Walt Whitman: Poet of Democracy. Cited in: BCL; LC68-1196. **548** Cloth $8.50

＊FAY, Edward Allen
Concordance of the Divina Commedia. 2 Vol. (1888). Cited in: BCL, L; LC68-26352.
183 Cloth $28.50

FERRALL, Rose N.
The D.X.V. Prophecy—Dante and the SABBATUM FIDELIUM (1938). An introductory study in the allegorical interpretation of "The Divine Comedy." **MS 90** $2.95

＊FINCK, Henry Theophilus
Wagner and His Works: The Story of His Life, with Critical Comments. 2 Vol. (1893). Cited in: BCL, L; LC68-25287.
189 Cloth $28.95

＊FISHER, Herbert Albert Laurens
Studies in Napoleonic Statesmanship — Germany (1903). Series of studies on the states of the Rhenish confederation. Maps. Cited in: BCL, AHA, L; LC68-25230.
939 Cloth $12.95

FITZMAURICE-KELLY, James
Cervantes in England (1905). MS **29** $1.75

FLEISSNER, Robert F.
Dickens and Shakespeare (1965). A study of the histrionic contrasts of Shakespearean influences in the novels of Dickens. LC65-28337. **549** Cloth $7.95

FLETCHER, Jefferson B.
The Religion of Beauty in Woman (1911). Essays on Platonic Love in Poetry and Society in the writings of Benvieni, Cavalcanti, Dante, Spenser and others. LC68-925. **550** Cloth $7.95

FLETCHER, Robert H.
The Arthurian Material in the Chronicles of Great Britain and France (1906). Over 200 Chronicles are discussed from the Sixth to the Sixteenth Centuries. Cited in: CBEL; LC68-2114. **551** Cloth $9.25

FLINT, William W.
The Use of Myth to Create Suspense in Extant Greek Tragedy (1921). MS **30** $3.95

FLORES, Angel (Ed.)
Ibsen: Four Essays (1937). A Marxist Analysis by Engels, Lunachaisky, Mehring and Plekhanov. **MS 91** $3.95

FOX, George G.
The Medieval Sciences in the Works of John Gower (1931). Study of the 14th Century Poet and his Writings. Cited in: CBEL; LC65-21089. **553** Cloth $6.15

*FRANKLIN, Benjamin
The Writings of Benamin Franklin. 10 Vol.
(1907) Collected and edited by Albert H.
Smyth. Illus. Vol. I—Bibliographical introduction and the "Autobiography." Vols. II-
X—Writings and correspondence arranged
chronologically. Vol. X—The "Life" by the
editor (Smyth) and list of correspondents
and full indexes. Cited in: BCL, GSUSA,
AHA, L; LC68-24976.   194 Cloth

FRIEDLAND, Louis S.
Spenser as a Fabulist (1937). Cited in:
CBEL.   MS 31 $2.95

FRIEDMAN, Lee M.
Zola and the Dreyfus Case (1937). 22 Illus.
                             MS 92 $4.95

FUESS, Claude M.
Lord Byron as a Satirist in Verse (1912).
Cited in: BCL, CBEL; LC12-21992.
                             554 Cloth $4.95

FURNESS, Clifton J.
Walt Whitman's Estimate of Shakespeare
(1932).   MS 32 $1.85

*GARDINER, Samuel Rawson
The Thirty Years' War, 1618-1648. (1903).
Illus. Maps. Though liberal and protestant
in its bias, deserves a place in any general
bibliography. Cited in: BCL, L, AHA;
LC68-25233   940 Cloth $10.95

*GARDINER, Samuel Rawson
What Gunpowder Plot Was (1897). Illus.
Cited in: BCL, L; LC68-25234.
                             941 Cloth $8.95

*GARDNER, Edmund Garratt
Dante and the Mystics: A Study of the
Mystical Aspect of the Divina Commedia
(1913). Cited in: BCL, L; LC68-24952.
                             271 Cloth $10.95

*GARDNER, Edmund Garratt
Dukes and Poets in Ferrara: A Study in the
Poetry, Religion and Politics of the 15th
and Early 16th Centuries (1904). Illus.
Cited in: BCL; LC68-25235.
                             943 Cloth $15.95

*GARDNER, Edmund Garratt
The King of the Court Poets: A Study of
the Work, Life and Times of Lodovico Ari-
osto (1906). Illus. Cited in: BCL, L;
LC68-24954.   944 Cloth $13.95

*GARDNER, Ernest Arthur
Ancient Athens (1902). Illus. Cited in: BCL;
LC68-25236.   945 Cloth $16.95

*GARLAND, Hugh A.
The Life of John Randolph at Roanoke.
11th Ed. 2 Vol. (1856). Illus. Cited in:
BCL; LC68-24977.   159 Cloth $19.95

*GARRISON, George Pierce
Westward Extension, 1841-1850 (1906).
Illus. Maps. A vivid portrait of a turbulent
and crowded decade. Although the emphasis is on expansion, the book is largely a
history of the U.S. during the years covered. Also discussed are party struggle
and the domestic problems of the Tyler
and Polk administrations. Cited in: BCL,
L, GSUSA; LC68-24978. 946 Cloth $12.95

GASKIN, Robert T.
Caedmon: The First English Poet, 3rd Ed.
(1902). Illus.   MS 33 $2.95

GAYLEY, Charles Mills
The Charles Mills Gayley Anniversary
Papers (1922). A Festschrift, originally
published in 1922, and long out of print,
containing 16 papers ranging from "12
Andamese Songs" to "Coleridge's Estimate of Fielding," together with a list of
Gayley's published writings from 1881 to
1920. LC67-30814.   715 Cloth $10.95

GIBBON, John M.
Melody and the Lyric (1930). Song and
Poetry from Chaucer to Dryden. 200 Mu-
sical Illustrations. LC65-15882.
                             555 Cloth $7.25

GILBERT, Rudolph
Shine, Perishing Republic (1936). Robinson Jeffers and the Tragic Sense in Modern Poetry. Cited in: BCL; LC65-15883.
                             556 Cloth $7.85

GILL, Frederick C.
The Romantic Movement and Methodism
(1937). A study of the Evangelical Revival
and English Romanticism. Begins with the
Wesleys and goes through the Pre-Roman-
tics to Wordsworth and Coleridge.
LC68-1308.   660 Cloth $7.95

*GILMAN, Lawrence
Aspects of Modern Opera; Estimates and
Inquiries (1909). Cited in: BCL, L;
LC68-25288.   302 Cloth

GINGERICH, S.F.
From Necessity to Transcendentalism in
Coleridge (1920). Cited in: CBEL.
                             MS 34 $2.75

*GIRALDUS
The English Conquest of Ireland A.D.
1116-1185 (1896). Cited in: BCL;
LC68-25237.   947 Cloth $8.95

GIRVAN, Ritchie
Finnsburuh (1941). Discussion of the Anglo-Saxon Poem. Cited in: CBEL.
                             MS 35 $1.00

GISSING, George
Critical Studies of the Works of Charles
Dickens (1924). Edited with a Bibliogra-
phy of Gissing by Temple Scott. Cited in:
CBEL; LC65-26454.   557 Cloth $6.50